THE GENERAL CALLED TSUNAMI

MEMOIR OF A SAPPER

THE GENERAL CALLED TSUNAMI

MEMOIR OF A SAPPER

Lt Gen BS Dhaliwal, PVSM, AVSM, VSM (Veteran)

THE BROWSER
www.thebrowser.org
Publishers & Booksellers

The General Called Tsunami: Memoir of a Sapper
by Lt Gen BS Dhaliwal

ISBN – 978-93-92210-05-1
Edition – I

Published in India by –
J.G.S. Enterprises Pvt Ltd
Imprint: The Browser

Publisher's Address –
SCO 14-15, Sector 8-C, Chandigarh 160 009
Email – service@thebrowser.org
Website – www.thebrowser.org

Printed in India
Cover design, typesetting & layout by 99beagles.com

THE BROWSER
www.thebrowser.org
Publishers & Booksellers

CONTENTS

ABBREVIATIONS

2IC	Second-in-Command
AAG	Assistant Adjutant General
ACE	Additional Chief Engineer
ACR	Annual Confidential Report
ADC	Aide-de-Camp
ADG	Additional Director General
ADGTE	Additional Director General Technical Examiner
Adm	Administration
AE	Approximate Estimate
AEE	Assistant Executive Engineer
AGE	Assistant Garrison Engineer
AMIE	Associate Member of Institute of Engineers
AOC	Air Officer Commanding
AOC-in-C	Air Officer Commanding-in-Chief
AQMG	Assistant Quarter Master General
ARAE	Amateur Rowing Association East
ARTRAC	Army Training Command
ASI	Assistant Sub Inspector; Army Sports Institute
ATC	Air Traffic Control
AVSM	Ati Vishisht Seva Medal
BDF	Botswana Defence Forces
BER	Beyond Economical Repair
BGS	Brigadier General Staff
BLD	Brick Lined Defence
BP	Board Proceedings
B/R	Buildings and Roads
BRD	Base Repair Depot
BRDB	Border Road Development Board
Brig	Brigadier
BRO	Border Roads Organisation
BSO	Barrack and Stores Officer
Capt	Captain

CAS	Chief of Air Staff
CADO	Chief Administrative Officer
CBI	Central Bureau of Investigation
CBR	California Bearing Ratio
CBRN	Chemical, Biological, Radiological and Nuclear
CDM	College of Defence Management
CE	Chief Engineer
CEIJ	Combat Engineers Instructors JCO's and NCO's
CEME	Commander Electrical and Mechanical Engineers
CGI	Corrugated Galvanised Iron
CGDA	Controller General Defence Accounts
CI	Chief Instructor
CME	College of Military Engineering
CMP	Corps of Military Police
CNS	Chief of Naval Staff
CO	Commanding Officer
COAS	Chief of Army Staff
Col	Colonel
COS	Chief of Staff
CPL	Casual Paid Labour
CPM	Critical Path Method
CPWD	Central Public and Works Department
CS	Chief Secretary
CTW	Cadet Training Wing
CVC	Chief Vigilance Commissioner
CWE	Commander Works Engineers
DAC	Dense Asphaltic Concrete
D&M	Driving & Maintenance
DAMS	Deputy Assistant Military Secretary
DASI	Directorate of Air Safety Inspection
DC	Deputy Commissioner
DCB	Ditch-cum-Bundh
DCWE	Deputy Commander Works Engineers
DDG	Deputy Director General
DGBR	Director General Border Roads

DGMT	Director General Military Training
DGSD	Directorate General Supplies and Disposal
DGW	Director General Works
DO	Demi-official
DPC	Department Promotion Committee
DRDO	Defence Research and Development Organisation
DSSC	Defence Services Staff College
DWP	Defence Works Procedure
E-in-C	Engineer-in-Chief
EGIS	Enterprise Geographic Information System
E/M	Electrical/Mechanical
EMP	Earth Moving Plant
EODE	Engineer Officers' Degree Engineering
ERC	Engineer Regimental Commanders
ES	Engineer Staff
FE	Field Engineering
FIR	First Information Report
FY	Financial Year
GBM	General Body Meeting
Gde	Grade
Gen	General
GIS	Geographic Information System
GM	General Manager
GOC	General Officer Commanding
GREF	General Reserve Engineer Force
GSO 1 (Ops)	General Staff Officer Grade 1 (Operations)
HAA	High Altitude Area
HBTC	Heavy Bridging Training Camp
HMP	Hot Mix Plant
HOD	Head of Department
HQ	Headquarter(s)
IAS	Indian Administrative Service
IATT	Indian Army Training Team
IB	Inspection Bungalow
IC	Indian Commission

IDSE	Indian Defence Services of Engineers
IEI	Institution of Engineers
IMA	Indian Military Academy
IOC	Indian Oil Corporation
IS	Indian Standard
ISI	Inter-Services Intelligence
IT	Information Technology
J&K	Jammu and Kashmir
JCB	Joseph Cyril Bamford
JC	Junior Command
JCO	Junior Commissioned Officer
JE	Junior Engineer
KLP	Key Location Plan
KRA	Key Result Area
KVA	Kilovolt-amps
LCN	Load Classification Number
LMC	Low Medical Category
LO	Liaison Officer
Lt	Lieutenant
Lt Gen	Lieutenant General
LWE	Land, Works and Environment
Maj	Major
Maj Gen	Major General
MEA	Ministry of External Affairs
MES	Military Engineer Services
MG Adm	Major General Administration
MGGS	Major General Staff
MGO	Master General Ordnance
MI	Medical Inspection
MH	Military Hospital
MO	Military Operations/Medical Officer
MOD	Ministry of Defence
MP	Military Police
MS	Military Secretary
MWP	Major Works Programme

NABCL	National Accreditation Board for Testing and Calibration Laboratories
NCC	National Cadet Corps
NCO	Non-Commissioned Officer
NDA	National Defence Academy
NDC	National Defence College
NGO	Non-Government Organisation
NH	National Highway
NOAI	National Optimist Association of India
NSA	National Security Adviser
OC	Officer Commanding
OHP	Overhead Projector
OIC	Officer in Charge
OP	Observation Post
Ops	Operations
OR	Other Ranks
OTM	Other than Married
PA	Personal Assistant
PAR	Plinth Area Rate
PBOR	Personnel Below Officer Rank
PCDA	Principal Controller Defence Accounts
PCN	Pavement Classification Number
PMC	President Mess Committee
PMT	Project Management Team
POL	Petrol, Oil and Lubricants
PPET	Physical Proficiency Efficiency Test
PQC	Pavement Quality Concrete
PT	Physical Training
PVSM	Param Vishisht Seva Medal
QMG	Quarter Master General
QPR	Quarterly Progress Report
QR	Qualitative Requirement
RCC	Road Construction Company
RFI	Rowing Federation of India
RHQ	Regimental Head Quarters

RMO	Regimental Medical Officer
RO	Reviewing Officer
ROP	Road Opening Party
RSI	Rajendra Sinhji Institute
SA	Small Arms; Surveyor Assistant
SASE	Snow and Avalanche Studies Establishment
SD	Staff Duties
SERC	State Electricity Regulatory Commission
SHO	Station House Officer
SI	Senior Instructor
SM	Subedar Major
SO	Staff Officer
SODE	Signal Officers' Degree Engineering
SOP	Standard Operating Procedure
SP	Superintendent of Police
SRO	Superior Reviewing Officer
SW	Surveyor of Works
SSW	Senior Surveyor of Works
SSR	Standard Schedule of Rates
STD	Subscriber Trunk Dialling
STE	Superintendent Technical Examiner
T&P	Tools and Plants
TBRL	Terminal Ballistics Research Laboratory
TESO	Technical Equipment Store Officer
TF	Task Force
TS	Technical Secretary
VC	Victoria Cross
VCAS	Vice Chief of Air Staff
VCOAS	Vice Chief of Army Staff
VCNS	Vice Chief of Naval Staff
VIP	Very Important Person
VrC	Vir Chakra
VSM	Vishisht Seva Medal
YAB	Young Officers and Advance Bridging Wing
YO	Young Officer

PREFACE

It is written about humankind that the race is not to the swift or the battle to the strong, nor does food come to the wise or wealth to the brilliant or favour to the learned; but time and chance happen to them all. (The Bible: Ecclesiastes 9:11). Life is not meant to be easy; it is meant to be lived, sometimes happy, often rough. But with every up and down, you learn lessons that make you strong.

I had never imagined that I would write my memoir. I, for one, thought that, since as I had passed on my knowledge and experiences to those who served under me during my military career, penning my memoir would serve little purpose. What little I did during my military career was done as a task to improve the organisation I served in. I have not kept copies of official documents to support some of the actions and incidents mentioned in this book. I always believed that official papers should remain in the office files. However, I have tried to record what I remember of the incidents faithfully. Some dates and other minor details may not be quite accurate. I hope that the reader will make allowances for this and bear with me. No matter how modest one's achievements may appear to oneself, their record is of interest to succeeding generations.

Further, I had been picked up for an assignment immediately after my superannuation from the Indian Army, as the Engineer-in-Chief. I was selected as Advisor (Technical) to the Hon'ble Chief Minister of Punjab.

This last assignment was more stressful than the military; there was no spare time to even think of writing a book. After putting in eleven plus years of continuous dedicated service with the Punjab Government (with two political governments), when my resignation was finally accepted in January 2019, I took a week's rest and thereafter got back to my hobby – reading. During this period, I got to read the book *Dying Empty* by Todd Henry. The line in that book that impacted me most is: *'Do not go to your grave and carry inside you the best that you have; always choose to die empty.'* It highlights that:

If you have an idea, perform it.
If you have the knowledge, give it out.
If you have a goal, achieve it.
Love, store and distribute; do not keep it inside you.

I consider myself fortunate to have been able to achieve more than what I sought in life. I have also been fortunate to have come across officers who imbibed in me the principles of punctuality, ethics, discipline and a never-give-up attitude. Further, those who came in contact with me in this journey of life know that I have distributed knowledge; yet I would die empty unless I could benefit coming generations from my experiences and methodologies adopted by me during my military career. With this purpose, I share my thoughts on the journey of my life in the Army so that my words could become a page in someone else's career guide. Sharing knowledge is an important facet of life so that others do not make the same mistakes. Hence, an endeavour is made in this book to narrate some anecdotes during my military career from which lessons were learnt and which became my 'success mantras'. These, the readers may consider for emulation.

It is truly said that excellence is an art achieved by training and habit. We do not act rightly because we have virtue and excellence, but because we have acted rightly. We are what we repeatedly do. Excellence is then not an act but a habit. Nothing will change in your life if you do not do something different from what you have been doing. Train yourself to find the blessing in everything. Don't give up just because things are hard.

Nothing teaches us better than our own experiences.

Before I narrate the events in my life and what gave me success, it would be appropriate to mention my heritage briefly. My father was from a humble background; born in a small village in a backward area of Punjab and was the only child of his parents. He lost his mother when he was an infant, and his father and grandfather had brought him up. In the village, hardly anyone was educated, yet his grandfather was very keen that he obtain an education. My father topped the Matriculation Examination (10th class) in Punjab by sheer grit and hard work. He got a scholarship for admission to the prestigious Government College, Lahore, where he did his Masters in English and Mathematics. After that, though he topped the written IAS examination, he was not selected. He never told us the reason for this. Contrarily, he always said that he was not selected as God had better things lined up for him, i.e., a commission in the Indian Army (The Dogra Regiment). Later, because of his mathematical background, he was transferred to the Regiment of Artillery. He took early retirement in 1968, after raising and commanding 169 Field Regiment. He had participated in the 1965 operations in J&K, where he earned a 'Mention in Dispatches' for his role during the war.

Throughout my childhood, I was greatly influenced by my father, who was a self-made man. He instilled in me an inner compass that always pointed towards correct things. In those times, since the strength of the Indian Army was less than what it is today, the Regiment was one big family. Hence, my personality was also influenced by the officers who were posted in the Regiment my father was serving in. I vividly recall one incident during a visit to the office of my father's CO. I saw and read *The Serenity Prayer* displayed on a beautifully painted board hung on the wall. It read:

God grant me the serenity
To accept the things I cannot change;
Courage to change the things I can;
And wisdom to know the difference.

The CO, addressed as CO Uncle, explained the meaning of this prayer to me. Later, when I became an officer, I displayed it in my office. Many refer to it as a prayer; others consider it contemplation, meditation or a talk to someone Unseen. The only investment is attentiveness. Recognising the truth and power of letting go is perhaps part of the wonder of that timeless flow that we undergo under the spell of a prayer.

While the writing of this book has been a slow and rewarding process, I acknowledge with deep gratitude the help and guidance I have had from various friends in this effort. The list is rather long, but not naming them does not undermine the fact that they know who they are. I also confess that any errors of commission and omission in this endeavour are mine alone.

Finally, I must acknowledge the great contribution of my wife, Jasbir, and my daughters, Anureet and Divas, to my life and career. They have been pillars of strength and my anchor.

Chandigarh
September 2022

Lt Gen BS Dhaliwal

THE SILVER GRENADE IGNITES

53 Engr Regt (Jan 68 — Dec 68)

The Corps of Engineers is one of the oldest arms of the Indian Army. The origin of the Corps dates back to 1780 when two regular pioneer companies of the Madras Sappers were raised. Subsequently, the Groups of Madras, Bengal, and Bombay Sappers were formed and later merged, on 18 November 1932, to form the Corps of Engineers in its present form. It consists of four major constituents – Combat Engineers, Military Engineer Services, Border Roads, and Military Survey. The Sappers utility in the military has been recognised over the ages. First and foremost, they are soldiers, capable of fighting as fully trained infantry-men; they have the expertise in all aspects of field engineering, and they are tradesmen with the skills necessary to enhance the general and civil engineering capability of the Corps.

It is with this fervour and spirit that I had opted to join the Sappers and looked forward to active soldiering. I was commissioned in the Corps of Engineers (Bengal Sappers) on 25 December 1966. After attending the Young Officers' Course at the College of Military Engineering at Pune, I was posted to 53 Engineer Regiment located at Jalandhar, where I reported for duty, in early 1968. I had stood first on the YO's Course and been awarded the 'Silver Grenade' for being the best all-round officer of the Course. I looked forward to serving with pride, confidence, and enthusiasm.

My First Interview with the CO

53 Engineer Regiment was then commanded by Lt Col S Mazumdar, who later rose to the rank of Lt Gen and superannuated as the Adjutant General. On the second day of my reporting to the Regiment, I was interviewed by him by being marched into his office. In those days, all officers' up-to-the rank of Captain were marched into the CO's office by the Adjutant. No chair was ever offered and the officer being interviewed had to stand at attention throughout the interview. It was an experience filled with some trepidation.

After welcoming me, the CO glanced over some papers and, in a stern voice, stated that he was unhappy with my course report since I had not worked hard enough to get a 'Distinction' grading. He added that, in future, he wanted me to put in my best in whatever task I was assigned. This admonishment took me aback as I was a topper on the course and expected to be complimented for my performance.

Later at night, as I reflected on his remarks, I realised that what he said was true. Due to peer pressure, a day before the final examination of the course, I had gone to town for a late-night movie with friends, due to which I made a few silly mistakes in the paper, which would never have occurred had I got a good night's sleep. I wondered how he was aware of this.

From this experience, I learnt that:

> As a senior officer, it is your bounden duty to lay down a very high standard for your command. You will attain the standard you expect, provided you set an example.
>
> Everyone can improve, provided his senior keeps coaxing him till he achieves the standard expected from him.
>
> There are no short cuts to attain a high standard except from consistent and dedicated hard work and practice.

Advice given by a senior officer should always be taken positively and in the correct spirit. Feedback should never be taken negatively or be allowed to demoralise you.

Train your mind to be stronger than your feelings. Don't compare yourself with other people; compare yourself with who you were yesterday.

First Assignment by the CO

Immediately after being marched out of the CO's office, the Adjutant, Capt JL Sharma (who later retired as a Col) told me to report to him the next day, at 0900 hours, to meet the CO once again as there was a special assignment for me. He gave no hint as to what the task might be and I could not summon the courage to ask. That night I kept wondering what the CO had in store for me.

The next day, I was marched into the CO's office once again. Lt Col Mazumdar enunciated that it was essential to determine the type and quantity of natural resources available in Punjab to know what can be tapped during a war if the need arises. He wanted me to find out how much; what type; in what quantity; and where timber would be available during the campaigning season in Punjab. He wanted a detailed report to be handed over to the Adjutant, by 0930 hours, after two days. He asked if I had any questions. My immediate response was, "No Sir." In truth, I had no clue how to go about the task assigned and how I would have the report ready by the laid-down time.

The CO also mentioned that he would not be able to provide me with a vehicle to move around for this task. At that time, I had little knowledge of Punjab as my father during his service was never posted in Punjab. Perplexed, while walking to the Officers' Mess at 1400 hours, I heard my name being shouted by someone familiar (as he was calling out to me by the name by which I was known at the NDA). It was a pleasant surprise to see that it was a coursemate, 2/Lt MD Sunder, who had joined the Corps of Signals. After the usual hug and banter, he told me that he was moving early next morning, towards Amritsar for reconnaissance for a forthcoming Exercise with troops and would be returning in the evening. I requested him for a lift to which he readily agreed.

After a good night's sleep, I took a lift in his vehicle at 0700 hours the next day, on a cold winter morning, without actually knowing where to go. It was en route that I told him of my assignment and, God bless him, he advised me to get down at Beas where a huge government factory for creosoting of wood was located. Hopefully, I could get some information from there.

At Beas, I sat down at a *dhaba* for a hot cup of tea. The *dhaba wala* told me that the factory would open at 0900 hours and the General Manager (GM) would come in any time after 1000 hours.

I was in uniform and as the Army is greatly respected in Punjab, the *dhaba wala* refused to give me a bill for the sumptuous breakfast he served, despite my repeated requests. When the factory opened, after thanking the *dhaba wala* for his hospitality, I went across to the Timber Treatment Factory. I was politely guided to the GM's office and again served tea and snacks.

The GM turned up soon after and apologised for having kept me waiting and asked the purpose of my visit. When I explained the requirement, he was highly impressed with the fact that the Army plans for all contingencies. He went all out to provide me with the data. Wherever he did not have the requisite information, he obtained it by telephoning the appropriate officers. He also gave me a list of officers who could be contacted for updating the data, when required. Once it was compiled in the format I desired, he assisted me in preparing a draft report. Needless to add, I was fed a sumptuous lunch. This gesture reflected the typical Punjabi hospitality.

I left his office at about 1700 hours, after thanking him profusely, totally satisfied that I had succeeded in getting all the data for my report sitting at one location. As I intended to write out the report at night, I also took half a ream of paper from the GM as I anticipated the offices of my Regiment would have closed for the day when I returned, and I did not have any transport to go to the town. Sunder dropped me back in my room at 1900 hours.

After a refreshing hot bath, I began to write out the detailed report. I did not go for dinner as I was sated from the heavy breakfast and lunch that day. Working non-stop, I completed the report by 0300 hours. It was complete except for its binding and the cover sheet, which was done by the Draughtsman Cell of the Regiment. I handed over the report, to the surprise of the Adjutant, half an hour before the scheduled time. At 1300 hours, I was called by the Second-in-Command, Maj V Wadhawan (who later rose to be a Brig and the Centre Commandant), to be told that the CO had expressed his appreciation on the report and that, in future, he expected a similar standard of me.

In the first assignment in my regimental life, I learnt the following:

> Hard-working people are lucky and fortunate. Take a deep breath and remind yourself there is always a solution.
>
> No task is impossible. God helps those who help themselves.
>
> There is an imperative need to interact with and have good relations with the local authorities, wherever one is posted. Good networking acts as a force multiplier.

My First Interaction with the MES

After a week in the Regiment, I was told by the Adjutant that, being the junior-most dining member in the Officers Mess, it was my responsibility to ensure that the washroom is maintained at the best, at all times. I had a look; it needed improvement. Not knowing where the MES is, I asked the Mess Havildar. He gave me the directions to the AGE's office. After lunch, as I had two hours to spare, I decided to do the assigned task.

On reaching the AGE's office, the peon informed me that the AGE was on a site inspection, and if deemed fit, I could meet the Superintendent (JE) sitting in the next office. As there was someone already sitting there, I showed my face and did not enter. When I was not called for over five minutes, I again showed my face; this time he called me in, offered a chair and asked what he could do? I explained my request.

The Superintendent (JE) asked me to sit in the AGE's office while he got someone to accompany me to have a look at what is required, and thereafter take up the work. The peon brought me a cup of tea. By the time I had a few sips, the person who was sitting in the Superintendent's (JE's) office walked in and said, "Let us go to the site and see your work."

I immediately got up, leaving the cup of tea, and walked with him to the cycle stand. We both quietly cycled to the Officers Mess.

When I showed him the washroom, I could sense that he was trying to hold back his mirth, but he asked, "What else?"

I replied, "That's it."

He asked what I wanted the walls to be painted with? I said any material that looks white and smooth (at that time I did not know all the types of material which could be used). He next asked me the surface I wanted for the washroom. I showed him the anteroom and dining room and asked him to better that.

He then said, "Okay, I have understood what you want and I will get the task done in the next two days."

I thanked him and asked what it would cost.

He smiled, and said, "A cup of tea."

By then, hearing us, the Mess Havildar had walked in; I told him what had occurred and to arrange tea. While having tea, the person told me that he was a builder working with the MES and enquired how important the work was to me, personally. I said that it is very important, as our CO accepts only very high standard work and my *izzat* was at stake. He smiled and, while departing said, "I am impressed at your simplicity and dedication. I will help you."

Not knowing what he meant, I thanked him.

The next day, as I was away on some out-station duty, I did not go to the Officer's Mess. The day after that, at lunch, I saw the work done. It was really impressive.

After the next party in the Officers Mess, Lt Col Mazumdar complimented me in front of all the other officers on the good work done. I realised that while an officer receives compliments, the good work is executed by tradesmen. This incident remained with me and played a huge part in having the highest standard in all works, thereafter. I have also come across a large number of good persons, who worked for free when they were requested sincerely and humbly.

Informal interaction with the CO

A fortnight later, around 1800 hours, I was lying in my bed with a quilt, and reading a Harold Robbins novel, when I heard a knock on my door. I wondered who it was.

I shouted, "Come in."

In walked my CO and I jumped out of the bed, attired in my boxer shorts, and stood at attention. I was caught with my pants down. Lt Col Mazumdar smiled and said, "At ease, son."

He then added, "Are you not going to offer me a chair?"

I rushed to give him a chair to sit. As there was no other chair in my room, I kept standing. Lt Col Mazumdar, realising my dilemma, asked me to sit on the bed. I hesitated and when he repeated it, I quickly sat down. He then asked me to show him the book I was reading. I felt embarrassed, but having been caught, I handed it over to him.

After glancing at the book, he emphatically said that the days to read such books are over; now is the time to read military history books and he mentioned the names of about ten. He then gave me a monologue on soldiering and how complex it was, and the need to be updated at all times. It can only be achieved by reading the correct type of books.

Lt Col Mazumdar left after about ten minutes. I was so intimidated that I did not complete the novel that I was reading. Furthermore, I stopped sleeping in boxer shorts and commenced wearing my pyjamas. Lt Col Mazumdar did not come to my room again, however, the fear that he may do so made me keep my room always neat and tidy.

Towards the end of my stay in the Regiment, I was told by the Adjutant that the CO wants me to accompany him for his evening walks. Suitably attired, I was at his house at 1830 hours.

During the walks, he spoke of many issues which I had never thought of. The walks with my CO widened my horizons and afforded me a new perspective on my life and career. Through the narration of a number of anecdotes, he stressed that opportunities are always flying past; however only the courageous catch them.

Some lessons I drew from the experience are:

> Walking with a senior/junior is an excellent opportunity to know the person better. This was followed by me in each of my appointments later in life, and it paid excellent dividends.
>
> To be courageous one has to be knowledgeable and be physically, mentally and spiritually fit at all times. The brave never gives up; they develop perseverance and are in a better position to achieve the goals they set for themselves. This is only achievable when one is honest in thoughts and in deeds.
>
> Never forget where there is a will there is a way.

Pay Parade

In those days, disbursement of monthly pay to soldiers was a properly organised parade. It was a full day affair. From 0800 to 1130 hours, all entries in the pay books of all the *jawans* were checked and updated. In case any Part II Order had not been published, it was done. Thereafter, from 1130 to 1230 hours, the Platoon Commanders were tested on whether they knew their command. For this, two *jawans* held a groundsheet and one of the *jawans* from the platoon, selected by the Company Commander, stood behind the ground sheet and was told to speak a sentence or two. The Platoon Commander had to name the soldier. In case the identification of the individual was correct, then he had to give all relevant details of the soldier. To pass this test, one had not only to work and play games with the men but treat his platoon as his own extended family. It appeared tough in the beginning; however, once an officer knitted with his command it came naturally.

Meeting the Army Commander

In the summer of 1968, after the wheat crop was harvested, a full-scale Exercise with troops was held. One of the many tasks assigned to my Regiment was to construct helipads where the Army Commander and the Corps Commander could land. I was deputed the task of preparing one such helipad, with a section of troops and the requisite earthmoving plant to complete it in ten days.

I moved out with my task force and set up camp close to where the helipad was to be prepared. Soon an old man from the village nearby came over. He had brought a jug full of refreshing *lassi* and enquired why I had brought the earthmoving plant. I told him that I have to construct a helipad and mentioned the qualitative requirements of a helipad. After patiently listening, he took me to a site on the outskirts of the village where the school children played rural hockey. The size of the ground was a little more than what was required for a helipad. The soil was stable and level, but it was dry and dusty. The old man advised me to prepare the helipad on this ground for which I would not require any of the plant machinery that I had brought along. He advised that we should first sweep the field properly. Thereafter, we should mark the helipad area and water it three to four times a day. After the first day of watering, we should sprinkle urea on the marked area and keep watering the helipad area for the next three days. On the fifth and subsequent days, rather than watering, only sprinkle water on the helipad area. The advice seemed workable to me and this was authenticated by the senior NCO (who was from Punjab.) We did exactly as the old man advised. Lo and behold, on the fifth day the helipad area started looking green from a distance and the green patch increased exponentially every day.

On the day the Army Commander, along with the Corps Commander, were to land on the helipad, my CO and many other senior officers turned up half an hour earlier.

After receiving Lt Col Mazumdar, I stood with the Guard Commander and Fire Fighting Party Commander, at the edge of the helipad. Everyone was highly impressed with the green tabletop and was complimenting my CO and opining that it would have taken a month to prepare it in the hot summer. After the Army Commander landed, he asked my CO as to who had prepared this helipad. Lt Col Mazumdar replied that his Regiment had done it. The Army Commander then said he would like to meet the officer who had been tasked for the work. My CO shouted my name and I ran across wondering what had gone wrong. I was introduced to Lt Gen Harbaksh Singh, VrC, who shook my hand and asked, "Son, have you made this helipad?"

I replied in the affirmative. He then said, "Well done!" and asked how long did it take and how I made it a green top.

I told him that I had prepared it, based on the advice given to me by an old man from the nearby village. I also mentioned the step-wise procedure we had followed and the time it took. I can never forget what the Army Commander said before leaving, "Son, never hesitate to take advice from the sons of the soil, as they know the land much better than us in uniform."

This experience taught me the following:

> There is no alternative to knowing your command thoroughly.
>
> Empirical knowledge has to be applied in the field and not blindly followed from manuals. However, it depends upon several factors viz. environment, time available and what will look appealing.
>
> An engineer must never disturb the soil that has been stabilized by nature. No machine can do what nature does over the years.
>
> Never hesitate to take the advice of the locals for any engineering tasks as they have much more knowledge about their land and local resources.
>
> To stand out, there is no choice but to do things differently.

Attachment with the Corps Headquarters

A new bridge known as the 'M4T6 Bridge' had been newly introduced into the Corps of Engineers inventory. As I had learnt about this bridge at the YO's Course at CME, I was directed to brief Lt Col PS Roy who was officiating as the Chief Engineer at the Corps HQ. (He later retired as the E-in-C). After I had explained all I knew about the bridge and how it could be employed, he had me attached with the Engineers Branch for nearly three months, as no other officer was available with this expertise and since there was no other officer posted in his office. I took on the duties of a Staff Officer and observed how a Corps HQ functions.

I learnt from Lt Col PS Roy on how to work diligently, systematically and intelligently. He highlighted to me repeatedly that as a rule never carry work to the next day, even if it meant working late hours. He also stressed that one must always find time to exercise/walk/play games on all days of the week and socialize at least once a week. Finally, he explained the necessity to remain professionally updated at all times.

One day, while I was showing slides behind the screen, during a Formation Commanders conference in the operations room of the Corps HQ, I heard the then Corps Commander, Lt Gen PS Bhagat, VC respond to a question asked by an Independent Brigade Commander. The question was regarding our operational plans being based on a seven-day warning period, and what would happen in case we did not get the requisite seven-days 'warning'.

The Corps Commander emphatically replied, "Sit down! A stupid question. In case I do not give the 'warning' in the laid-down time frame, it would mean that I have not performed my duty which, gentlemen, will never be the case."

Thereafter, there was pin-drop silence. This taught me that a commander must always, and at all times, act as a commander. This is only feasible if the commander knows his job and is confident.

Retrospect

I was extremely fortunate to get the best grooming possible in the best unit (53 Engineer Regiment was declared as the best unit in Western Command that year) with an opportunity to work directly under two icons of the Corps of Engineers, who later rose to the rank of Lt Gen.

Though both were different personalities, they instilled in me many virtues of leadership and soldiering. From them, I learnt that excellence is never an accident. It is always the result of high intention, sincere effort, and intelligent execution; it represents the wise choice of many alternatives. Choices, not chance, determine your destiny.

Amongst the other officers in the Regiment who left a lasting impact on me were Maj V Wadhawan – a pleasing personality and a voracious reader (later retired as a Brig); Maj Macsuedon – a mature, calm officer who never lost his cool (later retired as a Brig); Maj Gurdeep Singh who had the guts to call a spade a spade and always gave good advice to youngsters (later retired as a Col); I am still in touch with all of them. Also, 2/Lt Maninder Singh Brar, who was six-months junior to me, remained a good friend.

THREE YEARS IN PARADISE

EODE at CME (Jan 69 — Dec 71)

It is during one's formative years that many indelible impressions are created on the canvas of one's life. Some of them become invaluable and remain lifelong. An important thing I learnt is if you believe it will work out, you'll see opportunities. If you believe it won't, you will see obstacles. The possibilities are endless when you work hard and never give up.

After a hectic year, that was full of learning and hard, dedicated work in the 53 Engineer Regiment, in January 1969, I was detailed to attend the three-year EODE Course at the CME, Pune – a paradise on Earth. It was great to be once again with my coursemates.

The first month went in discussing each other's experiences of regimental life. On courses of instruction, perhaps one learns more from one's peers than from the instructors and classroom interaction. From the beginning of the course, I had made up my mind that I would not aim for the top position in academics but would limit myself to obtaining an honourable grading. In the time thus saved, I would try to excel in one sport and take up other hobbies.

In retrospect, to a great extent, I achieved both the aims I had set for myself.

Rowing

During my YO's Course, I had been introduced to rowing and had developed a liking for the sport. Rowing is extremely demanding, physically and mentally, and calls for a combination of aerobic and anaerobic energy. It requires a keen sense of discipline, and a willingness to devote time. I sacrificed a term break of a month's leave to stay on at CME to practice rowing and building up my stamina and strength. This effort not only got me the recognition I desired in rowing but also motivated me to remain physically fit.

I recall an incident that occurred before one of my rowing training sessions. During lunch, I got into an argument with a coursemate over a trifling matter. I was so upset that my training session in the afternoon was a total waste of time and energy, as my mind was elsewhere. My attention had been diverted and I was extremely dejected. That night I read a book by Swami Vivekananda, *Powers of the Mind.* It beautifully articulated that, in case you permit your mood to be spoilt, and then the person who upset your mental balance would succeed in his mission. In case you block your mind and do not permit the event to spoil your mood then the other person would be the loser. I was extremely impressed by these words and, after that, I practiced developing this attitude and was able to master it. Since then, I never let my mood get spoilt because of any individual, the environment or any event. Despite things going wrong, I have always kept my cool and my thoughts positive. It ensured that I could take appropriate decisions and overcome ugly situations always and every time. Also, I was able to work long hours without ever getting tired. However, as a caveat, every human being is different and one must stick to what works for one's temperament.

Another book that I read several times was *The Third Eye* written by T Lobsang Rampa. It is a hauntingly beautiful and deeply inspiring Tibetan story of a journey of awakening within. It discusses the opening of the all-powerful, all-knowing, third eye. I started practicing the techniques described in the book but, after three months, I thought of giving it up. I somehow overcame this urge and went on to learn with more sincerity and gusto. Progress commenced in a year, slowly and steadily. I quietly went about doing my daily practice to keep mastery on my third eye. It greatly assisted me to gauge people correctly; I could easily discern who was lying to me and who may get the organisation or unit in trouble.

Hiking

During the monsoon season, on Sundays, to keep officers from indulging in gambling at the Race Course, hikes were organised. It involved trekking a distance of over 10 kilometres on the hilly tracts of the Sahyadri hills around Pune. Thereafter, a hot lunch was served to all participants. Besides, the first ten officers who completed the hike got a chilled bottle of beer free, as an incentive. I enjoyed these hikes and would always be amongst the first ten. Further, by returning in the first bus after lunch, and a refreshing hot water bath, I could get a well-deserved rest and, later in the evening, go for a movie in the open-air theatre.

Once, I decided to walk with a group that was the slowest. They took unnecessary breaks, cribbed throughout the hike and I failed to fathom what enjoyment they were getting. At the finish point, to my horror, there was practically no worthwhile lunch left and no beer was available. Those who had reached before us, and were waiting, cursed us for delaying the return home. We came back when it was dark, there was no water in the taps and with practically no lunch, we were famished.

Retrospect

The major lessons I learnt during the three-year degree course are:

> Learn to accept whatever comes your way, and the only important thing is to meet it with the best you have to give.
>
> One must never let any event or anyone spoil your mood. For this one has to master any technique which works for you.

Third eye is there. One must develop the same.

One must never ape anyone. One should always be himself and remember that, in the long term, only the methodology that works best for your personality should be followed. This does not mean that one should not improve one's weaknesses. Rather an extra effort should be made to remove them.

Our goal is not to be better than other people; it's just to be better than our previous selves.

It is always paying to do your best in whatever you wish to do in life. Shirking unnecessarily takes a toll and has a big price to pay.

Time is a limited commodity; it is very precious and has to be utilised wisely. Never let the environment or anyone waste your precious time.

On the EODE Course, together again for three long years after NDA, the 20 of us coursemates became lifelong buddies and had great fun. In retrospect, we did well to have four officers attaining a three-star rank (SP Raman became the VCOAS, Pramod Grover superannuated as COS Western Command, Rakesh Puri superannuated as DGQA and I became E-in-C). One officer attained a two-star rank (Anil Jain superannuated as Director Management Services in DRDO) and six officers attained a one-star rank (Pawan Kumar Kapur, Satish Kumar Sud, Mohan Swaminathan, Tej Mittal, Ashok Nagpal and Sudhir Kumar). From each of my coursemates there was something to learn.

KANCHENJUNGA CALLS

54 Engr Regt (Jan 72 — Jul 73)

The Posting

Towards the end of 1971, as the war clouds were looming for the impending liberation war of Bangladesh the various EODE courses, except my course, were terminated early and all officers were posted back to their regiments. Our course remained at CME, as we had only a couple of months to obtain our degree (though we too had requested to be sent back to our units). In early 1972, our postings were received. Most were posted back to their empanelled regiments, except a few like me. I was posted to 54 Engineer Regiment instead of 53 Engineer Regiment.

54 Engineer Regiment was part of the 27 Mountain Division. There was another coursemate, Capt Mohan Swaminathan, who was also posted with me. After a long train journey, we reached Siliguri where a JCO from the Regiment had come to receive us with a 1-ton vehicle.

Life in the Field Company

After a week's stay in the HQ, I was posted to a field company at a high altitude. Before that, there was a requirement to undergo acclimatisation. The schedule was that every day in the morning, after an early breakfast, we had to walk up to the company location and after lunch return to the base camp. Those who did not feel well at those heights, after the mandatory period of acclimatization, had to do it again.

In those days we had no radio, TV, or internet; only music on the gramophone, with vinyl records. All field companies had their libraries built up over the years, as all officers going on leave or any course had to bring a minimum of five novels/books (in English language only) and two albums of English music for the gramophone. It was a great opportunity to read several books.

My company commander, Major Nathan, was a voracious reader and had his own collection of music. Though only a few years senior, he acted as a true commander, mixing with the junior officers yet he kept his distance. He was a perfect role model and I acquired many good traits from him. Unlike many others, he was not a heavy drinker and we got a lot of time to read books which he would discuss with us before dinner. This ensured we all read the books in the right earnest.

Effect of Rumours

A rumour had spread amongst the troops that living in high altitude areas makes one impotent. One day, when I was officiating as the Company Commander, an OR was marched in for an interview and I asked him what his problem was. After a glance towards the Company Subedar, he stated that he wanted to speak to me alone. For a moment I was taken aback and did not know what to do. I looked at my Company JCO, who stood at attention, looking straight ahead. With no support from him, based on my gut feeling, I requested him to leave the office and close the door on his way out. He saluted and left. Thereafter, the OR stated that he had an apprehension that he had become impotent. When I asked him why he feels so, he replied he had just returned from a short casual leave. I was quiet for some time as I did know how to react, or what more to ask him. He brought the silence to an end by saying, "*Sahib*, you will not be able to advise me, as you are not married."

I immediately responded, "Yes, I am not married. Hence, I will not venture to give any advice; however, I will get you medically examined by a qualified doctor soon."

The OR then requested me not to tell anyone of his problem as he would become a laughing stock in the company. I assured him of confidentiality.

In the afternoon, when the Company Subedar was seeing me off, he could not resist asking what the OR wanted. As I was sure that this question would be asked by him, I had given it a thought. As nobody ever lies to his Company Subedar, I told him that the OR was having some minor problems with his family (in Army parlance, the family is wife). I also requested him not to question the OR of his problem. The next day I went over to the Brigade MI Room. When I narrated the incident to the RMO, he said that the OR's misgiving is correct and he also felt the same when he went on leave; however, after a few days things became normal.

I requested him to meet my company OR alone and after checking him up, to raise his morale and give him, for all I care, any tablets by which he feels cured. The RMO was much older than me and enquired if I was married. When I said no, he laughed and said he knows his job and I should refrain from advising him on how he should treat his patients. I immediately apologised. He asked me to send the boy over to him the next day and he would surely cure him.

The next day I took the *jawan* to the RMO. The doctor made him sit and asked me to leave. However, he immediately changed his mind and asked me to sit down also. The RMO, in his style through simple questions, got the *jawan* to tell him the complete story. It emerged that the *jawan* had got married during his previous leave of 30 days and had spent less than 10 days with his wife. In the Company, he had heard that staying at high altitude makes a man impotent and, before going on leave, men normally visited the red-light area at Binaguri to check their virility. He too had done so but after the tryst he felt that he had become impotent. Consequently, he decided not to go to home on leave and returned to the Unit from Binaguri. The RMO then asked me to leave and examined the OR. When I was called back the RMO informed me that as suspected the OR had got a venereal disease from contact with a prostitute. I must have looked extremely worried but the doctor told me not to worry as the malady was curable with antibiotics, and he would not report the case. I thanked him profusely and returned to the company.

Thereafter, I had a long talk with the Company Subedar and decided that there was a need to get all the men examined by the doctor, in stages. I also explained to the *jawans,* through one of the senior NCOs, the drawbacks of going to prostitutes and the perception that one becomes impotent at high altitude is false. During the medical check-up, we found that two ORs (both recently married) had venereal disease and we were able to have them cured without reporting the matter.

The lessons I learnt while serving in a field company, in HAA, are:

> It is imperative that commanders, at all levels, always keep a finger on the pulse of their command. The perceptions of the men cannot be removed by an order or even by a 'pep' talk.
>
> These are best removed by straight talk either by a senior NCO or a JCO, who can explain things to them in the manner they understand.
>
> A proper interview of all persons proceeding on leave or duty is a must. A similar interrogation after they return from leave/duty is equally essential to be aware of the problems which they may have faced or are likely to face.
>
> Never forget the dictum that the unit is your extended family. Always find time for their problems.
>
> It is important to develop the habit of reading. It lifts us from the harsh realities of life into the world of imagination. Reading gives intellectual satisfaction.

Becoming the Adjutant

My stay in the field company came to an abrupt end, after just seven months when my Company Commander received orders on the telephone to send me to the Regimental Headquarters (RHQ) to take over the duties of the Adjutant. I was extremely downcast to leave the field company as I was enjoying my stint with the men. However, a choice is rarely given in the Army and I quickly settled down to the imports of my new appointment.

The RHQ was located on a hilltop with an excellent view of Kalimpong town. The entire office complex was in temporary accommodation, constructed under operational works. The CO's office was made of wood with CGI sheet roofing. Nearby was the RHQ Officers complex building with the offices of the 2IC, Adjutant and FE. Further away was the RHQ Clerical Complex. These buildings, too, were made of wood with CGI sheet roofing. With dedicated, methodical, and sincere work, I got the office staff working like a well-oiled machine, and developed an excellent rapport with the Divisional HQ staff, other formations and neighbouring units.

Blast in Office

In November 1972, Lt Col Bhagwant Singh, the CO was away on leave and the 2IC was also away on temporary duty for coaching the formation Staff College aspirants. Maj Kuldip Bhanot, who was the Field Park Company Commander and senior-most officer present in the unit was officiating as CO. Capt Swaminathan, the FE, was away to participate in the Command Squash tournament. As most of the officers of the RHQ were out, we decided to improve the office complexes by giving a fresh coat of paint to the CO's office, providing a false ceiling in the RHQ Officers Complex and constructing an additional room for the Duty Clerk.

On 10 November 1972, I decided to finalise the invitees list for the forthcoming Corps Day celebrations and complete the invitation cards. I told the Head Clerk not to disturb me unless there was an emergency. Through a series of telephone calls, I commenced checking the availability of all invitees, the correct spellings of their names and their decorations. I completed this task at 1000 hours and then walked over to the CO's office to check on the progress of the painting being done by the civilian labour employed for the task.

At the exact moment, I was entering the CO's office, there was a deafening blast. The painter on the roof fell from the ladder. The wooden wall of the CO's office, facing the RHQ Officers Complex, totally vanished. The painter's neck was severed by a CGI sheet resulting in his instantaneous death. I had no injury as, at the exact time of the blast, I was fortuitously in between the wall/door to the CO's office. Had I been a step ahead a flying CGI sheet would have certainly got me too. I was shocked and perplexed as to what had happened.

When I stepped outside, I saw that the RHQ Officers complex had completely vanished leaving a big crater. There was a lot of smoke and total confusion. The waiter who was bringing tea for me had fallen on the lawn but was saved from a flying CGI sheet by the tray he was carrying. The cane orderly too was safe as, at the very time I went to the CO's office, he had taken the *dak* folder from my office to the Head Clerk. No one in the Clerical Complex was hurt, except for one individual who had a fracture in his arm caused by a falling purlin. The four civilian labourers, working in RHQ Officers Complex office, were not to be seen and were later confirmed to have died due to the blast. The limbs of these labourers were found spread over an area of 100 to 300 metres.

Hearing the blast, Maj Kuldip Bhanot who had gone with the SM on an inspection of the unit lines, as well as other officers, JCOs and ORs of the Field Park Company rushed to check what had happened. I had got back my composure by the time Major Bhanot came. He was happy to see me and he gave me a bear hug and asked me to narrate what exactly had happened. The SM kept the onlookers away. I narrated the incident from the time I had come to the office in the morning. After hearing my story patiently, he directed me to take charge of the situation while he drove down to the Divisional HQ to report the incident. We jointly decided that he would attend to all activities outside the Regiment, while I should take charge of all actions in the Regiment and we would keep each other updated on all activities as often as we can.

Once Maj Bhanot left, I asked the SM to collect all the men, who were being kept away from the site. After they lined up in an orderly manner, I addressed them briefly, explaining what had taken place, and the likely casualties and that the circumstances of the explosion were not known. Our immediate task was to check if anyone else had been injured, collect the dead bodies with total humility and respect and keep them in a designated room. The debris was also collected. For this, the SM was directed to form separate teams to carry out proper marking and fencing of the crater area, detailing additional sentries for round-the-clock security and to construct a temporary office for me to function from.

Once all were put on their tasks, I reported the incident to all concerned initially on the telephone and thereafter in writing, as per the laid-down orders and instructions. We were thus able to get the situation in control in the least possible time. All officers and PBORs were briefed and this stopped rumour-mongering. Before the men went for lunch, I again addressed them saying that God had been kind as nobody from our Regiment had died or was seriously injured. I also stressed that the circumstances of the explosion were being investigated and if anyone had any clue the SM or I should be informed.

By the afternoon, a Court of Inquiry had been convened by HQ 27 Mountain Division. The Presiding Officer and a member of the court of inquiry team visited the site at 1500 hours. By then the limbs of those who had died in the explosion had been collected and the body parts properly listed. Similarly, all places where the remnants of the office complex were found were marked with the name of the item(s) located.

We also contacted the families of the deceased and established liaison with the civil and police authorities and briefed them on what had occurred. They were very cooperative and impressed to see how we were treating the dead with the utmost respect. They also permitted their cremation. The last rites were performed late in the evening with due honour and dignity. The local press was also briefed and they greatly assisted us by reporting it at a low key.

What perplexed the Presiding Officer of the Court of Inquiry was how I was saved when my office was blown up by the explosion. When they were told the sequence of events from 0900 to 1030 hours, they verified it from the telephone exchange and the timings tallied. They were wonderstruck at how providence had saved me and other military personnel. The Court of Inquiry was to investigate how & why the explosion took place and what triggered it.

As there was a lot of pressure on the Court of Inquiry to come up with early answers, they decided to conduct a check of the 'accountable documents' that same night. Fortunately, the steel almirah in which these documents were kept in the Adjutant's office for safe custody was found over 100 metres away, though badly dented. All documents were found safe and complete. Similarly, the operational works documents too were found to be complete in all respects.

The next day, the Court of Inquiry team visited the close-by ammunition dumps to check if there were any deficiencies in the holding of explosives. Here, too, everything was found to be in order. Similar checks were conducted in the ammunition dumps of a few field companies and everything there too was found to be in order.

While these checks were on, questioning of all personnel who used to enter the office complex every day – the sweepers who used to clean the office every morning, the cane orderlies and the clerical staff – continued to ascertain whether they had observed anything out of the ordinary. When this drew a blank, the names of those who were close to my hometown was drawn up as well as those I had punished for any reason or anyone who had any possible grudge against me. The Regiment was flooded with a large number of 'Sherlock Holmes' and each one had his theory on the occurrence of the blast. We were shaken by the round-the-clock questioning for three days. On the day of the incident, I had given orders for the morning PT and Mandir-cum-Gurudwara parade in the evening every day to continue. Both of these activities kept everyone fully occupied.

After two days, a telephone call from the FE, Capt Swaminathan, was received after he came to know about what had occurred in the Regiment. He informed that he had kept some Pakistani mines in the drawer of his office table. He was ordered to return to the Regiment forthwith. When he arrived and saw what had taken place and what we were going through, he immediately met the Presiding Officer and told him that he had drawn the Pakistani mines for a training-cum-demonstration planned in the annual training programme. After the demonstration, as he had to go for the squash tournament, due to the shortage of time, he kept the mines in the drawer of his office table rather than return them to the ammunition dump.

A check confirmed that two Pakistani anti-personnel mines and four anti-tank mines drawn by him were not there. He explained to the Presiding Officer that the Pakistani anti-personnel mines have an inbuilt fuse. In other words, the mine would blast in case any load was put on it. Further, by the blast of the anti-personnel mines, the anti-tank mines lying close to them would also have exploded due to sympathetic detonation. Once the actual reason for the blast, and how and why it took place, was verified there was a huge sigh of relief and normal life resumed.

Needless to add, the due process of law followed – completion of Court of Inquiry proceedings, recording of Summary of Evidence and finally the court-martial of Capt Swaminathan. The court decided that, as the culpable officer had spoken the truth, he was to be awarded two years loss of seniority only. He later rose to the rank of Brigadier.

I need to mention that my *sahayak* was from Bihar and on the day the blast occurred, without telling me, he took the invitation card from the Unit Gurudwara, having the photograph of Guru Nanak printed on it (which was lying on my study table) and framed it himself and hung it on the wall. I recall asking him why he had done it. He replied, "*Sahib*, since you have His blessings, no harm can ever come to you". I never can forget this wonderful gesture of his and the framed picture has travelled with me everywhere; rather I still have it with me.

The above incident taught me the following:

Wherever human beings are involved something can always go wrong.

When accidents or unfortunate incidents occur, one should never panic. Rather, one should take charge and become the leader you are expected to be.

To keep rumours/wrong perceptions at bay, remain truthful and brief your men from time to time on the actual situation.

Always remember that, in the end, the truth will prevail. Lies can only lead to many more lies. Never forget that the regiment and the men you command come first – always and every time.

Close and continuous liaison with the civilian and police authorities are essential as they provide immense assistance, in case you have been decorous with them. They are more mature and experienced in handling such situations than us in uniform.

Capt Mohan Swaminathan, by speaking the truth, won over the Presiding Officer, the Members of the Court Martial and thus got the least feasible punishment for his dereliction.

You cannot control everything that happens. You can only control the way to respond to what occurs. In your response, is your power.

Postings in the Army should always to be accepted in the right spirit.

The *sahayak,* in those days, looked after an officer with total sincerity and dedication (a quality which is only there in Indian troops). Concomitantly the *sahayak,* in his own way, ensured that the officer was able to devote more than the best to the unit and the men.

In August 1973, my posting orders were received for 53 Engineer Regiment, which was deployed in Sikkim on the Gangtok-Nathu La road. My CO, Lt Col Bhagwant Singh, had been extremely happy with my work and wanted me to stay on. When pressure from the higher HQ to move me forthwith came, he was constrained to send me on posting. The SM and the men of 54 Engineer Regiment, with whom I had developed a good rapport, gave me a grand send-off with a *'Vidai Man Patar'* (which is only given to the CO of the Regiment). I spent only 19 months in this regiment.

Retrospect

The officers who made an impression on me during this tenure were Col Bhagwant Singh, my CO, who had full faith in me and taught me to independently take all decisions on behalf of the Regiment; Maj Kuldip Bhanot (retired as a Col), for his mature and well-considered advice; Major Nathan (retired as a Col) for inculcating the habit of reading in me; Maj AD Nargolwala (retired as a Maj Gen) for his well-mannered, cultured and disciplined approach to life; Maj Harinder Singh (retired as a Col) for his frank and friendly advice; and Capt Mohan Swaminathan, (retired as a Brig), my coursemate, for his moral integrity.

RELEARNING THE BASICS

53 Engr Regt (Aug 73 — Nov 75)

On my posting to 53 Engineer Regiment, I moved, on 10 August 1973, in two jeeps (one each from 54 and 53 Engineer Regiment). The move was a short one from Kalimpong to Mile 13 on the Gangtok-Nathu La road. Throughout the trip, I was wondering what was in store for me in the Regiment which I had joined on being commissioned.

The next day, I reported to the CO, Lt Col SS Randhawa, in his office and he welcomed me back to the Regiment. I can never forget his first talk with me. He said, "I do not know you, but your spoken reputation is good. I have had to fight to get you back to the 53 Engineer Regiment. From today, you will be my Adjutant and you will have my total support in all the decisions you take on my behalf. However, remember that the decisions you take should only be in the interest of the Regiment and not for any individual's benefit. I sometimes lose my temper, but I would like you to remain cool under all circumstances." His words were terse and crystal clear. I could see that I was in for a lot of hard work as I had to live up to his expectations and my reputation.

Fortunately, I knew the SM, Gupteshwar Singh, who was a Naib Subedar in my earlier stint in the Regiment. He was an outstanding and smart JCO and we had a long talk. I learnt that the Regiment was due to move to Amritsar in a month and several tasks had to be completed before the move, which was less than a month away. I got down ensuring a smooth handing/taking over and a safe and comfortable movement of the Regiment by train to Amritsar.

Amritsar

After moving to Amritsar, the Regiment quickly settled down under HQ 15 Infantry Division. Lt Col SS Randhawa, my CO told me that he would be spending most of the time visiting other formations and the operational area. The entire office and day-to-day work thus fell on my shoulders. He wanted me to tackle all issues without disturbing him and he would reply only to letters on operational matters, from the GS Branch. He also added that he would not like to see any reminders, under any circumstances.

With the onus of office work on me, I learnt the importance of time management, and the methodology of replying to important letters, after due thought and care. From the CO I learnt that all letters should be written with brevity, yet their contents should convince the reader of your point of view.

To ensure that there were no reminders I had to come prepared to the office (after doing a lot of homework) every day. It essentially meant listing out the points on which action had to be taken, in detail. The points were split into categories – points on which letters had to be initiated, and the list of letters that had to be replied to. Most times I carried such letters home so that a draft reply could be prepared without any distractions. A list of points which had to be conveyed through telephone or personally or through meetings was also prepared. Finally, the points on which progress had to be obtained were listed out. Initially, this task took up to an hour every day. However, having done my homework, I could enter my office confidently and prioritize the schedule to complete the day's work easily and with surety. The training which I got on office work under the CO stood me in good stead as I climbed the ladder of higher ranks.

Life in a peace station is different from that in a field area. At Amritsar, routine assignments, errands and favours kept me on my toes. As a rule, I never said no to any task unless there were genuine reasons for saying so. It was optimal to do them in the best possible manner as they were in the interest of the Regiment. Probably, for this reason, no one has ever said no to me for anything throughout my life. The small things reflect a positive attitude and one gets paid back with gratitude.

At Amritsar, there was always a shortage of manpower. Sportsmen had to practice and family men had to be given time for their domestic needs. Also, operational works had to be done on priority. Liaison/errands are specialised tasks that can be done by those with special traits. One Sunday, I had a meeting with the SM and the company Subedars and selected two individuals each, at JCO and OR level, for tasks like a liaison with the civil administration, arranging cinema tickets, coordination with the police, MES, railways, visit Sri Darbar Sahib and other tourist places etc. They had to possess some prior relationship with the concerned authorities and had to be extremely good in their association management. I briefed them on their responsibilities and stressed that they should ensure that the work allotted to them was done under all circumstances. The best man was given the task where he had the expertise and there were no comebacks; success was guaranteed. These unsung soldiers were a major force multiplier for the Regiment.

A Fiasco Over a Deserter

A soldier who does not return to his unit after his stipulated period of leave is normally punished for over-staying his leave. When the period of absence is over 30 days, he is declared a deserter and his unit writes a letter to the police authorities of his area to apprehend him. Once apprehended, the police hand over the delinquent soldier to a nearby military unit, for custody in the quarter guard, till an escort party from his parent unit comes and takes him back to face trial for dispensation of justice.

In 1975, the complete Regiment had to move out on an Exercise with troops. The RHQ also moved to the operational area. One night I got a call from the OIC Rear Party, at about 2000 hours, that a deserter who had been brought in by the police, had escaped from our unit quarter guard. Immediately, I rushed in a jeep to Amritsar to meet the

Superintendent of Police (SP), whom I knew. The SP lived in a palatial house and there was a party on when I reached there. As I was in uniform and I did not want to disturb him at the party, I was escorted to a guest room. I requested his *munshi* to convey to the SP that I wanted to meet him urgently. When the SP came, I apologised for disturbing him and told him about a deserter escaping from our unit quarter guard and I desperately wanted to get him back into our custody. He smiled and said, "For this small thing there was no necessity to come to me. The *munshi* would have easily done the work."

He also invited me to join the party. I thanked him but refused, as my mind was still on apprehending the escaped deserter. The SP directed his *munshi* to pass on his message to the concerned SHO.

As I had not informed my CO about the incident, I was very anxious. I decided to go to the SHO's office to ensure that he implements the SP's orders. I reached the SHO's office at about 2330 hours and he confirmed that the SP's orders would be implemented 100 percent before 0500 hours and I should stop worrying and go back to my regiment. However, as I knew I would not be able to sleep till the deserter is back in the prison cell of the quarter guard, I decided to stay on. At 0030 hours, an ASI with a police party moved in a jeep to the deserters' village and stopped in front of a house and knocked on the door. An old man came out and, seeing the police, he started trembling. His younger son then turned up to check what the commotion was about. The ASI asked where his elder brother was. He replied that he did not know. The police, in a stern tone, told him to call his brother's wife. After some time, a young girl turned up and the ASI ordered a constable to open the young girl's drawstring with which she had her *salwar* tied. I was shocked and scared that I would get involved in a rape case. I ran to my jeep and told the driver to drive back to the Officers Mess.

On reaching the Officers Mess I told my *sahayak* to wake me up at 0500 hours. I had just about changed and got into bed when there was a knock on the door and the *sahayak* told me that the police ASI wanted to meet me. I opened the door reluctantly. The ASI saluted and told me that the deserter had been put in the quarter guard. I was bewildered by this swift action. I thanked the ASI and he left. I then told the sahayak to wake me up at 0600 hours and went off to sleep.

I was again woken up by a knock at the door at about 0330 hours. My *sahayak* said that the ASI wanted to meet me again. I wondered what had taken place in less than two hours. The ASI saluted and apologised for waking me up again but the quarter guard commander was not accepting the actual deserter. The person he had brought in earlier was the deserter's younger brother. I was perplexed as to what was going on and asked them to wait till I changed into uniform.

We went to the quarter guard and asked the man in the prisoner cell whether he was the deserter. He replied in the affirmative. The ASI then pushed his elder brother forward and said, "Now tell me who is the deserter?"

His reply was, *"Janab, jainu tusi kahon, vohi bhagora ban jauga."*(Sir, whoever you say will become the deserter).

Then the ASI told me that, as I had run away when they were scaring the deserter's wife, they got worried that I may go and report the case to the SP; they decided to take the deserter's brother in place of the actual deserter and put him into the quarter guard till the actual deserter was caught. Accordingly, they followed me in their jeep and delivered the deserter's brother to the quarter guard. The ASI explained that the actual deserter had spent less than a week with his wife, after his marriage, so he did not return to his unit after his leave and became a deserter. He was at home with his wife but, when he heard the police inquiring about him, he ran out from the rear door and hid in a sugar cane field. Subsequently, on hearing that the police were going to undress his wife he gave himself up. The ASI added that this would not have occurred, had I not panicked. I felt sheepish and had no answer. Despite tackling the blast incident in Kalimpong well, I had panicked. In hindsight, my anxiety ensured the police getting the deserter back expeditiously. The police have their methodology to solve cases and we, in the military, are greenhorns in this respect.

An interesting sidelight of the Amritsar tenure was that our regiment was also involved in the repatriation of Pakistani prisoners of war, at the Wagah border. The regiment excelled in all facets of soldiering. We won all sports tournament in the division and the inter-unit competitions in our Group tournaments too. On the operational side, we executed a large number of operational works and also developed numerous improvised aids for the crossing of tanks through boggy ground. The 'Sukhi Boat', named after our CO, was a major innovation for assault crossings, which drew appreciation from the Army Commander, Lt Gen IS Gill. The regiment was also involved in arranging the Investiture Parade for Western Command, which was highly appreciated.

Retrospect

The tenure at Amritsar taught me the following:

For a staff officer to be ahead in office work there is no alternative to putting in additional work at home. Only then can you ensure that what you want to achieve in the office on that particular day is done.

Drafting a letter is a technique that has to be mastered by practice. The earlier you master it, the less is your workload.

Every individual has some strong and weak points. As a commander, you have to exploit the strong points of each individual and cover their weak points.

As a rule, one should never say no to any request/task assigned. I am of the firm belief that before a senior officer assigns any task to you/unit, he has gone over it in his mind and only then given the task. You should take it up smilingly, without cribbing, For doing various errands in peace environment, one has to carefully select the best person for the same. It is then alone you have the surety it will always be executed.

Wherever we are posted, the need to develop excellent rapport with the police authorities and all other authorities is essential.

> An officer has to learn the art of multi-tasking and time management. Regretfully, acquiring these traits is not everyone's cup of tea. However, they can be mastered with practice.

After spending two years plus at Amritsar and when everything was finely tuned and the regiment had fully established itself in all spheres, my posting orders were received, in December 1975, as Instructor Class C at the CME. A week later, my CO's posting orders were also received for the CME. Ten days later, a company commander of the regiment, Maj DS Bajwa, was also posted to CME. All of us were posted to F Combat Wing. Maj DS Bajwa and I decided to leave on the posting, a day after the CO, Lt Col SS Randhawa, was dined out and the new CO, Lt Col SC Thareja, had taken over command.

My CO, Lt Col SS Randhawa, (who superannuated as a Maj Gen) advised me to perform my duties fearlessly, to the best of my ability and with integrity. During my tenure in the Regiment, I served under three 2IC's – Maj D Ajwani (rose to be a Lt Gen and retired as QMG), Maj SK Sondhi (retired as a Brig) and Maj AB Alekar (retired as a Col) – who, in their respective ways, guided me. Capt RB Inamdar (retired as a Brig) and Capt SN Mukherjee (retired as a Maj Gen) served as FE and IO in the RHQ. We functioned as a well-knit team. Incidentally, both these officers went on to command the regiment. We remain in touch with each other.

TEACHING IS A NOBLE PROFESSION

F Combat CME (Dec 75 — Nov 78)

Within a week of reporting to the CME, in December 1975, an interview was scheduled with the Commandant, Maj Gen PR Puri (who later superannuated as the E-in-C). For the interview, we three officers from the same regiment went in turn, according to our seniority. My turn came last. The Commandant welcomed me warmly, asked me to sit down and then enquired where I was coming from.

I replied, "Sir, 53 Engineer Regiment located at Amritsar."

The Commandant merely nodded and then my words sunk in. He said, "Are you telling me you are from Col Randhawa's Regiment as well as the Major I just interviewed before you?"

I said, "Yes, Sir."

The Commandant then reacted, "How the hell has the CO managed to get his company commander and his adjutant with him?"

I sheepishly said, "Sir, my posting orders were received first, thereafter the CO's and finally the company commander's; however, we left together after the CO's dining out."

I (having done the Advance Bridging Course with an Instructor's grading) was posted in the YAB Wing under Lt Col SS Randhawa, who was posted as the CI. The Commander of F Combat was Col PS Roy (under whom I had worked as a subaltern at Jalandhar).

Experiences in F Combat

One day, I was taking a class on 'improvised means for the crossing of water bodies' for the all-arms course for officers. I initially explained what was meant by the term 'buoyancy' and then went on to explain the methodology of calculating buoyancy, for which the symbol π was used in the formula. While solving an equation I put the value of π as 22/7. While solving another equation, I put the value of π as 3.14. Immediately an NDA coursemate from the infantry, who was a student in the class, raised his hand and enquired, "Please clarify what is the value of π; is it 22/7 or 3.14?" For a moment I thought I had made a mistake, and requested him to repeat the question. He repeated it more confidently. I did not know whether to laugh or tell him that 22/7 is the same as 3.14. I decided not to confuse the class and told them that the value of π is 22/7. I observed a smile on the face of my coursemate. It surprised me that no one in the class said 22/7 is equal to 3.14.

Bringing up students falling in the below 50% category requires special effort. For them, I took afternoon classes twice a week. I also took the help of the bright students who willingly came for the afternoon sessions. I observed that they were able to put across the subjects in a much better manner than I could, as they knew the weak students' capabilities better. Peer learning is an important part of any course. The weak students always acknowledged the extra effort I put in for them. I realised this later when I met some of them who had risen to higher ranks and they shared reminiscences with me. Truthfully speaking, I recognised only a few of them. As far as I was concerned, I only performed my duty and am grateful that it paid great dividends.

The important lessons which I learnt, as an instructor, are:

> In any class, there are only a few bright students. The mode of instruction must be in keeping with the knowledge and understanding of the larger majority.

Classroom training, to be made interesting, requires an out-of-the-box methodology. This was something the students also look forward too. More, about this later.

A teacher who loves teaching earns the right and the ability to help others to learn.

Nothing will change in your life if you don't do things differently.

Liaison Officer to Lt Gen JS Dhillon

About five months into my tenure at CME, I was at HBTC, Marve, at Mumbai for training the CIJ course on tidal water bridging, when I was told by my SI that I should go back to Pune and report to HQ CME at 0900 hours, the next day. He had not been informed about the reason for my being called back. The next day, I reported to the Col GS, who took me to the Deputy Commandant, then Brig HK Kapoor (who later rose to be Maj Gen). I was told that he had selected me to perform the duties of LO to Lt Gen JS Dhillon (Retd) who was visiting CME, after four days. He enquired whether I knew the General Officer or had met him earlier. I replied in the negative and said that I only know that he is a Bengal Sapper with a very tough reputation. The Deputy Commandant mentioned that it was for this reason that he had selected me for this prestigious duty and I must, in the next three days, tie up all loose ends. He gave me permission to incur any essential petty expenditure; however, I was to make sure Lt Gen JS Dhillon leaves CME happy. I said I would do my best. The Col GS warned me to check everything personally otherwise I would be in for a high jump. He also gave me a detailed programme for the visit.

Lt Gen JS Dhillon was spending the maximum time of his stay in his room in the Mini Guest House. I went and checked it and, at a first glance, everything looked good. In the evening, I told my wife the reason I had been called back from Marve. She inquired about the duties of a LO.

I said that I have to make sure that the General Officer is comfortable and escort him to all the places he is scheduled to visit. She then asked if I had seen the guest room where he was to stay. I said that everything seemed to be in order. She commented that it is not possible to check a guest room without actually staying or sleeping one night in that room. I thought about it and she was right, as we had a bad experience in CME itself when we moved into temporary quarters allotted to us and there was no running water available.

I decided to spend the night in the Mini Guest House and went there at 2100 hours on my scooter. The guard recognised me from my morning visit and opened the guest room. I got into the comfortable bed with the air-conditioner on and quickly fell into a deep slumber. At about 0330 hours, I was woken up by a loud noise, which appeared to be coming from the roof. On checking, the sound came from the water flowing into the overhead tank at high pressure. Later, when I bathed in the bathroom, I observed that the wastewater was not flowing fluently into the drain and there was some choking problem.

At 0900 hours, I went to meet the AGE (E/M) regarding the problems I had observed in the Mini Guest House. I requested him to look into the problem of wastewater getting blocked in the bathroom; a plumber to ensure that water flows into the overhead tank without making noise; an electrician to check all electrical points; and a skilled technician for the air-conditioners.

The AGE (E/M) was very kind and he detailed the best technicians to look into the problems. When the team arrived, at about 1100 hours, at the Mini Guest House I arranged a hot cup of tea with biscuits for them. Thereafter, I explained the faults that I had observed. Since they were experts in their respective fields, they got into action immediately and did a professional work. The AC mechanic cleaned the filter and put in a flex board to ensure there would be no vibrations; the cooling in the room improved dramatically. The electrician checked and rechecked all the points and changed a few condensers and other items and confirmed that nothing would now go wrong. The cleaner cleaned up the choked pipe and the water flowed out smoothly. The plumber, however, could not comprehend the problem. After a lot of explanation, when he understood the cause of the noise, he asked me to get two metres of white cloth with which he made two bags and tied them to the inlet of the main pipe. He put some sponge inside the inner bag and said that this would now work and there would be no/little noise when the water gushes in at high pressure in the early morning. I was not fully satisfied that his improvisation would function. I requested him to stay the night with the guard and food would be provided to him and we would check whether the noise continued in the morning or not.

At night, I once again slept in the Guest Room and was fast asleep when I was woken by the doorbell ringing at 0330 hours. The plumber was waiting outside and asked me to check whether there was any noise when the water gushed into the overhead tank. The improvisation worked beautifully. I returned to my house at 0500 hours without having a bath as I was totally satisfied that everything in the Mini Guest House was now functioning well. During the day, I tied up arrangements at the places Lt Gen JS Dhillon was to visit inside and outside the CME.

I received Lt Gen JS Dhillon at Pune railway station and we walked to the car waiting outside. The MP, whom I had brought along, opened the car door for the General Officer and I got into the front seat. When the driver turned on the ignition nothing happened. Embarrassed, I jumped out of my seat and told the driver to open the car bonnet. I thumped the battery; spark plugs and the ignition and then told the driver to start the car. The engine immediately revved. I closed the bonnet and returned to my seat. This took less than a minute, but it appeared to be a very long minute. Lt Gen JS Dhillon was silent till we were on the main highway towards the CME. He then asked me what the orders are, in case a General Officer's car develops a defect. I kept quiet. He then mentioned that, when he was the Central Army Commander, his car developed a problem only once. He had then directed his Chief of Staff that all personnel who were responsible for his car's maintenance should be brought down by one rank. Thereafter, his car never ever had a fault. I apologised and said it would never happen again. He smiled and asked me what I had done to set the car right.

I replied, "Sir, since the ignition did not make any noise it was obvious that there is a gap in the electrical connection. Accordingly, I just gave a thump at the appropriate place."

He then enquired how I had this knowledge.

I replied, "Sir, I am D&M and Earth Moving Plant qualified."(I did these courses back-to-back in 53 Engineer Regiment as a 2 Lt, when I was attached to the Corps HQ).

He laughed and said, "Son, you better make sure that there are never any loose connections in my car in future."

The Deputy Commandant was present at the Mini Guest House to receive Lt Gen JS Dhillon. After exchanging pleasantries, the Deputy Commandant left but Lt Gen JS Dhillon asked me to stay on. I was waiting for another rebuke but, to my pleasant surprise, he asked me to tell him all about myself in a couple of sentences. He was happy to know that I had served at Jalandhar, where he was the Corps Commander during the 1965 war. After a cup of coffee, I left with instructions to come the next morning at 0600 hours for a walk with him. I accompanied him every day for an hour's walk in the mornings and the evenings on each day of his visit. During these leisurely walks, he told me the history of the Bengal Sappers from 1947 onward, when he was the Commandant of the Bengal Sappers Centre at Roorkee; how he commanded the first Republic Day Parade; and his role in the 1965 war in Punjab. He spoke in great detail and was never annoyed when I asked him what may have appeared to him to be stupid questions. He also talked about physical and moral courage; the need to take difficult decisions in the nation's interest, for which a cost had to be paid; the importance of knowing the terrain on your side as well as the enemy area; how to convert a losing proposition into a successful mission and other issues which had me spellbound.

His three-day visit passed off quickly. When I saw him off at the Pune railway station, I had a lump in my throat as he had made a distinct impression on me. His final words were, "Always perform the duties assigned with sincerity and dedication till it becomes second nature and God will help you to do well."

I also received a pat on my back. For the first time, the Commandant CME received a laudatory letter from Lt Gen JS Dhillon in which he had thanked him for the courtesies extended and the magnificent work done by his LO.

It is to my eternal regret that I could not keep in touch with Lt Gen JS Dhillon, till I was appointed the Colonel Commandant of the Bengal Sappers, many years later, and went to call on him with my wife. He was very old at the time and, though they had their beds in their drawing-room, his wife and he were formally dressed to receive us. He recalled his visit to CME when I was his LO. I apologised for not keeping in touch with him as the exigencies of service kept me too busy. At his advanced age too, he gave me sane advice and told me to take it easy and not emulate him for being too strict with his command. I was very fortunate and blessed to get an opportunity, at a young age and service, to interact with him informally. The interaction left an indelible mark on me. His life is a fit case for study by junior officers.

After this duty as LO, I was detailed for similar duties for a number of dignitaries visiting CME. Each was an experience in itself. The following lessons were learnt by me as LO:

> Flaws in any guest room can only be gauged by staying in the guest room for at least one night. I always did this in my future assignments too and it paid huge dividends.
>
> The need to go into minute details needs no elaboration. In the rush of work, this is missed out.
>
> Interaction with senior and foreign dignitaries not only enhances knowledge but also makes one a better person.

Training Team

I had done less than one year as Instructor Class C and had picked up the nuances for teaching when the Commander F Combat, Col PS Roy, got a new Wing sanctioned as Training Team. Its role was to conduct trials of all combat engineering equipment (both inside and outside CME); liaise with units for modifications being made on the equipment, and to keep a record of all improvisations made. The Training Team also had to publish a quarterly journal regarding new developments in combat engineering for which we had to read a large number of Indian and foreign professional journals. I was nominated as the first OIC Training Team. This assignment was in addition to my duties in YAB Wing. Incidentally, in July 1977, I was promoted to a Major.

The Training Team also had to conduct 'Rapid Reading Courses' for all newly-posted officers to CME and officers from Southern Command. I was made responsible for this course. I had attended one such course earlier and found it interesting and engrossing. With three months available, I went over the instructional material a number of times and modified it to my way of teaching and also gained further knowledge on the subject. I also worked to improve my own reading speed and achieved a reasonable standard. When the course was to start, I was confident about the subject.

The course was of two weeks duration and conducted for one and a half hours, in the afternoons, for three sessions each week. To my utter surprise, I was told two days before the course was to commence that the Army Commander, Lt Gen AM Vohra, would also be attending the course. The Commandant CME, Maj Gen PR Puri, received him. Commander F Combat welcomed the course and then handed it over to me for conducting it thereafter. I gave an excellent introduction to the subject and by the time I finished it, I knew I had the interest of all the students.

After the tea break, I played a psychological game with the students. I repeated a number of times that the average reading rate of an educated Indian was between 300 to 350 words a minute. I then placed an article, which had 521 words, in front of each of them along with a stopwatch. I asked them to determine their own rate of reading by reading the article silently and noting down the time taken to read it, in minutes. Then, they were to divide 521 with the time taken in minutes, to determine their speed of reading which would be anywhere between 300 to 350 words. Everyone did the exercise and wrote their rate of reading on the article boldly, as I had requested. As expected, everyone mentioned their speed of reading was between 301 to 340 words per minute.

I then said that I was sorry and that I would not be able to conduct the class any further as they had all fibbed in calculating their speed of reading. The moment I said this, the Commandant gave me a stare and I realised that the Army Commander was also present in the class. I quickly added, "Except the Army Commander who had calculated it correctly."

Thereafter, I told the class that I, too, had misled them in repeatedly telling them that the average rate of reading of an educated Indian was between 300 to 350 words whereas it was actually between 175 to 250 words per minute. I added that I had done this after taking prior permission from the Army Commander in the tea break. I then asked the entire class to read another article and they should truthfully calculate their rate of reading. After the class had done so, I told them not to inform anyone, including me of their rate of reading. I assured them that, by the end of the course, their rate of reading would be anywhere from 1.5 to 2 times more than their present rate. Thereafter, the course went off smoothly and everyone was able to enhance his rate of reading.

In the Training Team I learnt that:

Rate of reading plays a very vital role in life, in general. In official work too, once destiny took me to appointments where I had to do a lot of reading, I exploited it to the hilt. Mastery in this subject enabled me to finish my office work in the shortest feasible time frame.

The opportunity to take classes of senior officers taught me that a subject has to put across to them in a totally different template. Needless to add, one has to be totally prepared to take tricky questions and answers have to be politely worded, yet firmly put across.

The learning of rapid reading or correct reading also taught me to conduct classes in a way to make it easier for the students to comprehend. More, on this later.

Rowing

In the first year of my instructional tenure at CME, I could not get any time to look after rowing per se, but I did find time to row. In the Inter-Course Officer's competition, the staff team also participated. With me as the main rower, the staff team easily won all the events, as none of the student officers had put in the effort required to learn from the coach. The Commandant, Maj Gen PR Puri, who had been a keen rower during his younger days, called me to his office and directed me to go all out to form the Rowing Federation of India (RFI). He also wanted me to select and thereafter train suitable officers attending the EODE courses to participate in the nationals as and when they are held. With a clear directive, I went upon this assignment with enthusiasm.

To form the RFI, I did a detailed study to prepare a draft memorandum. It was approved by the Commandant and then sent to the Lake Club, Calcutta, and the Madras Rowing Club, at Chennai. We, at Pune, formed the Maharashtra Rowing Association (MRA) with two member clubs – Pune Engineering College Rowing Club and CME Rowing Club. The Corps of Engineers Rowing Association (CERA) was also a full-fledged member of the RFI. Simultaneously, the Lake Club, Calcutta formed the West Bengal Rowing Association (WBRA) and the Madras Rowing Club, Madras, formed the Tamil Nadu Rowing Association (TARA). Thus, the RFI was born in 1977 with its founder members being WBRA, TARA, MRA and CERA.

For selecting and training students from the EODE courses, I went around all the classrooms and selected physically fit and sports-loving students and requested them to report to the Rowing Club. They came, but I knew that unless I make them bite the rowing bug they would go back to their original sport. For this, I had to befriend all of them. When I got their classes excused from the Commandant up to 1000 hours, everyone put their heart and soul into the sport. For experience, I took them to participate in the First Nationals at Calcutta one of the student's officers fell sick and I had to row in his place. We did well, compared to previous years, but did not win any medals. I must mention that this participation was only after three months of training which was very less.

I, was, however confident that, the next year, the same team would win the gold and silver medals.

After the First Nationals, I requested the Commandant to permit me to bid for the Second Nationals to be conducted at CME, to which he very kindly consented. We then went all out, not only to train hard but also to improve the infrastructure for conducting the event. The Second Nationals was a resounding success and the EODE officers participating, both from the CERA and the MRA, won the gold and silver medals. The rowers from WBRA and TARA were totally shaken as they never anticipated that CME would make such an improvement. It was possible by sheer hard work. Before the races began, I had the President of Rowing Association promise that in case CERA and MRA beat WBRA and TARA teams, the post of Vice President would be given to the Commandant CME, Maj Gen PR Puri. I made sure he was unanimously elected.

The results in rowing were achieved after putting in an extreme effort. In my last year in CME, there was a change in F Combat. Col PS Roy handed over to Col MPS Kandal who had his own priorities. Being a tough taskmaster, he accepted no mistakes in any task. I was working in YAB Wing and was also OC of the Training Team. Rowing, too, took a lot of time as, in addition to coaching officers in the morning and evening, I had to organise the conduct of the Second Nationals for which I had to interact with the Commandant and Deputy Commandant often. I practised multi-tasking and time management which paid me good dividends later in life. The year thus passed on a trot.

The following lessons were learnt by me in rowing at the CME:

> All goals are achievable provided you put your heart and soul into them.
>
> Whatever the mind can conceive and believe, it can achieve. Keep believing and your vision will carry you through.
>
> There is no shortcut to consistent hard work in case anyone wants to excel in any sport.

Good sportsmen make good officers. All the officers whom I selected and trained in rowing did very well in their career. Most of them became General Officers. Some of them are Lt Gen Vishambhar Singh, Lt Gen Vijai Sharma, Lt Gen AT Parnaik, Maj Gen VK Bhatt, Maj Gen AK Chaturvedi, and Maj Gen Prakash Panjikar. Maj Gen MA Naik, Col Praveen Oberoi and Col Bhanwala won laurels in this sport and were Arjuna awardees. All of them have remained true friends throughout my service and after my retirment too.

Civilians have their own personal interest and these days all sports bodies have lots of funds. The army way of thinking does not gel with the civilians. One has to tackle them with tact and maturity. Since I always behaved correctly with them, they too gave me due respect. When I took over as Commandant CME, in 2004, I was appointed as the Executive Vice President of RFI and I held this post till my superannuation.

INTEGRITY ALWAYS GETS REWARDED

MS Branch Army HQ (Dec 78 — Sep 80)

Three months after the successful conduct of the Second Nationals, by the CME, I had to take the rowing team to Sri Lanka to participate in the Amateur Rowing Association of the East (ARAE), in December 1978. Prior to the trip, my posting orders were received as OC of the Engineer Plant Unit, at Jalandhar. My wife was extremely happy as her elder sister was married to an Army officer commanding his Artillery regiment there. I too was happy as I was going to command an independent unit. The date of reporting also suited us, as it was a week after the trip to Sri Lanka.

Our joy vanished soon. Three days later, the posting order was cancelled and I was directed to move to Delhi for an attachment with the MS (Military Secretary's) Branch at Army HQ. I was to move before the trip to Sri Lanka. Till then, I did not know what MS Branch was, as postings up to Captain rank, in the Corps of Engineers, were handled by the Centre Commandant those days.

I met the Commandant, CME and requested him to get my attachment cancelled as I would not be able to take the rowing team to Sri Lanka. The Commandant advised that it is a very prestigious assignment and I should move to Delhi and forget the independent field company (where he would get me posted, after the MS Branch assignment, in case I still wanted it). As regards going to Sri Lanka, with the rowing team, he said he would get the move to Delhi delayed by 10 days. This was done and I got an opportunity to visit a foreign country at a very young age.

Thereafter, I moved to Delhi and reported to the MS Branch. It was the first time that I entered the South Block and was lost on the first day. A new Section had been raised for boarding out low medical category (LMC) officers, on compulsory discharge, in consonance with a decision taken by the previous COAS, Gen TN Raina. The other officers in this newly-raised Section were a Lt Col (as AMS) and two Majors from the infantry (as DAMS). Just as we began functioning and had sent one Armoured Corps officer on compulsory discharge, the new COAS, Gen OP Malhotra, cancelled the Army Order. We thus became surplus to the MS Branch and, before 89 days of attachment were over, the Lt Col and the two Majors were posted out to the QMG, SD and WE Branch respectively. In my case, I was sent back to CME for three days with instructions to report back to the MS Branch again. The reason was not told to me.

On return to Delhi for the second attachment, being a surplus officer, I was moved around to more or less all Sections of the MS Branch to officiate in place of any DAMS who went on leave. One day, while functioning as DAMS 2, I got a chit from the SO to the MS to examine a case for posting an officer to Jaipur. However, no application of the officer was attached to the chit. Based on the officers' profile, I examined the case and prepared a noting sheet for the AMS. Just as I had completed it, I got a call from the SO to the MS asking whether I had examined the case. I replied in the affirmative. He then told me to take the case file to the MS, Maj Gen Kundan Singh and put the phone down. I rushed with the case file to the SO and found that he was not in his office. My intention was to inform him that the AMS had not vetted the case, as he was on leave. As I came out of the SO's office, the cane orderly of the MS said *"Sahib, aap andar ja sakte ho"* (Sir, you can enter).

I entered the office of the MS, Maj Gen Kundan Singh, for the first time. He was busy poring over some letters and, without looking up, pointed at the chair and asked me to sit down. After finishing his work, he said "Yes, what is it?"

I told him, "Sir, I am officiating as DAMS 2B and I was told by your

SO to show you the file regarding an officer's request for posting to Jaipur."

He took the case file from me and after glancing through it enquired, "Where is the slip from the Defence Minister?"

I replied that I had not received it from the SO. He then asked me the basis on which I examined the case. I said that it has been vetted based on the officer's profile only. He seemed annoyed and asked me a number of questions on the officer's profile. I could give correct answers as I had gone over the officer's dossier minutely. When he received appropriate replies, he asked me, "Since when are you in MS Branch?"

I replied, "Sir, I am on attachment and today is the first day I sat in the DAMS 2B office as he and the AMS are on leave."

"No wonder I did not recognise you," he responded and his tone of voice changed.

He directed me to get hold of the slip sent by the Defence Minister, addressed to him, and then re-examine the case and bring it to him the next morning. The next day, I took the file to him, at the appropriate time. He went over it and said, "Good work! Thank you!"

A fortnight later, my 89 days of second attachment were coming to an end. I was sent back to CME and told that I would get my posting orders soon. For the next three days, I was tense as I did not know where they would post me; though I was quite sure it would not be in the MS Branch, which already had its authorized strength of Corps of Engineers officers. Also, none of the officers in the new Section had been attached to earlier, had been retained in the MS Branch. On the fourth day, in June 1979, I was pleasantly surprised to see that I was posted to MS Branch as DAMS 3C. After my dining out from F Combat, I reported back to Delhi.

At the MS Branch, once a month, a tea was arranged for all officers posted in or moving out on posting. It was attended by all officers and those posted in or out were introduced to the MS. I was standing quietly in a corner during the tea, as all the officers present were senior to me. Just then Lt Col V Raghavan, the AMS1, loudly said to the MS, "Sir, will you believe me when I tell you that we have an officer amongst us, who did not want to be posted to the MS Branch?"

The MS said that he cannot believe it. Lt Col Raghavan then called out my name and directed me to step forward. I never felt so embarrassed in my life. After the tea, I got an opportunity to shake hands with the MS who said, "I sincerely hope that by the time you leave, you change your impression about this Branch."

I came to know later how I was posted to the MS Branch. From the DAMS upwards, everyone had recommended that the E-in-C's Branch be directed to absorb me in their office as the quota of Corps of Engineers Officers was already full in the MS Branch. Also, the QR for the appointment of DAMS 3C, which was falling vacant, was tenable by an infantry officer. However, the MS had ruled on the noting sheet, "No, absorb this officer as DAMS 3C."

I wondered why this was done as he did not know me. I had only met him once during my attachment period. Maybe, he was impressed by the manner I could answer all his rapid-fire questions or perhaps Lt Col V Raghavan ensured that I was posted to MS Branch as he had learnt that I was not keen to be posted there.

DAMS 3C dealt with the postings of officers to the NCC; ADCs to the President of India downwards; postings to RAW; and postings of officers requested for deputation by the PSUs. It was a challenging assignment.

NCC appointments were in cities and towns all over India and these were not being filled up. When I took over, 46% of the appointments were vacant. To tackle this issue, I first went over to the Surveyor General's office and obtained maps of all the States of India. With the help of these maps, I ensured that I posted officers close to their home station and not to their actual home stations. By this strategy, we were able to fill a large number of posts lying vacant for a long time. (For posting of an officer to an NCC unit, the criteria were that the officer should be acceptable to the DG NCC and not be posted to his home station). The officers whose postings I organised were able to perform their duties much better as they knew the local language and customs. In nine months, I filled up close to 80 percent of the vacancies. This was greatly appreciated by the DG NCC and the MS. On a lighter note, I used to attach the map while sending the posting proposal showing where the officer was being posted and his home station. When the first posting proposal went to the MS he remarked, "I thought I had got a file from the MO Branch to comment upon."

I also realised that there were representations on 60–70 percent of the posting orders issued by my Section. This led to infructuous work and very little time for planning postings. I had a long brainstorming session with my team. It took a lot of time to convince them to strive to have no representations on posting orders issued henceforth. However, I reiterated, that under no circumstances would any laid down norms be broken. I also highlighted that it would be in our interest and in the organisational interest too, as the officer would be able to put in his best at his choice station. A proper procedure was worked out and put into action. The new methodology took some time to be fine-tuned but it worked well. The DG NCC was extremely happy as his organisation had more officers and, more importantly, they were able to function more effectively.

Working with Civilian Staff

It was for the first time that I was working with civilians and found that they were very difficult to motivate and would not work at my pace. Initially, I was unnecessarily hyper until a civilian clerk put me in my place.

One day, I had to take a noting sheet for the COAS, to the MS, on the need to enhance the service limit of officers being posted as ADCs to the President of India. It was typed by a civilian clerk who, despite my repeated requests, did it at the last moment. Without checking the noting sheet, I ran down the steps, as I had got a call for bringing it to the MS for his signatures. The MS signed it and then looked up at me. There was a spelling error. 'There' was typed as 'Their'. I apologised for the lapse. The MS corrected it and told his SO to send it immediately to the COAS's Secretariat. When I came out of the MS office, the civilian clerk who had typed the note was standing there and said, "You must have been rebuked for the typing error. Do not ever confront me in the future, as you alone will suffer and not me."

I learnt a lesson that civilians have to be tackled differently and I changed my style of working. Later, my Section worked on Saturdays also to ensure there was no backlog and every civilian used to turn up on time and there were never any typographical errors. The experience in MS Branch greatly assisted me when I served in the MES and BRO later. I hold the firm opinion that civilians are essential in the MS Branch; otherwise, the present comparatively fair system may not exist. I learnt the following in handling civilian staff:

> Accept the fact that they are more experienced and mature (as they have worked there for a much longer time than those in uniform).
>
> You have to work very hard to learn as much as they know, rather more than they know. There is no alternative to this.
>
> After gaining the necessary knowledge, one still has to win over their minds and hearts. This has to be done by being friendly, fair, straight-forward, and humble, yet firm.

Issue of a Wrong Posting Order

In those days, the DG NCC was shown the dossiers of the officers being proposed for induction into the NCC. After his approval the posting of the officers to suitable posts remained the responsibility of the MS Branch. One day, when the DG NCC was in my office and we were showing him a large number of dossiers while sipping black coffee, he told me that one of the officers I had posted as OC of a Girl's Battalion at Ahmadabad was a bad example to the girls. The officer was a Sikh who cut his hair, and in the evenings, he moved around the girls' hostel without his turban and he smoked too. The DG NCC desired that he be moved to the NCC HQ at Ahmadabad and another officer be posted in his place.

I obtained the approval of the AMS and issued the posting order of the officer, in consonance with the request of the DG NCC. Two days later, the officer came to meet me. I told him about the feedback the DG NCC had given about him. He replied that the truth was not what the DG NCC had said. He had caught the DG NCC's niece (who was an NCC officer) in a corruption case and he was being made a scapegoat. I was shocked and told the officer that I would see what could be done.

I decided to take the advice of the MS (X) – a senior civilian officer with whom I used to interact for posting ADCs to General Officers. I went to his office and explained the entire case. After giving me a patient hearing, he advised me to never decide a case after hearing one side of the story only but always hear both sides. I apologised for my lapse and requested advice to settle the case. He said one option is to keep quiet and only the Major posted out may curse you for some time and no one in the MS Branch will know anything about it.

I said, "Sir, this my conscience does not permit."

He then asked me to leave the case file with him. I thanked him and left his office.

Five days later, he called me and gave me the case file. I opened it and saw that he had written, "I have verified the case and it is in order" on which the MS had written, "Approved." I again thanked him and he smiled and said, "Major, keep this attitude always." I said, "Roger, Sir," and left his office.

The MS (X) had checked the facts of the case from the GOC at Ahmadabad and then got it approved from the MS.

Thereafter, I showed the case file to my AMS and he remarked that, since I had changed the posting on the DG NCC's directions, the case could only be rectified by MS (X) as he alone could check the DG NCC's version (on behalf of the MS) and not me.

Deputation to Botswana

After a year of dedicated and sincere work, my Section was working like a well-oiled machine. We had streamlined procedures, adding a humane element to requests, provided it also served the organisational interest. Infructuous work reduced drastically. This new approach became a topic of discussion in the MS Branch. The teamwork which I could develop with the civilians posted in my Section in MS Branch was unbelievable. They even came in on my request to work on weekends. This was feasible as we all were enjoying our work and it was being appreciated too.

Just when everything was falling in place, my NDA course-mate in MS 5, told me that, as I lacked command reports, the basic critéria for any posting on a foreign assignment (at my service level), he was unable to clear my name, though I made it in the merit in two delegations which went to Iraq and Mauritius. I spoke to my AMS about it. He was fully aware of the circumstances.

During the monthly officers' tea, the MS pointed towards me and enquired from the AMS1, "Why is this officer staying on in MS Branch when he does not have mandatory command reports?"

The AMS1 replied, "Sir, we shall decide the officer's case in a couple of days."

That night, I told my wife to get ready for an immediate posting; where I did not know. Three days later, I was pleasantly surprised to see my name in the list of officers being sent to Botswana on deputation. We got only fifteen days for the move and a large number of administrative arrangements had to be completed. My tenure with the MS Branch came to an abrupt end, albeit on a positive note. The assignment at Botswana was to be for two years, extendable by one year.

Retrospect

While serving in the MS Branch, I learnt that:

> One must forget one's ego while planning the posting of any officer. The posting should be strictly planned in conformity with the laid-down rules and regulations, yet taking into consideration the officer's choice, problems he faces etc. The aim is that the officer is posted to an appointment and a

station where he can give his best to the organisation. One must never act as God.

Representation of a posting order is infructuous work. It should and can be reduced by staying within the laid down parameters.

Officers who were posted as ADCs to Governors of the State would always try to extend their tenures through various means. To stop this practice, I always spoke to the concerned officer four months before he was due for posting and explained to him why he should move. In some cases, I met his request (provided it did not clash with his career interest). This drastically brought down the representations on posting orders of the ADCs to the Governors.

NO LEGACY IS AS RICH AS HONESTY

IATT Botswana (Oct 80 — Dec 83)

In October 1980, I was part of a team of 20 officers moving to Botswana in the Indian Army Training Team (IATT) there. For administrative convenience, the team moved in four sub-groups in a week. I led the first sub-group, which had five officers with their families. Our flight from Bombay to Nairobi, Kenya was at 0100 hours. We reached the airport and were checking in when there was an announcement on the PA system that Major BS Dhaliwal should report to the reception counter. The entire sub-team held their breath, fearing that the trip was being called off. This had happened with two earlier teams going abroad. They requested me not to go to the reception counter. When the announcement was made for the third time, I had to go and check why I was being called. I was pleasantly surprised to see my MS Section civilian clerk, Mr Raman, near the reception counter. He had come from Delhi with a bouquet to wish me 'bon voyage' on behalf of the staff of DAMS 3C. I was touched by their gesture and profusely thanked him.

He also told me that, in addition to an 'Adverse Career Certificate', a 'Career Protection Certificate', signed by the COAS, had been filed in my dossier. In other words, I would not be 'Rejected' for deficiency of command reports but would only be 'Deferred' by the Promotion Selection Board, when my name for promotion was to be considered. I cherish the memory of such individuals for displaying such loyalty and friendship. When I told my team that a clerk from MS Branch had met me, they heaved a sigh of relief. Finally, when the plane took off, I observed a big smile on the face of each member of the team. In those days traveling abroad was a great accomplishment and, in the Armed Forces, very few got such an opportunity at our service level.

The air journey was comfortable and enjoyable as we were all traveling First Class. We finally reached Gaborone (in Botswana) our destination, where we were well received and taken to a four-star hotel to stay till married accommodation was allotted to us. A new gated colony was constructed for us. The accommodation was spacious and built to good specifications. All officers got their accommodation in this colony except Maj J Gonsalves and myself. We both got independent bungalows in an area where only white people lived. Probably they thought we too were whites. I came to know this later when I saw that my name was wrongly spelt as *Dhaliwath* (a German name). The bungalow had a servant quarter; however, no electricity was provided to it. They probably did not want the locals to forget how to live in the bush (their rural areas).

Botswana is a beautiful, clean country with a temperate climate, neither too hot nor cold. The locals were very friendly, simple, and respectful. The weekends were free. Officers of the rank of Major and above had a Rover jeep each with a driver. The work timings were from 0900 to 1630 hours.

Construction of an Obstacle Course

After nine months of stay in Gaborone, one day the Deputy Commander of the Botswana Defence Forces, Brig IAN Khama asked me whether I could design, plan and construct an obstacle course with a small arms range for them. I confidently replied that I could. In a week's time we prepared the project report based on the laid down principles and parameters for our obstacle courses in India. Once the planning was done, I got it approved from the Brigadier.

With the type of obstacles to be constructed decided upon, along with Capt AS Rautella from the Corps of Engineers (who was the only other Sapper on the team) we listed out the stores required (based on the drawings) for each of the obstacles to be constructed. Pricing of the items was not difficult as they were fixed and similar in the city. Thereafter, a detailed list of tools and plants was prepared. The BDF personnel posted in the Combat Engineer Company were tradesmen – carpenters, masons, electronic engineers, etc. To assist them, labour was required. In Botswana, the prisoners in the city jails were used as a labour force in the BDF. I requisitioned the prisoners weekly, based on the progress of work.

A detailed note was then prepared for the Deputy Commander BDF, through their Finance Cell. I spent half a day explaining how I had worked out the relevant details. They were extremely happy to see that there was an optimum utilisation of resources to minimise the cost. The noting was approved by the Deputy Commander BDF, with a maximum variation of plus 25 percent, whereas we had requested for a variation of only plus five percent.

We were free to procure the stores from any of the stores (for which a list was provided) and select any 'make' of the item and place the requisite order on behalf of the BDF. The payment was done by the Finance Cell. The procedure was simple and clear, precluding any need for obtaining price quotations etc. We ran a five-day course for the BDF Sappers. We deliberated on how each one of the obstacles would be constructed by each of the tradesman. The BDF Sappers were keen learners and all the tradesmen had received good basic training and never cut corners.

Working diligently, we got all the obstacles constructed a fortnight before the due date. The Deputy Commandant kept a close check but he never came to the site during the working hours nor did he ever ask the progress – something not followed in India. We stopped work an hour earlier each day, in order to leave the site spotlessly clean. The prisoners, who came as labourers, were outstanding workers despite the crimes they may have committed. I never saw anyone shirking and they seemed to enjoy the construction work. They were also very respectful. One of them was a Civil Engineer and he guided us on local issues and we gave due consideration to his inputs. We made him in-charge of quality checks and he did his duty sincerely.

After the work was completed, we got the 'Obstacle Course and SA Range' inaugurated by the Commander BDF. He was lavish in his praise and thanked the IATT for going beyond the call of duty to complete the task. A couple of days later, I was called by the Deputy Commander BDF who asked me the total net cost of the project. I mentioned that he could get it from the Finance Cell. He again said, "Please work it out and let me know the total net cost of the project."

I wondered if he had some suspicions on the cost submitted. Upon reassessment, we reduced the cost by excluding the tools which had been bought as permanent assets and the return of all the unused items. When it was re-submitted, again he said, "Major, I want to know the net cost of the project. Please rework and intimate it to me."

I was perplexed, and discussed it with the Team Leader, Lt Col VN Wadhwa. He thought for a while and then advised me to again check if any bill had been added twice.

The third time, when I entered the Deputy Commanders office, he asked me to sit down. Without any preamble, I blurted out, "Sir, we worked for the last six months to complete the obstacle course on time. Further, we kept the total expenditure well below the estimated cost. I do not know why you are still telling us that the expenditure is on the higher side."

He remarked, "Oh! It is for this reason you are agitated. I have never asked you to reduce the cost. I only told you to work out the net cost of the project, which meant including your consultancy and supervision charges. I am fully aware of how hard you and your Captain have worked on this project."

For a moment I was perplexed. I had never imagined that he was asking us to actually increase the cost. Once this sank in, I replied that we are in uniform and we get our regular pay; we cannot charge the BDF any professional fee-cum-supervision charges. The Deputy Commander replied, "In our country, nothing is taken gratis. You put in extra work and you get paid. This norm is universally followed."

I knew I could not win the argument and left his office after asking for some time to work it out.

I then walked over to Lt Col VN Wadhwa, our Team Leader's office and told him exactly what had transpired. He laughed and asked whether we want any professional fee-cum-supervision charges. I replied in the negative. Later, the Finance Cell told us that the Deputy Commander had requested six embassies – USA, USSR, Germany, UK, France and Italy to give a rough estimate to construct the obstacle course with a small arms range for them. Their costing was 15 to 20 times more than ours. I realised that their costs would be higher as they would have to fly in a team of experts, arrange for their boarding and lodging at Gaborone, and the civilian firm would charge their professional fee and overhead charges.

Respect for Water

Botswana is known for its Kalahari Desert. The country gets very little rainfall. They have named their currency *Pula* which means water. Gaborone, the capital city, had its water supply from a freshwater lake which was fenced 100 metres away from the waterline and no human being was permitted anywhere near it. We were not allowed to conduct any bridging and outboard motor training on this lake. We in India are blessed with surplus water; however, in the garb of development we have polluted most of the surface water, natural streams and rivers. In the urban space, freshwater is never wasted in Botswana and the punishment for this is very severe. We must remember that water is a very important resource – we drink it, wash in it, play in it, generate power with it, irrigate crops with it, travel and transport goods on it, fight fires with it, and worship it too.

Maintenance of Government Assets

The house given to us was an old bungalow; however, it was very well maintained. The punishment for not looking after any Government asset is very high in Botswana and everyone maintains them as their own. An officer who left after two years stay in Botswana had to pay a good portion of his month's pay for the discrepancies noticed in his house. My wife always believed in leaving a house we occupied a shade better than it was when it was handed over to us. A retired British corporal came to take over the house. We were told he takes a cup of black coffee with cream, which my wife gave him. He went around the house and did not charge us any penalty; rather he complimented my wife for looking after the government property very well. Most officers had to pay fines, and any negotiations would result in doubling of the fine, which was non-negotiable. I wonder when we, in India, will learn to look after government property with due care.

Retrospect

My three-year stay at Botswana was enjoyable yet full of learning. I also got an opportunity to widen my horizons by visiting several other countries during my annual leave. The major gains for me were:

I developed a more confident personality.

My vision and attitude to life changed for the better. Since we became financially sound, on return to India, we could concentrate on the work in hand, as there were comparatively fewer worries on the financial side.

Having seen how various countries tackle common place issues differently (according to their culture, traditions and the prevailing environment) I also perceived that it would be foolish to apply them blindly in India as all countries are different. We have to find home-grown solutions in keeping with our environment and the prevailing socio-political conditions. However, I did pick-up options which can be modified to adapt to Indian conditions.

In all the countries I observed, they take due care of the government property as their own. I succeeded to a great extent in applying this wherever I was posted in India.

I applied the school education concepts which I observed in Botswana, with a twist, on return to India when I was Commander Diploma Wing and Commandant CME and succeeded in improving the methodologies of training.

For minor offences, like coming late, not being properly dressed etc, the punishment was by of fines, which had a more deterrent effect. I tried this in a different format later in India and it worked.

I learnt how they value water and on return to India I did my utmost to stop wastage of water in all the stations I was posted to and took action to conserve water.

Out of the 20 officers who went to Botswana, the team leader, Lt Col VN Wadhwa, Raj Rif, Maj AJS Sandhu, Arty and Capt TPS Bakshi from the Dogra superannuated as Maj Gens. Maj PK Chakarvarti, from the Armoured Corps, Maj GJ Gonsalves, from the MLI, Capt Jasbir Singh, from the Kumaon, and Maj SC Dua of the AMC superannuated as Brigs. We remain in touch.

BACK TO SOLDIERING

53 Engr Regt (Jan 84 — Sep 85)

In December 1983, after a three-year stay in Botswana, it was time to return to India. Though we had an extremely comfortable and enjoyable stay there, towards the fag end most of us were homesick and wanted to return to our motherland. As expected, I was posted as 2IC of 53 Engineer Regiment, at Abohar (in Punjab) under 16 Infantry Division. I was overdue for my command reports so a posting to Regimental duties was a *sine qua non*. The fact that it was to my empanelled regiment was comforting. My CO was Lt Col DS Bajwa for the first year and thereafter it was Lt Col DN Nawani.

The Divisional HQ and divisional troops were strung along on the banks of the Abohar Canal. The troops were on one bank, while the officers and the families lived on the other bank. When I joined the Regiment, it was scheduled to move in the next ten days for training followed by a formation-level Exercise, near Suratgarh. I quickly settled my family in a *basha* (a house made of mud and a thatched roof, covered with a tarpaulin) and moved with the advance party to the Exercise area.

In the Exercise area, the Regiment initially was involved in housekeeping tasks – construction of an underground operations room, conference room, water point, electric lighting with DG sets, track work etc. for the formation HQ. Thereafter, we practised the anticipated tasks for the Exercise with troops – trail-blazing, bridging, mine laying, mine breaching etc. The two-and-a-half-month period spent in the Exercise area was extremely useful for me as I could quickly develop a rapport with the officers and PBOR. Having polished our drills, during the Exercise all the sub units acquitted themselves professionally and we completed the bridge construction 35 minutes ahead of schedule for the armoured formations to move in. In summing up, at the end of the Exercise, our Regiment was complimented on its good all-round performance.

After the Exercise, we moved back and settled once again on the banks of the Abohar Canal. Maj Gen BC Joshi (who later rose to be the COAS) assumed command of the 16 Infantry Division. At that time, we had outstanding officers on the staff in the Divisional HQ. The Col GS was Col JS Dhillon (who later commanded 15 Corps and superannuated as the MGO). Lt Col Shantanu Choudhary was the GSO 1 (Ops) (who superannuated as VCOAS). Col MS Bhandari was the Col Adm (who superannuated as DG Artillery). There was a lot to learn from these officers through regular interaction. I continued my links with them during service, and even now, remain in touch with them.

Conduct of Reconnaissance

On assuming command, the GOC was briefed by his staff officers. After this, briefings from the COs of the supporting arms and services commenced. During these briefings, I observed that the GOC spoke little, but kept noting points for clarification later. Immediately after the briefings were over, the GOC's reconnaissance of the operational area was scheduled. The supporting arms COs had to accompany him for the next ten days. As my CO was on compassionate leave, as officiating incumbent, I was a part of this reconnaissance. It was a great learning experience.

The importance of reconnaissance needs no elaboration. It involved going into the minutest detail of the terrain on both sides of the International Border. As I had not done a reconnaissance earlier, I was caught on the wrong foot. Many, including myself, had not gone into the details which the GOC had desired, or thought essential. I kept noting the queries to which I was unable to reply. Every night, I used to interact with my officers to find answers I needed to know. The ten days were very hectic; however, it was a great learning experience.

Mine Laying Philosophy

While Col DS Bajwa was on a short leave, I had to attend a COs conference at the Bengal Engineers Group and Centre, Roorkee – the Group HQ. The GOC probably had a light schedule and decided to visit 53 Engineer Regiment to discuss the mine-laying philosophy. He wanted the CO and the company commanders to be present. When the GOC reached he learnt that the CO and 21C were away. Nevertheless, he commenced the discussion with the field company commanders.

Due to the short notice, the field company commanders had very little time to prepare for the discussion and were not on the same grid. When the GOC saw that the deliberations were not proceeding well, he walked out in a huff. Late in the evening, when I returned from Roorkee, I was told what had occurred. In the morning, after saying a silent prayer, I went to meet the GOC in his office. Fortunately, Maj Gen BC Joshi was in a good mood. I apologised for the faux pas in my Regiment on the previous day and requested a chance to explain to him the 'Formation Mine Laying Philosophy'. He replied that he had no time that day, due to prior engagements, but he would listen to it the next morning while driving to Bathinda, where he was going for a meeting with the Corps Commander.

I thanked him and rushed back to prepare. As it was for the first time in my life that I was to give a presentation, sitting in a car, I deliberated with my draftsmen as to how it could be done. There was silence for some time till one of them said we could consider using tracing paper overlays. As it appeared workable, I gave a draft to the draftsman to prepare. I then did a mental appreciation that, since the journey from Abohar to Bathinda would take about 35 minutes; I had to restrict the presentation to not more than 20 minutes.

The overlays prepared were self-explanatory and the presentation was made in the form of questions and answers. After 'hit and trial', I finally got it right. However, the draftsmen had to work till 0200 hours that night. The next day, I reached the GOC's residence and the ADC greeted me with a hot cup of coffee. The Col GS came five minutes later and was surprised to see me there. I told him the reason. Maj Gen BC Joshi came out of his residence on time and asked the Col GS to sit in the front seat so that he could listen to my briefing. When we were on the highway to Bathinda, he asked me to start my presentation.

I said, "Roger Sir! Before I give you our formation's minefield plan, I request a few confirmations and clarifications:

> A confirmation that the first overlay correctly depicts our formation boundary.
>
> If so, where do we expect the enemy's major and subsidiary thrust lines?
>
> What stopping power is desired on each of the thrust lines and by when, on a D-day basis."

Maj Gen BC Joshi, after comprehending what I was getting at, did try to upset me. However, I kept cool and got the appropriate responses. Slowly, as the presentation progressed, and the pages of overlays kept turning, the minefields too were displayed D-day wise. In the final overlay (with six hours as reserve) we had all the minefields, having been laid, were depicted with varying stopping powers, based on the most and least likely thrust lines as indicated by the GOC. By then, we were ten minutes away from Bathinda.

The GOC was extremely happy to see how I had covered the complex subject in an easy to comprehend manner. He directed the Col GS to call all the brigade commanders to the conference room at 1900 hours that evening when I would present the Mine Laying Philosophy-cum-Plan. On reaching Bathinda, I requested the GOC's permission to return to Abohar, so that I could prepare for the evening's presentation which had to put across with OHP slides. During the return trip, I mentally prepared the slides and could get them ready by 1800 hours. Fortunately, this presentation too went off well, especially as the GOC, in his introduction on the subject, had praised me.

In those days the Army Commander, Lt Gen K Sundarji, would hold discussions on operational subjects frequently. All subjects connected with combat engineering i.e., mine-laying, flooding, etc. were sent to us, and I had to give one-hour long presentations (which invariably extended to three hours) on the various plans. I normally got a week to prepare for these presentations. Having interacted with Maj Gen BC Joshi, I knew that the presentations had to preclude technical language. Further, they had to be thorough and pragmatic. It was a lot of hard work. I also learnt how to take on complex questions and not get flustered when I was not too sure of the answers. I usually requested for a day to give an appropriate response. The Col GS, Col Adm and my CO would also attend these presentations and I had to take on a barrage of questions from them too. These presentations made me a confident speaker.

Operation Blue Star

In June 1984, Operation Blue Star happened. Our regiment had more than 35 percent Jat Sikh troops. As 2IC, I was specifically tasked by the GOC and the CO; to keep a very close eye on all officers, JCOs and ORs to ensure they do not get affected by rumours and the ISI propaganda.

The SM and Regimental Havildar Major played a stellar role to assist in this sensitive task. We used to hold mini meetings, twice a day, at different locations and keep an eye on all so-called 'suspects'. The policy unanimously decided by us was to explain the truth and the actual situation to the suspects, through selected JCOs and NCOs who were close to them. We never met the suspects alone but interacted with them along with other troops. A nominated JCO or NCO kept a close eye on their movements and kept us fully informed of their activities. This approach worked and we succeeded in the regiment upholding the highest traditions of the Indian Army during the trying times. This paid me good dividends when I went to command 658 Engineer Bridge Unit later (where everyone in the Unit had more than two red ink entries). Additional activities to keep the troops busy up to midnight etc. were also carried out.

I also learnt how vital it is to act normal in disturbing circumstances, and no one should be marked/pointed out ever. Every individual conscience must be convinced to do the right thing as is expected of Indian Army soldiers.

Repair of Gurudwaras

Our Regiment was given the responsibility to repair the Gurudwara Sahibs at Muktsar and Malout. One day, I went to see how the work was progressing. On reaching there, I saw personnel of Assam Regiment were checking the rooms abutting the Gurudwara Sahib to ascertain if there were any hidden weapons in them. The young Captain, who was a Christian, found condoms in the *granthi's* house. He was in an awful mood and was shouting that a brothel was being run there. I called the officer aside and cooled him down. He just could not believe that, according to Sikh tenets, a *granthi* is permitted to marry and have children. I do not blame him as in Christianity the opposite is followed. There are things that are difficult for persons of other faiths to comprehend. Further, Christians go into their church wearing shoes, whereas in a Gurudwara everyone has to remove their footwear. Unfortunately, this is not known to some and sensitive issues can create problems, which are difficult to handle later. I was there by providence; while an officer from my regiment (a Hindu) was trying to explain this to the infantry officer, who was not prepared to listen.

Retrospect

I had a comparatively short tenure in the regiment; however, it was hectic. Respite is not a word one can cherish when serving with troops as life was on a perpetual run. A whirlwind of activities occurred in a short time where officers had to prove themselves at every step. I learnt a number of lessons:

> While giving presentations to senior officers, the subject has to be pitched at their level, without technical jargon or verbosity. If one is unable to answer a question, accept the fact, rather than resort to a fib. After you have got the answer, go back and clarify. Do not get browbeaten or lose your cool during a presentation. Slides must be self-explanatory in order to reduce the number of spoken words.

Do not carry any notes during the presentation. Practice many times till you require no aids; however, never memorise the script.

Tackling troops is a complex subject. Each situation is different and there is no cookie-cutter solution. Before deciding upon the course of action it is best to take the advice of senior JCOs and NCOs. In my experience, I always got good advice. Never show your fears or concerns during any grim situation; always remain cool and composed.

Interacting with the Divisional staff officers (all key appointments) who later rose to the rank of Lt Gen, taught me the nuances of completed staff work.

Last but not least, the manner of conducting reconnaissance for terrain evaluation and analysis was brought home to me.

In this tenure in the 53 Engineer Regiment, there were only a few officers from my earlier tenures. The new officers, whom I interacted with, have become lifelong friends – Majors Gautam Dutt, Ravi Kharbanda, Kumar Fulay, MP Singh, AK Singh, and Roshan Katyal; Captains A Matlotia, Sudhir Kelkar and PK Roy; and 2/Lts Biswajeet Ghosh and Piyush Bahugana. Gautam later become the E-in-C; Ghosh was my Technical Secretary and retired as a Brigadier. AK Singh, superannuated as a Maj Gen. Kelkar retired as a Brigadier. Those who did not attain flag rank, have/are doing extremely well in their second careers. I cherish my association with them.

In this short tenure I served under two COs, nearly a year under Lt Col DS Bajwa and nine months under Lt Col DN Nawani (both superannuated as Cols). I remain in touch with both of them.

FATE FAVOURS THE SINCERE

HQ 16 Corps (Oct 85 — May 86)

The qualitative requirement (QR) for an officer to be considered for posting on deputation to Botswana clearly spelt out that he should have earned his mandatory command reports. However, as mentioned earlier, the MS Branch had cancelled my posting as OC Earth Moving Plant at Jalandhar, where I would have earned my command reports. In the MS Branch, I had informally learnt that my name was at the top of the merit list for a foreign assignment. The QR probably would have been waived by the MS. However, I had to sign the mandatory 'Adverse Career Certificate' before going to Botswana.

As it happened, my name was in the 'Deferred' list and not 'Rejected' list, when the results for the No. 4 Selection Board for promotion to Lt Col were declassified. The civilian clerk from MS Branch, Mr Raman, who had come to see me off at the Bombay airport had told me the truth. At that time, I was serving in the 53 Engineer Regiment. In order to be considered in the next promotion board, I had to be posted out immediately, so that my ACR of the balance period could be initiated and placed before the promotion board. When Maj Gen BC Joshi came to know this, he was kind and gracious to speak with the concerned officers, in MS Branch, to issue my posting orders. Three days later, in October 1985, I was posted as SO-II (Engineers) in the Engineers Branch of HQ 16 Corps at Nagrota, with directions to report thereafter in five days.

I reported at Nagrota, leaving my family at Abohar. The first three days passed off in interviews at various levels. Having worked at HQ 11 Corps, as a subaltern, I was generally aware of how a Corps HQ functions; however, HQ 16 Corps was much larger as compared to HQ 11 Corps. After the interviews were over, I requested the Chief Engineer, Brig Rajesh Mathur, for permission to go on a reconnaissance of the border areas since I had not been posted in the area earlier, to which he readily concurred. I made the necessary administrative arrangements and studied the maps of the areas where I intended to conduct the reconnaissance, for which I was allotted 20 days. (Due to logistic and other administrative issues, the period was extended to 25 days). I was thus able to carry out the reconnaissance thoroughly and professionally in the manner I had learnt from Maj Gen BC Joshi. It was tough and hard work. The days were taken up in traveling to the various posts and meeting various commanders and the sapper officers. Every night, I used to write copious notes on what I had seen. I was not hesitant or shy to clear my doubts. Most nights, I got little sleep as all the data had to be sifted and compiled under various headings. Before I knew it, the reconnaissance was over and I was back in the office.

After a day's break, I was detailed to assist the CE on a presentation for an 'Operational Works Conference' to be held at HQ Northern Command after ten days. Having been on the ground, I was absolutely clear of the requirements. After deliberations with the CE, I commenced preparing the slides, for his approval. After three days, when the first set of draft slides was ready, I was told that the CE had proceeded on 10 days of casual leave. The ACE, Col VK Khanna, told me that he would now go to the conference. The next day, when I went to see the ACE, I was told that he too had proceeded on casual leave due to a tragedy in his family. Next, the Corps HQ's (SD Branch), sent a note to the Engineers Branch that I would attend the conference at HQ Northern Command. As I had prepared the slides, I was more or less ready. However, in order to personally make the presentation, I reduced the number of slides to the bare minimum, re-worded some of them and prepared a fresh set of 'back-up slides' whose need may come up to clarify any queries which may arise during the presentation which was to be given to the Army Commander,

Lt Gen AK Handoo.

In the conference hall at HQ Northern Command, I was delighted to see Col RK Raichand, the Col GS (Ops). We had served together as instructors at F Combat CME. Ravi Raichand (who rose to be Lt Gen) asked if I had come to assist the CE. I replied that I had to attend the conference as both the CE and ACE were on leave. He then asked if I was confident to give the presentation. I replied in the affirmative. He said, "Good; do not get unnerved by the Army Commander."

I was wondering why he said that when Lt Gen Handoo walked in and all present stood up. The Army Commander went to the podium, looked around, and saw me – the only Major in the conference hall. Pointing towards me he said, "Out."

I was truly flustered and did not know what to do till Col Raichand told him that I was representing HQ 16 Corps as the CE and the ACE were away on leave due to extenuating circumstances. He further added that he knew me and I would be able to put across the 16 Corps requirements. Lt Gen Ashok Handoo replied, "If you think so, then get him on the stage and let us hear him."

Thereafter the Army Commander went and sat in his chair.

I would be lying if I say I was not shaken up. However, as I was totally prepared, I took a deep breath, got back my composure and walked up to the podium to give the presentation. Lt Gen Handoo did not interject for the first few minutes. When I was giving out the requirement for operational works for each of the posts, he had a long look at the slide. Thereafter began a barrage of questions, which could only be replied by someone who had gone to the sites and studied the requirement objectively. As I had been to the posts, I could answer most of his questions, with all relevant details. I also utilised some of the 'back-up slides' which I had prepared. However, for two queries, I was not too sure of the answer and stated that I would get back to the Col GS soon.

The Army Commander then asked, "Son, when did you last visit these posts?"

I answered, "Sir, 15 days ago".

He then cleared the HQ 16 Corps requirement of operational works in full. The other CE's, had a tough time, as they had not visited all posts in their respective areas. After the conference, Lt Gen Handoo directed his Col GS to convey his appreciation to the 16 Corps Commander, for the good work done by me. I was later complimented by the BGS, on behalf of the Corps Commander, Lt Gen M Mayadas. I never dreamt that I would have to give a presentation to the Army Commander. However, when the opportunity came, I was able to put my best foot forward.

Retrospect

The next four months at the Corps HQ passed off peacefully, as I had little work to do. I utilised the time to update myself on engineer requirements in the Corps Zone. In the evenings, I got time for hard physical workouts. In addition, once and sometimes twice a week I would climb up for a pilgrimage to the Vaishno Devi temple to pay my reverences and to check my fitness level.

I was approved for promotion in the next No. 4 Selection Board, in May 1986. Having spent only seven months at Nagrota, I expected to be posted in the theatre. MS Branch, however, surprised me by doing the opposite – posting me as DCWE (E/M) in HQ 137 Works Engineers at Dimapur, in Nagaland, in Eastern Command. I did not represent and accepted the posting order in the right spirit. In the extremely short tenure at Nagrota, lessons which I learnt earlier were reinforced:

> As they say, time spent on reconnaissance is never wasted. The techniques learnt on conducting reconnaissance and from the terrain evaluation and analysis done in the 16 Infantry Division was fine-tuned. Had I not put in the requisite hard work; I would have been castigated by the Army Commander.
>
> There is no short cut to dedicated hard work, intelligent and systematic working.
>
> Striving for success without hard work is like trying to harvest where you have not planted.

NO SHORT CUT TO LEARNING

137 Works Engrs (Jun 86 — Dec 88)

For the first time in my career, after putting in close to twenty years of service, I was moving to an MES establishment, in June 1986, on posting to HQ 137 Works Engineers as DCWE E/M. There was uncertainty in my mind but some officers who had served in the MES set my apprehensions to rest and told me to have a ball and enjoy myself.

HQ 137 Works Engineers was located close to Dimapur town, whereas the Corps HQ was located about 10 kilometres away. The CWE was Col RK Sharma for the first six months of my tenure. When he was posted out, Col KL Bhatia replaced him. The CE Zone was Brig Jagdish Narain (who later became the E-in-C). His successor was Brig Hira Singh. The area of responsibility of HQ 137 Works Engineers was vast. It had the following units:

GE 868 Engineer Works Section at Rangapahar (Dimapur).

GE 869 Engineer Works Section at Zakhama, with outstation AGEs at Chakabama and Leimakong.

GE 872 Engineer Works Section at Kumbhigram, with an outstation AGE at Agartala.

GE Silchar, with an outstations AGE at Aizawl and a Gde I at Lunglei.

On my very first day in the office, the CWE had a conference, which I attended. He enquired from me about QPR. This was Greek to me and I kept quiet. He commented, "I am sorry; you know nothing about MES."

I felt extremely embarrassed and tried to blame the system/organisation for not teaching me about MES, BRO and Survey, the other pillars of the Corps of Engineers. I only knew combat engineering. I did not sleep well that night. Upon introspection, I concluded that I had only myself to blame, as it was my duty to have learnt about MES and BRO in my service thus far, and should not blame the organisation/Corps for this shortcoming.

I resolved to master MES activity and worked like a man possessed to learn. The office timings were from 0700 to 1330 hours. In the afternoons, I had sufficient spare time to study. There was an MES officer as DCWE (B/R), Mr Gurdev Singh, a soft-spoken, bright and dynamic officer, who had come on his first staff appointment after successfully completing the GE's appointment. He relished teaching and gave me his updated MES Regulations, IAFW 2249, and other pamphlets to read. I read them over and over till I knew them thoroughly. We would daily go for two-hour walks and discuss only MES. During office hours, I never disturbed Mr Gurdev Singh unless there was an emergency to clear any matter. He not only cleared all my doubts but would take periodic tests too. It was a pleasure learning beyond the books from him.

House Keeping Points

I learnt about 'House Keeping' points from Mr. Gurdev Singh and the vital role each one of them play in the functioning of any MES office. Thereafter, I got the mammoth backlog of the Housekeeping points pertaining to E4 Section, which was under me, from all the GEs. It was a tough task to clear them as all were vintage cases. When Brig Jagdish Narain, the CE Zone, was informed about this achievement by Lt Col SS Dhanoa, his SO 1 (E/M). The CE sent me a 'well done' DO letter.

I also learnt about the 'House Keeping' points pertaining to the other Sections from the respective Section subordinates and I cleared my doubts from Mr. Gurdev Singh. I also grasped that, in case all Sections points are cleared, then the executives would have more time for their primary tasks and their chances of getting into any problem, at a later stage, reduces drastically.

Learning at Grassroots Level

To learn the technical intricacies (which are not taught in the engineering colleges) and how the MES personnel function at the grassroots level, I knew that I would have to move to the GE's and lower offices. Accordingly, I decided to visit all stations in the area of responsibility of 137 Works Engineers. Moving from one station to another was dangerous, due to the prevailing insurgency, and no one from the HQ ever wanted to go these distant outstations. I volunteered and the CWE permitted me, without a second thought.

Before I went on the visits, I always drew up a detailed plan on what I had to do and how it would be done. They were informed in advance so that there was no time wasted. I gathered all theoretical knowledge and all my doubts were listed on paper. During the visits, I learnt all details on desert coolers, geysers, water coolers, window and split ACs, water pumps, sewerage pumps, generator sets etc. I also gained knowledge of how they function, what are their makes, how they are tested and how to check their authenticity etc. I also became familiar with the functioning of electricity, water, sewerage and drainage supply systems; and how these works were executed on the ground.

My day would commence at 0430 hours (in the east it is bright sunlight by then) with a walk with the GE to see the water supply and drainage systems on day one, the electrical system on the day two and the sewerage system on the day three. We used to be back at 0700 hours so that the GE could attend his office at 0800 hours. After breakfast, I used to move on foot (in civilian clothes) once again with the concerned AGE and JE and check each of the systems, clarify all doubts and be back for lunch. Thereafter I used to interact with the concerned tradesmen and suppliers who had provided the equipment and the spares. By the time I completed my visits to all the outstations, my incertitude was removed and I knew all that is to know about each type of machinery, to the minutest detail. Very few officers posted in the MES go into these details and thus are not able to perform duties to their optimum capability.

My next set of visits to the outstations was to familiarise myself with how all works were being executed on the ground. The programme followed was more or less on similar lines as my first visit except, this time, I visited the high-power works on the first day. On the second day, I perused the maintenance contracts, job orders etc. I observed that most of the officers and the builders did not read the contract document thoroughly, the sites after finishing the day's work were not properly cleaned and there were variations in each of the GE's computations for similar works. I noted all the observations and would, on my return, discuss them with my gurus, Mr Gurdev Singh and Major Malshe who was the SW. With their experience, they would tell me the correct procedure to adopt and where corners were cut by the builders. It was a great learning experience. I also learnt how to go through a contract document quickly and note the important clauses. There was no short cut except to practice and re-practice until one mastered the technique. I got myself tested by the gurus and they were always happy with the hard work being put in by me. When Mr Gurdev Singh was posted out, his relief was another senior civilian officer, Mr OP Shrivastava, who generally did not like army officers. I dealt with him tactfully and learnt a lot from him too. I had no ego problems and we became good friends

Finally, my third set of visits to the outstations was to hear first-hand the user problems and settle their issues which were feasible and workable. I met the station commanders and ensured all genuine problems intimated to me were resolved at the earliest. For this, I would interact daily with the GE, AGE and JE till a confirmation was received.

It is pertinent to mention here that the entire knowledge could not be obtained after visit to a single GE's office/site. I obtained authentic information from either the executives, or the vendors, or the mechanics. Most of the officers did not have the requisite knowledge.

Retrospect

As a DCWE E/M, I learnt a number of lessons. Some of them were:

The MES is a mixed organisation of civilian and military personnel. As both streams come from different backgrounds and based on the type of training each has got, they naturally have a different approach to all issues. As officers in uniform are unable to grasp these basic issues, they find it difficult to adjust and function. An army officer in the MES has to forget his ego and own the organisation. Thereafter, the civilian staff will slowly but surely adjust to your way of working, provided it is not for personal interest/growth. This is the most vital lesson.

In a Army outfit, an officer is accepted as a leader straightway. Even if he is not good enough, the unit carries him on its shoulders. In the MES, the Army officer is only accepted if he has the requisite knowledge, keeps himself updated on the latest in the field, and more importantly carries his team along with him and owns the organisation.

Civilian personnel fall under Civil Service Rules. There is very little one can do against them. Army personnel, being under the Army Act, are liable for even the smallest offence. My tenure in MS Branch had taught me this difference. One has to change the style of working while handling civilians and they are as good as us in Army uniform, if not better in some cases, provided you accept them as they are and exploit their strengths and cover their weaknesses.

To function effectively in the MES, there is no short cut to the knowledge of engineering, in its true sense, and the various processes involved in doing any work. The knowledge gained in engineering colleges is not sufficient, by any stretch of imagination. In addition, there are unbelievable restrictions imposed by the government, yet work can be done provided one approaches it with a positive mindset.

Camaraderie is missing in the MES; however, it can be built, provided one is accepted as a leader.

In the MES, each appointment works independently; regretfully very few guide their juniors. This is due to the fear that, in case anything goes wrong, they could be held culpable.

MES procedures laid down are outstanding and have stood the test of time. Even the CWPD has adopted them. We however need to be reviewing them periodically in conformity with changing circumstances.

I learnt the importance of follow up and feedback to get the work completed expeditiously.

Every problem should be solved in conformity with the existing rules and regulations.

The two-and-a-half-year long tenure passed quickly as I was always busy learning and looking for procedures and systems to provide greater user satisfaction. It is pertinent to mention here that I also learnt about BRO by visiting Project Sewak nearby a number of times. I observed that the procedures followed in BRO are generally as per the MES except that there are less checks and balances vis-a-vis MES.

SUCCESS THROUGH HARD WORK

CWE Chandigarh (Jan 89 — Jun 91)

The Posting

The existing policy on postings clearly laid down that no officer can be posted to an executive appointment at his home station. As my home station is Chandigarh, I represented, in writing, highlighting this fact to the E-in-C's Branch. Nonetheless, it was communicated on the telephone that I should move as ordered and necessary approval of the competent authority for waiver of the rule had been obtained 'in service interest'.

My wife and daughters were, however, extremely happy to move to Chandigarh from Dimapur. After a warm send-off and a comfortable journey, we reached Chandigarh and settled down in the single officers' accommodation of the Air Force Officers' Mess.

I went to the office at 0900 hours, on the day I had to report for duty. No one was there. At 1000 hours, the staff began trickling in while I quietly sat in the CWE office, which had stacks of files piled up. I wondered what was in store for me. My PA (a lady) came in at 1015 hours and wished me. I asked her why there were so many files in the office. She said that, as my predecessor was not attending office, these were files on which action by the CWE, Col YP Singh, was still pending. She added there were many more files in her office. I heard her without responding.

At about 1100 hours, when all officers were in, I called them together and had a long informal chat with them and got a fair idea of the state of affairs in the office. On the first three days, I did not do anything in the office, as I did not consider it appropriate to telephone Col YP Singh or take formal briefings from the staff. On the fourth day, Col YP Singh came in at 1100 hours. He gave me the 'handing/taking over' notes and requested me to sign them; which I immediately did. We had arranged a farewell tea for him, which he declined. He left the office at 1135 hours, after wishing me luck in my new appointment.

Initial Actions

After seeing off my predecessor, I sat in the CWE's chair. I closed my eyes, said a minute's prayer and decided to take on the assignment by its horns. During the previous three days, while going over the 'handing/taking over' notes repeatedly and seeing the files piled in my office, I had decided on the schedule to be followed on taking over. My initial aim was to clear all reminders, alleged complaints and pending correspondence within a week. Without wasting any time, I called the Section Heads and Superintendents of all the Sections to my office.

In Stage-I, all 'reminders' were replied to. For this, all Section Heads were directed to put up a draft reply (hand-written in pencil) by 1700 hours, with the case file duly flagged. Further, where a reply was not feasible, then a date by when the reply would be submitted was to be mentioned. At night and the next morning, I re-drafted the replies and gave them to the Section Heads to read, amend (if essential, after obtaining my approval) and get them typed for my signatures. In all reminders, the first line had an apology viz. 'I on behalf of my office apologise for the delay with an assurance it will never happen again.' Thus, on the second day of my command, all 43 reminder replies were sent by hand to the concerned offices. In five letters, a date was given by when the reply would be submitted and I made sure they were submitted a day before the target date.

In Stage-II, similar action was taken with all the 56 alleged complaints pending for more than ten months. In their case, after the study, a format was made for each type of complaint and finalised after detailed deliberations. Once the format was ready it was easy for all to fill and the truth came out viz. the alleged complaint was baseless, false, malicious and devoid of any truth. 47 alleged complaints were recommended for closure. In balance nine, where there was a doubt, the investigation was ordered, and the higher HQ informed that the investigation report would follow in a week.

For the nine pending cases, a Board of Officers was convened under my signatures to investigate the specific allegations with a site check and with a direction to submit their report in three days. Thereafter, where the individual had faltered, I visited the site to check the documents to confirm whether it was an inadvertent error or a willful act. On completion of the investigation, I recommended a specific course of action, administrative or disciplinary. In all the cases, the Command HQ concurred with my recommendations. This sent a clear message to all under my command that there would be no escape for willful defaulters. Incidentally, HQ Western Command issued directions to all zones that alleged complaints, in the future, would be replied in conformity with the CWE Chandigarh format.

Acceptance/Rejection of Tenders

On the fourth day of my command, I was to clear my doubts on handing/taking over notes with my staff officers. They were informed a day earlier and, as scheduled, E1 Section was present in full strength at 0830 hours. The previous night, I had compiled the list of clarifications I wanted. During our deliberations, I was also giving instructions on the manner to proceed further. It took 30 minutes more than planned. After a five-minute break, we commenced with E2 Section, when the SW, Mr Popli, came in with seven folders addressed to me, by name, with 'Urgent' written on top of them. With the previous CWE's powers having been withdrawn, these were seven tenders that had been sent to the CE Zone for according acceptance. Now, the CE Zone office had returned all of them with the cryptic remark that 'the present CWE may take action as 'deemed fit'.

Five tenders had only two days remaining and the other two had four days remaining for deciding whether to accept or reject them. I halted the briefing of the E2 Section and, in the remaining office hours, the SW gave me a detailed brief on the five tenders on which we had to make a decision by the next day (keeping one day in reserve). With the briefing, I was clear on the work and at home, I again did a detailed study on the tenders. All the hard work put in by me as DCWE E/M came to my rescue. In the noting sheet, I wrote down what all needs to be added, deleted and amended. I got only three hours of sleep that night.

The next morning, the SW Mr Popli accepted most of my suggestions and, before lunch, I accepted four tenders and rejected one, and ordered its recall. Since it was my first executive appointment, the SW did ask me how I knew so much. I told him about my gurus who had taught me. I shudder to think about what I would have done had I not done self-study in my previous posting.

Standing Orders and Standing Operating Procedures

I also decided how we would tackle all tenders in future. We streamlined the procedure to bring in transparency and laid down a time frame for all activities. Simultaneously, I prepared 'Standing Orders' for them and gave it to the SW for the issue to all GEs for compliance. A copy was also endorsed to the CE Zone.

Over the next two days, I continued with the briefing of my Section Heads, while the Standing Orders and SOPs on all important facets were being prepared. Where essential, copies were sent to the CE Zone office for approval before issue. It took a month for all of them to be finalised.

Standing Orders after Acceptance of Tenders

Three days after a tender was accepted, the builder along with his GE, AGE and JEs had to meet me in my office. During this meeting, not exceeding 20 minutes, the scope of work and all relevant details were broadly given out by the concerned GE. Since I too had studied the tender, I used to intervene at important points. Most of the builders would look shocked, wondering how I had got the time to read the contract so minutely. After another three days, a meeting at the site would be held and all problems/doubts of the builder were cleared. This meeting too was limited to 20 minutes. In these three days, a pragmatic and workable CPM chart was prepared by the GE, corrected by the SW and finally by me, before it was handed over to the concerned JE. Every week, on Sundays, all work under progress was reviewed with each of the GEs on the telephone. This continued till I knew all the relevant details on each work. By constant monitoring, before the end of six months, all works had more or less caught up with their schedule. A clear message was sent out to the builders that, in case they wish to earn their money, they must finish the work before the due date.

Interview with CE Zone

A week after taking over as CWE Chandigarh, I realised that I had not met my CE, Brig Kanitkar. In our first meeting, he advised me that, as I stood approved for promotion to the rank of Colonel, I must learn to make my own decisions, rather than bothering seniors for any inadequacies. He further added that I should only telephone him in case I had achieved anything outstanding and NOT repeat NOT for advice on how to sort out my mundane problems.

While returning to my office after the short interview, I reviewed the advice I had been given in my mind. Initially, I thought the CE was wrong; however, later I realised it was a great piece of advice.

Brig Kanitkar stayed for less than three months and Brig Siddique took over. I never spoke to Brig Kanitkar after my initial interview; yet during his farewell party he said to me that he had been hearing a lot about the good work being done by me and asked me to keep it up.

One must only perform one's duty sincerely and never bother seniors with problems. Solving them is part of one's duty. The greatest pleasure in life is doing what people say you cannot do.

Interaction with the Staff at the CE Zone office

Though I had little or no interaction with the CE Zone, I did develop an excellent rapport with the ACE's at the CE Chandigarh Zone and all the other staff officers. I would telephone each one of them as often as I could. I also met them whenever I could spare time. In these interactions, I listened and acted on the good advice, if any, given by any level officer. This rapport helped me tremendously as no case was ever stuck in the Zone.

It is pertinent to mention that the entire officers and staff of the Zone were talking about how I was able to answer all the reminders and complaints within three to four days of taking over as CWE Chandigarh. They advised me to take it easy as it may affect my health. I was humble and told them I hardly did anything; it was the staff who had performed par excellence.

I also went to see the local works under execution. As I could not go during office hours, I inspected the local GE's work from 0630 to 0830 hours and be in my office at 0900 hours. For inspecting the outstation GE's work, I used to leave Chandigarh at 0500 hours, to be at the MES IB, Patiala at 0545 hours. For an hour, I would discuss each work at the MES IB and from 0645 to 0745 hours; I would inspect the works on the ground. After a quick breakfast, I would leave Patiala and be in my office at 0900 hours. Each station had to be visited a minimum of four times to understand its external services viz. water supply, electric supply, drainage and sewerage system. After these visits, I knew all that was essential about the station; which all works were going on; their progress etc.

Office Correspondence

My responsibilities and schedule meant a lot of homework. By this, I got my SOs to send all replies on time. I could also improve progress on all reports and returns and be aware of all pending cases. In the mornings, when the *dak* went to the Section concerned, the reply to the letters had to be put up in pencil (double space) and I would send the file back as quickly as feasible, duly amended, for an issue to be put up or to go under my signatures. In a month's time, everyone had picked up my style and all SOs realised that it is best to do work on time.

House Keeping Points

To clear the mammoth backlog, I gave the responsibility to all AGEs. Initially most faltered to achieve their respective targets. Thereafter, I commenced calling the officers, who did not achieve their respective targets, to my office at 0800 hours. As everyone detested to report at this hour, accordingly the targets set began being achieved. I also observed that, once the first target was achieved and a 'Shabash' was given to the concerned individual, progress thereafter improved exponentially. This exercise continued till 100% progress was achieved in each of the 'House Keeping' points.

Meeting with the Users

The third week went in meeting all the GEs and their staff and inspecting all works under them. In those days a CWE's area of jurisdiction was based on a geographical area and he had to look after all users in that particular area. Nowadays, CWE's are not geographically-based but on the service viz. Army, Navy and Air Force units they serve. CWE Chandigarh had a variety of users – Army, Air Force, TBRL, SASE, DRDO. Each had different requirements and priorities. The ACR channel was based on which service had the maximum workload. I never neglected any of my users. Rather, I paid special attention to each.

After a month, when I was confident about my tasks and responsibilities, I went to meet the senior-most officers in each of the stations under my jurisdiction. I prepared for all the issues they were likely to raise. I listened patiently and invariably said that I would brief them on how I intend to tackle each of the issues, in a week. On the due date, using an OHP slide presentation, I frankly put across the issues and thereafter briefed them on how I intended tackling each of them, with timelines. Normally, a day before the timeline given by me in the presentation, a completion report was given by the concerned GE. In order to achieve this, progress on each of the targets was reviewed with the concerned GE, on a daily basis or even twice a day.

The lessons learnt by me, as DCWE (E/M), on the importance of feedback and monitoring were fully tapped. It became my style of working.

Once this was over, rather than the user telling us, I used to tell them of the anticipated problems and the actions being initiated by me. They were surprised that I, as the CWE, was telling them what needed improvement in their respective stations. All my major users – both the Air Force AOCs and the GOC 1 Armoured Division – thereafter had no complaints on MES matters; only praises.

An Altercation With an MES Union Leader

About three months after I had taken over, the GE (Air Force) was replaced by a newly-promoted civilian MES officer, Mr Babjee. He was from Andhra Pradesh and knew little Hindi and no Punjabi. One day he had a problem in his establishment. An NCO who was a JE, again newly-posted, had stopped the union leader (a six feet two inches tall and mean-looking Sikh electrician) from committing theft of some aluminium parts from a BER aircraft. The NCO, who was in civilian clothes, was beaten up by the union leader. The NCO ran and told his GE what had taken place. The PA, who knew limited English told the GE what his JE was trying to say. The GE had no alternative but to call the union leader to his office and, in a soft tone, told him that he should not have used force and he should apologise to the JE. The union leader, who was drunk, then threatened the GE, that he would kidnap his wife and his two daughters, that night, in case he even thought of taking any action against him.

When the PA translated the threat, the GE got very scared and rushed to my office in his car. He was so shaken that he kept repeating only one word – 'Resignation'. He just could not tell me what had occurred. Since I knew about his language problem, I spoke to his PA and learnt the full story. I asked him to send the union leader to my office. The PA somehow convinced the union leader to meet me and sent him on the scooter of the office peon. When the union leader walked into my office, I saw that he was intoxicated and could not even stand straight. He had probably been briefed by his friends and spoke politely, "*Sahib,* it is not your case so please stay out of it. I will sort out the matter with my GE."

When I did not say anything, he made the mistake of threatening me by saying that he had come to my office with his shoelaces open, hence I had better listen to him. The insolence of the man, his tone of voice and language was a direct affront. In a reflex action, I got up from my chair and calmly walked up to where he was standing and hit him hard on his solar plexus. The union leader fell flat. My peon rushed in, picked him up, and gave me a 'thumbs up' signal, smilingly. The union leader, after getting up, shouted, "Tomorrow morning from 0600 hours there will be a total strike and it will not end till you are posted out." He then left my office.

After the union leader left, my mind went blank and I cursed myself for what I had done. I knew he would never tell anyone that I had hit him, as that would go against his image. The moot point now was how to stop him from ordering a strike/tools down. My mind was still fuzzy when I heard the horn of a VIP escort vehicle blowing. My peon rushed in saying that it appears to be a CBI raid. Before I could react, two policemen barged in, one went towards the door of the washroom and shouted 'all clear'. The other placed a chair in such a position that the person sitting on it could see both the front and rear doors and me. He then went outside and guided an SP (in uniform) to the chair. The SP, who had revolvers in both his hands, sat down and introduced himself as SP Patiala.

He apologised for disturbing me and stated that they were constrained to follow protocol/SOP as their life was always in danger. Once I learnt that he was not from the CBI, I relaxed and asked him whether he would like to have tea or coffee. He said tea; the peon heard it and rushed to get the tea. The SP Patiala said that he had come with a request from the SSP Patiala Range for posting of a boy from E1 to E3 Section. I knew the boy as he had been recently posted to my office and told the SP that I would get the needful done. When the SP was convinced that I was giving a genuine assurance, I told him that I too had a humble request. I told the SP Patiala that a union leader was creating problems and I would be grateful, in case he could advise him to behave.

The SP asked me if the union leader was around. I said that he must be outside as he was there before the SP arrived. He called his subordinate and told him what to do. The ASI shouted his name and threatened him to behave, otherwise, they would be constrained to teach him how to be a good citizen. He further added that they would henceforth keep a close eye on him. Thereafter the SP left with his escort vehicles. After a cool thought, I devised a plan to stop the strike. I called my PA for some work and she asked me why the police had come. I told her that when the union leader misbehaved with me, I rang up Mr KPS Gill (who is related to my wife) and he, on the radio set, had directed the SP to provide the necessary assistance. I further added that, if anyone knows the union leader, he should tell him to behave and meet me at the earliest. She said that she would get the information sent to him.

By then I had been allotted an independent bungalow in the 'N' Area which was 500 metres from my office. When I reached home, as usual, I never mentioned the incident to my wife though she knew something had occurred in the office from the tension on my face. She gave me a paracetamol tablet and I was not permitted to see any files. I put the alarm for 0400 hours and went to sleep. About 0100 hours, my wife, after keeping a hand on my mouth, woke me up. She whispered that someone is ringing the doorbell. I got up and saw from a slit in the curtain, that it was the union leader. I wanted to open the door but my wife would not allow it, saying he could be a militant. I told her that it was someone from my office and she should go back to the bedroom. She reluctantly did so. I opened the door and in walked the union leader, who was now sober. He took off his turban and put in near my feet and started weeping. I told him that I would tell him the truth about what had happened, after he left my office, provided he does not tell anyone else. He swore on his children, that he would never tell anyone. I told him what I had told my PA, as Mr KPS Gill in those days was a terror; people trembled on hearing his name. I said that an order had been issued to sort him out; it would therefore be wise for him to disappear from Chandigarh for the next few months, by when I would get the matter settled. He promised me repeatedly he would do exactly as advised and pleaded that his family should not be troubled. I gave him my assurance. He said he would ring me up before returning to work. Thereafter, I had no problems with the MES union or any of the officers and subordinates. I, however, started getting requests whenever anyone had problems with the police. All genuine cases were looked into.

Air Force Requirements

There are two Air Force stations at Chandigarh – 12 Wing and 3 Base Repair Depot (BRD). Both are independent stations abutting each other. Except for donning the Air Force uniform, they had nothing in common as their roles were different. Inside the Air Force station complex, only the operational and administrative units were located. The married accommodation for the officers warrant officers and air warriors was in the city. However, the AOC's and the CO's of the flights and a few key officers had married accommodation inside the Air Force complex.

12 Wing had fighter, transport aircraft and helicopters. Their priority was the upkeep of infrastructure required for their functioning – runway, ATC, blast pens, hangars, radar station etc. For obvious reasons, everything had to be at its peak efficiency at all times and any snag/fault had to be rectified in the least time. For this proper SOPs were in place. During the first fortnight, after assuming charge, I spent two hours every day before office started to see all the facilities and understand their role, functions and the engineering support required. This knowledge is a must.

The runway painting became due four months after my posting. The AOC had requested me to do a very thorough job as it had an important role to play in the safety of aircraft during landing and take-off and camouflage of the runway. I assured him that he would be more than satisfied. He wanted the job to be completed in all respects in three months. This came as a surprise as, in all previous works, four months had been given for its execution. I had not seen such a job is done earlier and got hold of the relevant IS Codes and the previous tender document for reading as homework. After studying them and deliberations with the GE and the SW, we decided to add a number of clauses in the tender document. The major ones were; the complete paint and accessories required for the entire work would be bought within 10 days after commencement of work. In the first 20 days, the previous paint was to be scraped off and the surface prepared for the primer coat; the paint would only be permitted to be applied after it was tested at a renowned laboratory. I was aware that builders normally do not read the contract fine print in detail. In the pre-bid meetings, we highlighted the new conditions in the contract agreement. We also told them they would need sufficient painters to complete the work in 90 days and gave the bidders a copy of each of the relevant IS Codes. There was one young builder who was paying a lot of attention during the pre-bid meeting. I checked with my SW who told me that he is a budding builder full of josh and always does good work and on time. This builder had quoted the lowest cost for the work. After he was allotted the work, I called him and the GE in my office for a discussion. During our interaction, I was pleasantly surprised and happy to note that he had read each clause of the Contract Agreement and the IS Codes. He had also planned how to execute the work.

With a good builder and the experts of Asian Paints (who were supplying the paint) we had no problems and the work was completed one day before time with 10% spare paint (as the wastage was reduced). The AOC used to come often to observe the progress of work. He told me confidentially that during his service he had seen the painting of several air airfields but none like this ever. Incidentally, Mr Varinder Kumar Garg, the builder, is today the CEO of M/s Varindera Construction Ltd that executes works both in India and internationally.

DASI Inspections

The Directorate of Air Safety Inspection (DASI) is a central team of experts in each facet of an Air Force station. Its officers are of very high moral integrity. The DASI, on behalf of the Air Chief, conducts three inspections of all Air Force stations three times a year. Two inspections are conducted after due notice and one is a 'surprise inspection' with just three hours' notice. The DASI came in for a 'surprise inspection' soon after the runway was painted and they were highly impressed with the work done. Their Head complimented me and requested the tender document and relevant IS Codes, which we gladly handed over.

All AOC's take the DASI inspection very seriously. So do the MES staff, and I made myself available 24x7 for any assistance during the inspection. I would interact and clear doubts, if any. The MES was always tested for the operational role of repairing potholes on the runway and its basic tasks. This was an excellent method to test the operational readiness of any Air Force station. It can be introduced in Army formations too, with suitable modifications.

Debriefing After All Visits/Inspections

Another procedure the Air Force strictly followed was that thirty minutes after a VIP was seen off, a review meeting was held with all COs of the units which the VIP visited/inspected. All aspects that went amiss or could be improved are deliberated threadbare, in a frank and forthright manner, and necessary instructions/directions issued for action. No one is pulled up for an inadvertent fault; however, if it could have been prevented or occurred due to a definite lapse, the concerned officer is duly warned. I was always invited to these review meetings and found them pragmatic and workable. I followed the same procedure in my office and in my higher appointments too.

Air Force as a User

Initially, and till one establishes a rapport, the Air Force appear to be tough users. However, their requirements are for operational reasons only; hence, I always went out of the way to fulfil them. Once they know you are sincere, they give you tremendous respect and honour. I was always introduced to all VIPs who came for a visit. They also always invited me to their social events.

3 Base Repair Depot

The BRD has technical officers who are experts in their respective fields of avionics specialisation. I observed that they always took their work seriously and continuously updated their knowledge. Most of their workshops are, regrettably, of old vintage and have their limitations. Unfortunately, this is something no one is prepared to listen to. In my first meeting with the then AOC, Air Cmde Gurnani (who later rose to become an Air Marshal), he mentioned that, while air conditioning in the Army and Air Force Stations is for the comfort of human beings, in the case of BRD it is an absolute necessity for calibration of the various aircraft instruments. If it is not done at the appropriate temperatures, they would show wrong readings, which may lead to accidents. This hit me hard and I assured him (without studying the problem) that I would solve it in a week. The AOC was kind enough to remark that I could take a month but do something.

I then had a meeting with the GE and AGE (E/M). They averred that all the air-conditioning plants at 3 BRD had outlived their life and were functioning at 60-70 percent efficiency, only due to the extreme care being taken of them. They opined that there was no way we could reduce the temperatures, as the load of the heavy machines and personnel working inside the workshops was very high. When I saw that both had raised their hands, I called off the meeting and gave the problem a cool thought. Once a solution came to mind, I went once again to check the air conditioning plants closely.

At the air conditioning plant, only the operator was there. He was surprised to see me, alone. I sat down and requested a cup of tea. He had a kettle and made me a cup, while I asked a few questions about him and his family. When I thought that the rank barrier had been broken, I got on to the subject I had come to discuss. I asked him the time when he switched on the air-conditioning plant. He said about 15 minutes before the tradesmen came into the workshop. I then asked what would happen, in case we switch on the plant two hours earlier. He replied that then it would be cold and lower than the temperature they needed. However, when all tradesmen were inside, and the machines were switched on, the temperature would slowly rise but would remain lower than the maximum permissible. It was difficult to maintain the requisite temperature for the last one to two hours of the shift.

I then met the OIC of the workshop. Being a technical officer, he quickly grasped what I was getting at. He agreed that they could do the critical calibration in the morning hours and, in the latter part of the day, do those tasks for which rigid temperature control was not required. The next day, I was there to get the air-conditioning plant switched on two hours in advance and when the tradesmen walked in, they were extremely happy to feel the cold environment. I checked with the OIC of the workshop who was extremely happy at the temperatures now being maintained.

I then called the GE & AGE (E/M) and directed them to draw up a proper maintenance schedule for the plants, with the assistance of the vendors who had provided them. We finalised a proper SOP for action before starting the plant and at intervals, as laid down in the maintenance schedule. Similar action was taken for the other plants. The AOC was informed by his Workshop Officer about how the temperature problem had been resolved. The AOC, in turn, rang me up and conveyed his appreciation for the unconventional solution. Thereafter, I developed a great rapport and it was a pleasure and an honour to rub shoulders with him in ensuring they could exceed their overhauling tasks. Their other problems were comparatively simple, as I had tackled them earlier. Whenever a senior officer visited the BRD, the AOC would introduce me as an officer who has a solution to any problem.

External Services

In 12 Wing and 3 BRD, the need for the least breakdowns in electrical services is vital. As opposed to 12 Wing, 3 BRD was supplied from only one main feeder. I interacted with the Punjab State Electricity Board and explained our need. They went out of the way to provide another connection from the VIP feeder. The AOC had the work sanctioned straightway and, with two feeders, breakdowns in the BRD reduced drastically and they got additional time for repair and achieving their targets. A lot of activities had to be done inside the BRD campus periodically to reduce breakdowns and give high power-factor electricity with nil voltage drop. My practical learning as DCWE (E/M) helped, along with assistance from the Punjab State Electricity Board. I remembered the saying 'Good, Better, Best! Never let it rest till your good is better and your better is best'.

Similar action was taken for water supply, sewerage and drainage. Only improving the drainage inside the campus was of little use till the water had a clear passage to flow into the drain. I learnt this the hard way after the first monsoon. The floodwaters could not flow out as the drains had not been cleared by the civic authorities. From the next year on, I used to borrow a JCB from an engineer unit and clear the drains so that the airfield water would not accumulate but flow into the drains and the airport was not flooded. This was also highly appreciated by both the AOC's.

Army Units

CWE Chandigarh, I had three GEs under me for the various formations as under:

> At Patiala. The GE (Project) was looking after the KLP of the Armoured Division – both married and OTM accommodation. The GE (Maintenance) was looking after the upkeep of the formations and units at Patiala, Nabha and Sangrur. The GOC for the first six months was Maj Gen Shanker Roy Chowdhary (later the COAS) and thereafter Maj Gen AS Sandhu (who later became the DGMO). Both were outstanding officers, having their own perspective. I learnt a lot from them.
>
> At Chandigarh. One GE was looking after the maintenance and new construction of 'N' and 'K' areas, the SF Battalion at Nahan and other units in and around Chandigarh - Ordnance Cable Factory, TBRL, SASE etc.

Construction of New Married Accommodation

I would like to elaborate upon the methodology adopted by me to make improvements in both the new married and OTM accommodation. The first step was to get one married accommodation sample quarter completed at the earliest. Thereafter, I used to take my wife, along with two other officers's wives, to show them the sample quarter. They were accompanied by an officer to answer their queries and arrange tea and snacks for them. This officer noted down all the changes suggested by them, from the functional point of view. The ladies gave excellent points and all the aspects, which were feasible, were listed out. Thereafter the GOC's wife and two ladies from the formation were requested to visit the site and the modifications recommended by them were deliberated upon and got approved. Additional suggestions were also considered and the final list of changes finalised.

The GE thereafter prepared the draft financial effect of each of the points recommended for modification to the Zonal office. This was mandatory as all these works were within the CE's powers. These points were then presented to the 'Planning Team' of the CE Chandigarh Zone. Once they comprehended the changes being recommended, then the planning team of the Zone was taken to the site and each point and its financial effect was deliberated upon in detail and a final decision taken. Thereafter, a formal letter was written to the CE Zone for his approval. With so much homework, the approval was received promptly and the requisite amendments made. The builders were kept in the loop throughout the process. This ensured the Plus and Minus Deviation Orders were made simultaneously, rather than at the end of the project. The users were extremely happy that they were kept involved at each stage of the project.

Other than Married (OTM) Accommodation

A similar procedure was adopted, except that the concerned CO and his men were shown the accommodation and their functional inputs were looked into. The officers were always shown the accommodation being constructed at various stages and, wherever feasible, all changes proposed were implemented. I also made it a point to meet and interact with the Project Management Team (PMT) as and when they visited. These interactions ensured that the 'users' were always kept in the loop on all aspects of the project.

Posting Out

Before I realised it, two and half years had passed and, in July 1991, I received my posting orders to CME Pune as Commander of the Diploma Wing. CWE Chandigarh was a very difficult and tough assignment; however, it was a successful tenure. I managed to enhance the image of MES with both the Army and the Air Force.

I also succeeded in keeping a harmonious relationship between the civilians and the military. Fate too played its role to come to my assistance when the chips were down at the beginning of the tenure. I was also honoured with a Commendation from the Chief of the Air Staff. CWE Chandigarh was declared the best CWE in Western Command for both the years of my command. Maj Gen VN Kapur, CE Western Command, who later took over as E-in-C, was extremely happy with the working of my office and was happy to visit our 'users' who always praised the MES cover being provided to them.

Retrospect

A large number of lessons were learnt by me, as CWE Chandigarh. The important ones are:

Before taking over any assignment one must plan the schedule in accordance with the inputs obtained.

As my office had gone into 'sleep' mode, I did the duties and work of my subordinates for the first fortnight. This may not be always desirable, but it paid great dividends in handling my staff.

The 'One-Minute Manager' principle was applied to all fairly i.e., one-minute praise or one-minute rap on the knuckles.

It is important to inculcate the habit of giving feedback to everyone. I was always updated to respond when any 'user' rang up to check progress on any point.

Good work needs no advertising; the 'user' and the staff automatically come to know the same.

Despite all the hard work one put in, things can still wrong. Fate has a role to play. When the union leader acted tough with me, destiny sent the police right on time. A situation that I exploited, by telling a lie, resulted in my having no union problems thereafter. Had destiny not sent the police at the appropriate time to my rescue, I really do not know how I would have tackled the situation.

When positive results are seen in any effort, everyone starts contributing. When targets are achieved on or before time, there is an adrenaline rush to work much harder.

When an office is run efficiently, others speak with respect and help you in your effort.

Whatever I did not like in the MES during my tenure as DCWE (E/M) I changed viz. introduced discipline, camaraderie, care for juniors, and work as a well-knit team

Within the constraints and restrictions, one has to provide the best service to 'the users' with a smile. Never quote the rule book to 'the users'. One has to do the task/assignment (provided it is not for any individual) within the framework of the rules.

Since my wife and I closely interacted with all the officers and their families, we realised we had a talented lot. At short notice, and with little practice or rehearsal, we could organise and hold our Raising Day celebrations, which was highly appreciated by 'the users' and the zonal officers.

It is important to have a good working relationship with the builders. All problems were deliberated upon and the correct approach chosen in accordance with the Contract Agreement. By this healthy relationship, all works got executed on time and with least/no cost overruns. It is pertinent to mention here that the President of the Builders Association of Western Command was Mr Jawahar Goel, a mature gentleman who readily assisted us to tackle the not so good builders and always gave well considered sane advice on how to tackle complex issues.

Two points which I stressed were builders leave a site tidy and clean every day and the finishes should only be executed by good/excellent tradesmen.

After I realized one should not disturb one's seniors with problems, the solutions to even the knottiest problems automatically came to mind when a sincere thought was given to them.

Officers who served with me at CWE Chandigarh and in CE Chandigarh Zone remain in touch with me. The IDSE officers were Mr AK Sharma GE (AF), who superannuated as CE Delhi Zone. (He later served under me as SOI (E/M) when I was CE Southern Command and as CE Delhi Zone when I was the E-in-C). Mr MM Bhatia, who was AGE (B/R), under GE Chandigarh, recently completed his tenure as CE (AF) Allahabad and won the 'Best Zone trophy'. Mr Deepak Agarwal, GE (Project) at Patiala superannuated as CE (AF) Nagpur. Mr Gurdev Singh, from CE Chandigarh Zone, rose to be CE Bathinda Zone. Col VK Sharma (also from CE Chandigarh Zone) superannuated as CE(Navy) Bombay Zone when I was CE Southern Command. Mr Atul Sikka, AGE under GE (AF), stands approved as CE. Mr Tejinder Singh, BSO and Mr Vig, at GE Chandigarh and GE (AF) Chandigarh respectively, achieved the highest rank in their cadre. Both were outstanding and reliable officers. I will be failing in my duty in case I do not mention Mr Popli my SW, a cool and knowledgeable officer who never got rattled, and his ASW, Mr Alok Kumar, who still remembers the excellent exposure at Chandigarh and thereafter he never looked back.

FORESIGHT IS FORESEEING THE UNFORESEEN

Diploma Wing CME (Jul 91 — Oct 94)

After the tenure as CWE Chandigarh, my family and I were extremely happy to move to CME, Pune. We bid adieu to Chandigarh on a hot and humid day, in July 1991, with a warm send-off where all officers from CWE Chandigarh and the CE Chandigarh Zone as well as the CADOs of 12 Wing (Air Force) and 3 BRD turned up. In MES establishments this is very rare. I was extremely happy to see the spirit of camaraderie displayed.

On reaching Pune, we made ourselves comfortable in the 'Honeymoon' block. During the train journey, I had given a deep thought on what I had to do, after assuming my new appointment. The first week passed in interviews, listening to presentations, interacting with old friends and acquaintances, and admission of my daughters to school. We could settle down quickly as we had earlier served in the CME.

Once we settled down, I commenced devoting full attention to my new assignment. In addition to performing the primary duty of Commander Diploma Wing, I had four other responsibilities – PMC of the Officers Mess, Vice Chairman of Holloway School & of the Church, and Secretary of the Rowing & Equestrian Clubs. I commenced with the briefings on the Officers Mess from the Mess Secretary, and on the Diploma Wing from each of the Heads of Departments (HODs). I also interacted with the students attending the Diploma Course.

After a fortnight, I set myself the following objectives to be achieved, in the first six months:

> Improve the Officers Mess kitchen, and refine the procedure for procurement of local purchase items. In addition, improve the preparation of all items in the 'bill of fare'.
>
> Make the Diploma Wing students, living in the barracks and married accommodation, as comfortable as feasible. Also, make a definite improvement in the cook house, dining hall and the general administration of the students.

Officers Mess

For two days, from 0530 hours to 0830 hours, I was in the kitchen carefully watching how the duties were being performed and noted all the changes/improvements required. Thereafter, all the points were placed under different heads, based on who was to execute them. I discussed the list with the Mess Secretary, Maj Gajendra Chauhan, the Assistant Mess Secretary, Capt Jaspreet Brar and the mess staff. After deliberation and discussions, a few additional points were included which had been missed by me. The exhaustive list of tasks was to be executed by three agencies - Diploma Wing students, the MES, and from the Officers Mess funds. Once this list was finalised, I gave it to Maj Gajendra Chauhan, to assess the cost involved, especially for those items which involved expenses from the Officers Mess funds.

Gajendra Chauhan, after a long look at the list said, "Sir, can I speak frankly."

I replied, "Of course!"

He took a deep breath and said, "You are wasting your time; we will never get the requisite resources to do any of these tasks. I too had tried to do them when I took over; however, very soon I had to give up as I got no support from anywhere."

I thanked him for his frank and forthright advice and asked how much money could be spent from the Officers Mess funds, under my financial powers. It was Rs 2,500 each month. Both Gajendra and Jaspreet initially wondered if I was a crazy man who would not listen to sane advice. Later, when they saw the changes being implemented, they commenced having faith in me and both gave me more than100 percent in effort and sincerity.

I then did a mental appreciation and decided that I would have to use the Diploma Wing students, after class hours, to the maximum extent. I would also have to request for essential earth moving plant and assistance from the E/M faculty. Last, but not the least, I needed a lot of assistance from the GE of the CME. To cut the story short, employing the Diploma boys and with the assistance of the GE, I got all the essential repairs done and gave a face-lift to the kitchen.

Before utilising the students, I discussed it with my officers in the Diploma Wing. They discouraged me saying that most of the students were educated and being from the clerical stream were not accustomed to fatigue work. Further, they would not hesitate to write long complaints on how they were being treated. I thought on the matter and then sent a note to the Deputy Commandant-cum-Dean, Maj Gen SS Randhawa, highlighting the importance of practical and application-oriented training for Diploma students. Further, it would also assist in obtaining recognition for our courses, as Government Diploma courses were for three years and the CME Diploma Course was for only two years. My note was approved by him and also put up to the Commandant for his information.

After the work was completed, the JEs (one from the Army and other a civilian) from the GEs office were requested to address the Diploma students. They took pride in explaining all relevant details. The combatant JE had passed out from CME three years earlier and he told the Diploma students that they were fortunate to go through this application-cum-practical-training capsule. During his time, since they did not receive any practical training, they had difficulties during their first posting to MES establishments. He advised them to try and do maximum practical works as that would assist them later in the MES.

Reduction of Pilferage

With the infrastructure of the kitchen improved, the next steps were to stop/reduce pilfering of rations. Through my SM, I selected two local students of the Diploma Wing, who had a good command of the local language and dialect, to mix with the Mess staff for three days and check from them where all pilfering, if any, was taking place. It was found that only sugar and tea was being purloined by the women who came to work. I stopped giving morning and evening tea from the Officers Mess to the student officers. They were requested to make their own arrangements for brewing tea in their rooms. They readily agreed as the tea prepared by the Officers Mess was not up to their standard. Also, everyone had his own timing for tea. Jaspreet was made personally responsible to ensure that the ration (free and payment) was up to the mark qualitatively and in quantity. This check made a huge difference.

Reduction in Messing Charges

I recalled the days when I was a student officer on the EODE course. A few student officers did not come for breakfast at all, as they got up late in the mornings. A greater number also did not have dinner in the Officers Mess as they either went out or attended a party in the Officers Institute at CME. On Saturday nights over 25% did not have dinner in the Officers Mess, as they went to the RSI at Pune, or somewhere else to eat. I checked with the stewards and they agreed with my assessment. Based on this, directions were issued to the Mess Secretary to provide rations based on the anticipated strength and not the posted strength of dining members.

The mess timings were strictly enforced. However, no officer was stopped from entering the Officers Mess for lunch & dinner. Nonetheless, as opposed to the menu in the bill of fare, the officer was offered an egg *bhujia*/chicken/*paneer* dish for which he was charged separately. This worked well; wastage of cooked food stopped and rations were saved. From the saved *atta*, rice and *dal* we were able to feed the Officers Mess civilian staff free of charge, after getting a no-objection from the student officers. The daily messing charges were also reduced from Rs 7 to Rs 3.

Reduction of Wastage

I had also observed that a large number of officers had the bad habit of filling their plates and leaving half of it uneaten. During my rounds in the dining hall, I explained to them that they were wasting food, while a large number of people in the country were sleeping with an empty stomach. By this regular talk, the wastage came to near zero and we could further reduce the quantity of meals to be cooked and the daily messing reduced from Rs 3 to Rs 1.70.

Improving the Standard of Cooking

To improve the standard of meals we again adopted a practical solution. We checked with the 300-odd Diploma students whether they had any relatives or acquaintance working as cooks in and around Pune. To our good fortune, four students did and one was a chef in a four-star hotel. We made them interact with the Officers Mess cooks. They gave simple and practical tips and also accepted our request to come to CME on their days off, to practically show our cook how to improve the dishes. This made a definite improvement in the taste of the food and also improved the presentation exponentially. The dining members immediately noticed the change, though the cost of dishes did rise marginally.

Maintaining the Standard of Infrastructure and Services

Improving the standard of infrastructure and services is comparatively easy; however, maintaining it at that level is difficult. Surprise inspections were conducted once a fortnight. One minute of praise and one minute of rapping knuckles of those who did not perform, worked. In addition, the most dedicated worker got a good gift from the Mess Secretary and the worst worker had to pay a fine. Fines, as I observed in Botswana, worked in India too.

Improvement in Accounting System

Once the Officers Mess started functioning well, we had enough spare rations to bake biscuits for the dining-in student officers every month. I then went on to streamline the accounts of the Officers Mess to ensure that the monthly bills were handed over to the members, on the first day of every month, whether they dining-in or non-dining members. For this, the date of the bill was amended to the 25th of each month. All members were reminded that the first cheque to be signed by anyone, in any month, should always be to the Officers Mess.

General Body Meeting

My first General Body Meeting (GBM) of the Officers Mess lasted exactly 24 minutes. It was a monologue by me and not a single comment came from any staff or student member. The then Commandant, Lt Gen CA Barretto, in his closing remarks said, "Thank you for this gift, as this is my last GBM." He was superannuating two months later and Lt Gen KC Taneja was to take over. Incidentally all GBMs, when I was the PMC, were always over in less than 25 minutes and with no comments. This was feasible as I was available to all officers 24x7 and met them formally and informally frequently. I always gave them a patient hearing. Whenever a point was raised that would benefit the majority, immediate action would be taken on it. In case it could not be implemented, for any reason, I would convince the member with logical reasoning.

Boundary Wall Connecting the 'In' and 'Out' Gates of the Officers Mess

In those days, there was no wall connecting the 'In' and 'Out' gates of the Officers Mess. I went for a drive on the Pune-Bombay road and took photographs of a number of security walls. I gave them to the architects of my wing and asked them to submit three designs for a wall to be constructed in front of the Mess. The design was to be such that it meshed with the surroundings. They did an excellent job and I went with the designs to the Commandant, who approved one. Initially, it appeared an easy project. The alignment of the wall had to be parallel to the Officers Mess. After a detailed survey, it was seen that we would have to shift one of the pillars of the 'Out' gate by 3.2 inches; then alone it would be parallel to the Officers Mess. This was done and the end product beautifully meshed with the surroundings and exists even now for all to see.

Preparation of the Front Lawns in front of the Officers Mess (Towards the Front Wall)

I was aware that the CME was to celebrate its Silver Jubilee, the following year. A season prior to the event, I decided to improve the lawns in front of the Officers Mess which were in a rundown condition. I checked with the officers under me whether they knew a horticulturist who could advise us on how to replant the grass. Good fortune struck; a civilian officer's cousin was working in the Maharashtra Horticulture Department. He came with his head gardener who was an expert in sowing grass. After seeing our lawns, he said it had too many weeds. In case, we wanted a good lawn we would have to remove all the existing grass and de-weed it by ploughing the area. Thereafter, we would have to manually remove all the weeds and top soil. In addition, he mentioned a long procedure to prepare the fresh surface by adding river sand and good soil to the black cotton soil. He stressed that, in case we work hard and can prepare the surface and plant the grass before the monsoon, there would be a very good lawn after the monsoon. The result was there for all to see.

Banquet for the Army Commander

A banquet was to be held in the Officers Mess after the Army Commander's annual inspection. Prior to this, dinner nights were the norm. The advent of banquets, which ladies also attended, soon became de rigueur. As it was an important function, at about 1700 hours, I went to check on the arrangements with the Mess Secretary. I was assured that everything was under control, but the manner he said it told me something is amiss. As I walked towards the kitchen, the Mess Secretary stopped me and said that John, the Chief Chef, had got drunk and they were getting him sober by making him drink lots of lime water to induce him to vomit. He expected him to be on his feet in an hour. The Mess

Secretary added that all dishes according to the approved menu were ready, only the dessert was yet to be prepared. I got worried and asked the other chefs if they would be able to prepare it without John. All kept quiet. I knew we had a problem at hand. I requested my wife to come to the Mess. When I told her what had happened, she said that she cannot prepare the dessert – 'Tipsy Pudding' – for all the attendees. I then cajoled her to prepare it for the main table only which she did hesitantly. We were back in the Officer's Mess early for a last-minute check when I got a call from the Commandant that, as some important guests of the Army Commander had come to meet him without notice, the dinner would start 45 minutes late. What a relief this call was!

When I went into the kitchen, I saw the Chief Chef on his feet. I told him that we had an additional hour so he could go about his task coolly. The Mess Secretary intervened to say that he had lied that all dishes were ready, actually two had yet to be cooked; but with the extra time available, they would be easily ready on time. I kept my cool and walked away.

The banquet went off very well. The Army Commander was Lt Gen Bipin Joshi (my GOC in 16 Infantry Division at Abohar). As the PMC, I received him with the Commandant. I had to be seated at the top table while my wife was seated at the table in front of the main table. When the dinner was over, the Army Commander while walking out, surprised everyone by going to talk to my wife and then leave, escorted by the Commandant. He recognised my wife during dinner and had walked over to say hello and exchange pleasantries as he had not met her in the ante-room, before the dinner. Such were the generals of yesteryears.

When we were seeing the Army Commander off, I heard him mention to the Commandant that after a long time he had tasted authentic tipsy pudding of his NDA days. He added he would send his cook to CME for learning the recipe. I never told anyone what happened.

As PMC of the Corps of Engineers Mess, I learnt a number of lessons. Some of them are:

> To improve any existing running establishment, one has to first comprehend the problems objectively and then to find a pragmatic and workable solution for them.

> Improving such institutions requires total involvement and cannot be done by issuing orders.
>
> Officers dining in the Officers' Mess have to be handled in a correct, yet tactful, manner.
>
> Mess bills commenced being paid on time when the fine was made exorbitant for any delay.
>
> Thefts and wastage can be reduced by appropriate methods. It also helps in reducing the daily messing charges.

Administration of the Diploma Wing

Before commencing actions to improve the administration of the Diploma Wing, there was a need to obtain a clear insight on what the students desired and what all could be done. For this, all the complaints submitted by Diploma students earlier were studied. They were mainly on pilfering of rations, poor hygiene of the cook house and unlivable conditions in their barracks. Some complaints were on delay in issue of their Part-II Orders etc.

Improvement of the Barracks and the Bathrooms

As usual, we took up the easiest task first, i.e., improvement of the barracks and the bathrooms. A check revealed that they were indeed poorly maintained and the distemper had come off in many places. We again did exactly what was done in the Officers Mess. We removed all the previous coats of distemper and thereafter distempered the walls and roof according to the laid down procedure i.e., preparation of surface etc. As the Diploma students were working in their own barracks and they were aware that 30 percent of the total marks in most subjects were for practical work, every student put in his best to score the maximum marks, in practical work. Simultaneously, the bathrooms and the surrounding areas were spruced up. The bathrooms took time as there were a number of wash basins, WCs and mirrors which had to be replaced. For giving a new look to the flooring we hired a vendor with a machine to grind and polish the mosaic/chip flooring. This vendor did an excellent job as he was given free meals and was permitted to stay in the campus till the work was completed.

It was essential to teach the Diploma students that top class work cannot be achieved by only utilising the best ingredients. Good tradesmen who had talent and good workmanship are equally essential.

Improvement in the Kitchen

As regards the kitchen of the OR Mess, those days the cooking was done with coal and firewood. The walls and roof were covered with soot. I tasked the SM and the Administrative JCO to take up this work. They were given a week to plan the work and permitted to commence work from a Friday afternoon, when 25 of the best students were excused classes on Saturday. As expected, the SM planned each activity meticulously, procured the materials, and arranged for the tools and plants required for the work. The Diploma students were impressed.

Prevention of Pilferage or Complaints on the Food Prepared

The next step was to ensure that there were no pilferage or complaints on the food prepared. After a deliberate thought, I decided to remove all the administration staff from the kitchen/*langar* and hand over the responsibility of the kitchen/*langar* totally to the Diploma students. For this, three Diploma students would be excused classes for one day. The SM was with me on this change; however, he requested that five Diploma students should be given this task for each day since the *langar* catered for a large strength. Further, the Diploma students could also be given the additional responsibility to look after their barrack, bathrooms and the garden in front.

This idea came to me from the fact that, when I did my degree course, rowers were excused classes up to 1030 hours every day for close to three months. Yet we all did very well on the course. The Diploma students were excused classes only for one day and a proper SOP of how they would take notes of the classes they had missed was promulgated and followed.

By making the Diploma students in-charge of their own kitchen, there were no complaints on its functioning, pilferage of rations and their administration. They also ensured that their barracks were kept spotlessly clean themselves. Cleanliness is a habit which can be inculcated, if enforced sensibly.

Married Accommodation of the Students of the Diploma Wing

The ORs married accommodation of the students of the Diploma Wing posed no problems. One of students living in the married accommodation, along with three selected additional students, was tasked to plan the project, and brief the SM of their requirement. The SM added additional points like clearing of the roof and surrounding areas. They did a splendid task, with total harmony and team work.

Day-to-day Administration

I selected the best-suited Diploma students for various administrative duties viz. getting works done from MES, to carry out market purchases, and to carry out liaison with the Administration Wing for issue of Part II Orders, as well as liaison with the Railways for booking travel tickets. These students, depending upon when assistance was required by any of them, were permitted to miss the afternoon practical classes. Since they had excellent liaison with the concerned people, they got the work done smoothly. The principle of best man for the job was applied, and there were no problems.

By the end of six months my immediate actions on all essential points of my duty as Commander Diploma Wing, were completed. The Wing had commenced reacting positively to all my orders. Further, these activities convinced them that I am their true leader and I was performing my duty and nothing more. Incidentally, I did not inform my seniors of all what the Diploma Wing had achieved. It was only when I was making major changes, that I obtained prior clearance.

Overall Championship Trophy

During my tenure, Diploma Wing always won the 'Overall Championship'. More important we beat Adm Wing in the 'Best Barrack Championship' for the first time and continued winning this trophy for three years.

Training Curriculum

Having served as a DCWE (E/M) and as a CWE, I knew exactly what duties a JE is expected to perform. These were clearly spelt out in the MES Rules and Regulations. I had a brain-storming session with the Heads of Departments. They were convinced that there is a definite need to change the syllabus. A revised syllabus was prepared which focussed less on theory and more on application and was practical-oriented. I had to repeatedly remind them that the Diploma course had to be tailor made for a JE to function effectively in the MES which services the Army, Navy, Air Force and other allied organisations.

I also met the Principals of the Diploma institutes in Pune. I learnt that the Diploma College at Pune was basically training personnel to fit into two firms – Bajaj and Kirloskar. They mentioned that their annual meet for syllabi of the Academic Council, in which representatives of Kirloskar and Bajaj, would attend was being held the next day. I obtained an invitation to attend. What surprised me, during the deliberations at the meet, was that the maximum changes in syllabi were being asked for by these two firms, as good training saved them time and money when the trainees were inducted into their firms. I too worked on this principle.

Once the syllabus was finalised, I had to take the approval of the Dean-cum-Deputy Commandant. He had never served in the MES, but was very happy to hear that the future JEs would be more effective and approved the syllabus. For implementing the revised syllabus, a lot of work had to be done by the Diploma Wing officers. During this exercise,

I came to know all my officers very well and also got to know of the inadequacies in their knowledge. By the time the revised lessons plans were prepared, each officer in my Wing gained additional knowledge too.

Feedback

In CME, a large number of extra-curricular activities keep a senior officer very busy. I had a gut feeling that many of my instructors were not teaching in a professional manner. Since I could not go to the classes on a regular basis, I had to find a method of showing them a mirror of what their students thought of them as instructors and of me as the Commander of the Wing. Accordingly, I prepared a single sheet 'Feedback' form which included a number of questions viz:

On performance of the Commander

—Are they comfortable in their barracks?

—Is there any pilferage of rations taking place?

—Are their administrative problems being attended to?

—Is the Commander performing the duties expected of him?

On performance of the Instructors

—Name three Instructors who come late to the class.

—Name three Instructors who do not teach properly.

—Name three Instructors who inform you the likely questions which may be included in the examination paper.

— Name three Instructors who are too lenient in marking the papers.

The students were not required to write their name on the form, however all questions had to be truthfully answered. A correct pen picture of each of the instructors was clearly visible. I then called each of them individually to my office and let them know what their students think of them. I also warned them that, in case I do not observe a definite improvement, I would be left with no alternative other than to attach the feedback form with their respective ACRs. I observed a definite improvement in all my instructors. I did permit the officers to read the feedback received on me too. This practice, though planned to be done every six months, had to be done only once again, when a positive feedback was received on most of the instructors.

Sunday Classes

On observing that some students were absolutely outstanding, and with my experience as instructor in F Combat, I introduced classes in the Diploma Wing from 0930 to 1230 hours, on Sundays (not on other holidays). On this day, the good students were nominated to takes class on topics in which the majority of students were observed to be weak and they could have their doubts cleared. This was a big success and there was a distinct improvement in results.

I also issued directions to all instructors to come on Sundays, any time between 1000 to 1100 hours, and go around the classes to clear doubts, if any, of their students. No instructor objected, though I could feel they did not like it. Surprisingly, I got calls from a number of officer's wives that this was a very good step initiated by me. During the one to two hours their husbands were away, they were able to complete their household chores without any disturbance. After visiting the classrooms, all instructors were advised to spend some time in the Officers Mess library to read newspapers and magazines and to draw books to read at home. Very soon, all instructors appreciated this step also as they enjoyed visiting the library. I had been performing this ritual in my previous tenure, and it was something I always looked forward to. It relaxed me from the daily grind.

AMIE for Outstanding Students

After nine months, I observed that a few students were extremely intelligent and always scored close to full marks. After checking five boys closely, I went to the Dean-cum-Deputy Commandant and highlighted their capabilities to him. I requested that they be kept in CME for two additional years, after they finished their Diploma Course and the Wing would assist them to appear in the AMIE examination to obtain an engineering degree. It was accepted 'in-principle' and a case was projected to the E-in-Cs Branch which approved the proposal. Before I left CME, three boys had easily cleared the AMIE examination and two of them had thereafter become officers.

Stopping Direct Entry JCO's into MES

To make up the deficiencies of JE's in the MES, direct entry for Diploma holders was permitted. Those selected, who had a Diploma in any field of engineering, after undergoing a basic soldiering course at the Group Centres were inducted into the MES, as JCOs. However, CME Diploma holders who underwent a tailor-made course for the MES at the CME had to stay on as NCOs, till their turn came for promotion. Further, all Diploma colleges in India were running tailor-made courses for entry into the Railways, Automobile Engineering firms etc. The students who attended a Diploma course, in these colleges, actually could not perform their duties in the MES. Initially, the Commandant did not accept my viewpoint. I felt that I had not put the point across to him properly. I told him that I too was of his opinion till, towards the end of my tenure as CWE Chandigarh, I met a Direct Entry JCO deployed as officer in-charge of an electric sub-station who was consistently failing to perform his duties. When I questioned him, he mentioned that he was a Direct Entry JCO who had done a diploma course in Automobile Engineering from a college in Gurgaon. The Commandant then understood the problem and consented to putting up a suitable case to the E-in-C's Branch. It was initially not understood there also. I was called to explain and present the case to the E-in-C personally. I went fully prepared with all facts and was able to convince him on the blunder made to induct Direct Entry JCOs into the MES.

Recognition of Diploma Courses Run by CME

With the changes made in the curriculum, and increase in the number of periods being attended by the students on application/practical training we were able to convince the concerned Regulatory authorities to recognise the CME Diploma for B/R and E&M. We also succeeded in getting the CME Diploma for Architecture recognised from the competent authority.

CME Golden Jubilee Celebrations

Having re-laid the front lawns of the Officer's Mess during the previous monsoon and constructed the front boundary wall connecting the 'In' and 'Out' gates of the Officer's Mess, I got involved in the CME Golden Jubilee Celebrations. As the total number of attendees was large, the only place feasible for dinner for such a large gathering was the Officer's Mess front lawns.

The COAS, Gen BC Joshi, was the Chief Guest. After seeing the Combat Demonstration, the COAS and the guests along with the hosts were to have dinner on the front lawns of the Officer's Mess. Temporary structures had to be fabricated to display the life of CME which had to be elegant and simple. I first put the existing tables in an E-shaped pattern. Thereafter, the stewards and waiters laid out the silver, cutlery and crockery. The cover overhead was designed with hollow pipes and a V-shaped roof. This structure was thereafter covered with white cloth and for lighting two temporary tube lights were fixed. Similar temporary pipe structures were designed for the bars. These well-lit structures looked attractive. The Corps colour awnings gave it a military look.

The Commandant, Lt Gen KC Taneja, was contemplating precluding the degree course students from the dinner, as he felt that it would become too large a gathering and difficult to manage. As I was responsible for the event I intervened and strongly recommended that the student officers be permitted to attend as they were the future and it was important for them to learn how to organise such events. I took responsibility for their good behaviour. The Commandant accepted my request.

As the Officers Mess waiters could only cater to the guests and senior officers, I selected suitable students from the Diploma Wing to perform duties of the barmen. They were attired in white shirt, black trousers and a black band to serve the EODE courses. The entire event up to the fireworks finale went off splendidly. After all the guests and senior officers left, totally impressed and happy, Exercise 'Close Down' commenced. This was planned systematically and to the last detail and a rehearsal had been conducted earlier. I stayed back till all the silver had been deposited safely in the 'Silver Room' where it was checked, rechecked and then sealed. All officers posted in the Diploma Wing were present and literally forced me to go home assuring me that everything would be done to my expectations. I told them I would come in the morning at 0530 hours to check. The Mess Secretary, Maj Chauhan, was there and he confirmed that except for one fork missing there was no loss either of the vendors or the Officers Mess crockery and cutlery. The liquor and soft drinks consumed had been worked out and the Noting Sheet would be ready by 1100 hours. He also told me that the Diploma Wing Officers and students were there till 0300 hours, till everything was silently and systematically put back at its original locations. Not a single vehicle was used as the guests were staying in the guest rooms on both sides of the Officers Mess. He added that but for them, the Officers Mess could not have been able to do this gigantic task.

The gardeners were on the Mess lawns at 0600 hours sweeping quietly to give them a clean manicured look. When the guests woke up, they were astonished to see the lawns immaculate and wondered how the paraphernalia was removed without any noise. Maj Chauhan added that the Officers' Mess was ready to serve breakfast. I was extremely proud of my team. Later, an officer from each of the EODE courses came to meet me at the Diploma Wing after their classes were over. I thought something had occurred during the dinner about which they had come to complain. When I called upon them to sit, they said that they had just come to thank me for having faith in them and to say that they had thoroughly enjoyed the 'Silver Jubilee Celebrations' and complimented me for organising it so well. I was speechless. It is then one realises that goodwill begets goodwill.

The Silver Jubilee Celebrations taught me a number of lessons:

Anticipating tasks, well in advance, and working on them makes things easier.

There is unbelievable talent available, one has only to locate and tap it. The Diploma Wing architects and students made such good cut-outs from thermocol sheets of the life in CME campus, at no cost. When we got stuck at the last moment for having black bows, two officers' wives helped and did such a marvellous job that saved us a lot of money.

We got an excellent vendor through the civilian chefs who had come to train our cooks and they were very professional. The vendor provided delicious fare at a competitive cost. More important the food was distributed warm, and quietly at the appropriate time which could not have done by us. By employing professionals, you get excellence on time, without any hassles.

Considering the age of officers doing the EODE courses and student attitude being what it is, things can get out of control. However, they become a force multiplier when they are treated maturely. On my superannuation, the officers attending EODE courses, when I was Commander Diploma Wing, had become Cols. During official get-togethers to which I was invited, they would tell me that they knew me since I was Commander Diploma Wing at CME.

Church

The CME church was a small building. For major occasions, we had to hold events outdoors for a stage, crib piers and wooden chassis had to be taken on loan from the Bridging School. It was a long and time-consuming procedure to do so. I arranged to build a permanent stage outside from waste material and cement. I was happy to see it existing when I was Commandant CME.

Holloway School

The school was efficiently run by the teachers employed from amongst the staff and student officers' wives. As it was in the CME campus, there were a large number of aspirants for the few vacancies of teachers; selection was always a difficult task. I recall a student officer's wife who was an MBA and B. Ed., who was not selected as she was considered, over-qualified to be a Nursery teacher. She was very upset and came to my office to argue her case. It took a lot of persuasion and patience to explain the situation. I felt sorry for her and got her a good assignment in Pune, for which she was grateful.

Equestrian Club

We had two ponies in the Equestrian Club and it was good fun going for a ride in the early mornings. One pony was really good and we trained her for a race to be held in the Pune Race Club. She won the Sub Area Commander's cup which was a first for the CME.

Posting

For the first time in my career, I had spent more than three years in one appointment. I had over 35 officers from the Army, IDSE officers (from different cadres) and GREF officers in the Wing. All of them contributed towards achieving the KRAs we had set for ourselves.

The results of No. 3 Special Selection Board for promotion had been declassified and I stood approved for the rank of Brigadier. However, my posting order came to command 658 Engineer Bridge Unit. I left CME on posting in October 1994, after an intellectually stimulating, socially satisfying, and professionally rewarding tenure.

I cannot end this chapter without expressing my gratitude for the guidance and total support I received from the Commandants I served under in this tenure at the CME – Lt Gen CA Barretto, Lt Gen KC Taneja and Lt Gen NR Khanna, all outstanding Sappers. Maj Gen SS Randhawa, Maj Gen WS Chona and Maj Gen TM John were the Deputy Commandants. Needless to add, during this long tenure at CME,

I met and made friends with a large number of officers though they were serving in other faculties and wings.

Before I end this chapter, I must mention how the IT building in the CME campus came up. Col Venugopal, an officer from the DRDO came on a visit to the CME and met Maj Gen SS Randhawa who was the then Deputy Commandant-cum-Dean. The General, during the interaction, mentioned a policy letter issued by the MT Directorate, a year or two earlier, that the DRDO could construct an IT Complex in any Class 'A' training establishment where a void in IT training was observed. Maj Gen SS Randhawa had served in the MT Directorate as a Colonel and as a Brigadier, and was aware of this letter. Col Venugopal did not know that such a letter existed and confirmed it from his office. A fortnight later, Col Venugopal got the construction of the IT Complex commenced in the CME campus. That was the power of DRDO. The building, unfortunately, was completed only after Maj Gen SS Randhawa superannuated.

DO NOT COUNT THE DAYS; MAKE THE DAYS COUNT

658 Engr Br Unit (Nov 94 — Jun 95)

The most difficult part of an army career is the unknown. Not knowing where you are going to be posted next and what the circumstances are going to be. I had been promised by the E-in-C, Lt Gen Jagdish Narain, that I would get command of an engineer regiment. Yet, after the hectic, yet enjoyable and satisfying three-year tenure as Commander Diploma Wing, I was posted as CO 658 Engineer Bridge Unit, at Guwahati. By then, telephonic connection with the East had considerably improved and I could speak to the CO, Col Ramesh Chander, and obtain a good feed-back on the state of the unit. I learnt that it was due to move to Nasirabad by early March 1995.

Based on this input, I mentally planned the actions to be taken during the handing/taking over the period and thereafter. I also decided to move alone to Guwahati leaving my family behind. This enabled my daughters to complete their academic year in their respective school and college at Pune.

On reaching Guwahati, in November 1994, the 2IC of the unit along with the SM received me and took me to the single officers' accommodation alongside the Officers Mess of the unit. I was the only officer dining in the Mess. I surprised the 2IC by requesting him to direct the head clerk to send me all policy and running files (less the files which the present CO may require) for perusal at night.

By the third day, in addition to the handing/taking over notes, I had gone over all the relevant files and heard the CO's briefing. All these inputs updated me on the state of the unit, and what all needed to be done before the impending move. As was my habit, I made copious notes to clarify and update my knowledge. When I took over command, the following facts stood out:

> 658 Engineer Bridge Unit, since raising 16 years earlier, had never moved out of Guwahati.
>
> In accordance with the OR posting policy, prevailing those days, a unit only intimated its deficiencies in various trades. The regiments had a choice to post anyone they desired of that trade to this Unit. To put it bluntly, all OR considered undesirable by the regiments were posted. Most of the personnel had red ink entries and a poor discipline record.
>
> The unit had to move out to its new location in three months. Prior to the move, it had to hand over 3,500 MT of bridging equipment to several depots, and close to 330 APBVs, most of which had outlived their life, to several ASC battalions. No action regarding whom the vehicles, bridging equipment and the accommodation were to be handed over had been initiated.
>
> The technical and administrative inspections for the current training year were due.
>
> The annual BPET, PPET and range classification were yet to be conducted. The annual CEME, small-arms inspection and other minor inspections for the current year were due.
>
> There was no packing materials collected to fabricate the boxes to carry unit loads.
>
> The Advance Party was due to move out one day after I took over the command.

On assuming command, I gave the following directions:

> PT parade would be held from 0500 to 0540 hours daily from the next day.
>
> Two personnel of the unit would accompany me for my morning and evening walk-cum-run every day. The list for this was to be

drawn up, seniority-wise, of JCOs, NCOs and ORs in the unit. This practice would continue till all personnel had been on the walk-cum-run with me. The Duty L/NK, every evening would hand over the names of the personnel detailed to walk with me, the next morning, when he comes to give me the 'All OK Report'.

A tentative block programme, with suitable dates after taking into account all relevant factors, was to be drawn up for the various inspections, handing over the vehicles, bridging equipment and preparations for the move of the Unit.

One officer was to be in charge of all the inspections along with two JCO's. The other officer would work directly under me for liaison and collection of allied items, stores, etc. These inspection teams had to work out the resources required for each inspection, in detail.

All Sundays were to be full working days till all the inspections were over.

I would hold conferences daily, at 1430 hours.

The first *sainik sammelan* was to be held at 0930 hours, the next day. After the *sainik sammelan,* I would go around the entire unit. All stores were to be kept open for inspection.

The previous CO was to be given a befitting farewell based on when he planned to move. The senior Capt would coordinate all activities and keep me informed.

The 2IC, along with the Advance Party would leave for Nasirabad, after showing me around the unit area, as given in the schedule.

It was clear to me that, to command such a unit, a different approach would have to be adopted. More importantly, to complete all the impending tasks, in the time frame available, a concerted effort had to be put in from the first day onwards and that too intelligently. With the 21C, Capt Sunil Mohril (with five years' service) moving out with the Advance Party, I would be left with only two young officers, Capt Anil Joon and Capt PH Sharma (with three years and two years of service respectively). Hence, I had to take hands-on charge.

The Discipline of Unit Personnel

This was my major concern and I had been giving it serious thought from the day I came to know about it. I concluded that I had to deal with this subject differently. The following steps were taken:

> All personnel were to be kept busy so that they are physically exhausted every day. The morning PT parade was to be compulsory and tough.

The two individuals who were to accompany me, every morning and evening, for a 7 to 8-kilometre walk-cum-run, would be used to speak about their problems, name the naughty boys and perhaps even suggest corrective measures. Through this interaction, I would know everyone in my unit and they too would come to know me.

The walk with the CO became a topic of discussion amongst the JCOs, NCOs and ORs. Since I was staying alone, in the evenings I would often go to the *langar* on the pretext of tasting their food. I used to go prepared with jokes to make them laugh and try and make them forget their tension and hard work. This worked beautifully for the first four weeks, and there was no disciplinary case.

The First Disciplinary Case

After four weeks, I decided to give a Sunday off to the troops, as they looked jaded and tired. That day, I spent the morning with two clerks, going over the actions to be taken for the move of the unit and studying the relevant Army Orders and Army Instructions. It all came back to me, as I had done this exercise earlier when I was the Adjutant of 53 Engineer Regiment for the move to Amritsar.

After a slightly heavy lunch, and a glass of beer, I planned to have my first-afternoon siesta. Just when I had nodded off, the telephone rang. The call was from the local police SHO to inform me that he had caught two boys from my unit, drunk and misbehaving with the local women. With the SM, I was at the police station in 15 minutes. I had met the SHO earlier; accordingly, he released the boys.

In the unit, I asked them to tell me what happened. The Sikh sapper told me that the police had put a bottle of liquor in their mouth and got them drunk. When I told him that he was in Assam and not in Punjab, he smiled and I knew he was lying. An extremely tough schedule from 0400 to 2000 hours was enforced for them. They were given only two *chappatis* and watery *dal* to eat for breakfast, lunch and dinner, with no tea. The punishment was carried out in front of other unit personnel so that everyone realises that it is not worth being undisciplined. What hit the ORs most was the food given to the defaulters. This I came to know later when interacting with them at the *langar.*

After three days, both defaulters had lost more than five to six kilograms of weight and were literally in tears. They were told to truthfully tell their story and as further punishment, they had to stand in front of the PT parade and apologise for letting the unit down and assure everyone that, in future, they would never do any action which would give the unit a bad name. Their further punishment was then condoned. The impact was so much that others, who invariably came late from leave, commenced reporting back a day earlier. Everyone appreciated the tough punishment given to the defaulters as against holding a court-martial. The creative solution worked.

A Zero-Accident Drive

A check of the records revealed that the unit had one or two accidents each month and a large number of them were fatal. After serious thought, a 'different' solution worked amazingly i.e., the drivers' conscience must dictate the imperative need to drive safely. For this, a list of all drivers was made state-wise along with the language the driver could read and comprehend. I recall there were a total of six languages. The clerks/personnel who could write in these six languages were then called in and asked to pen a paragraph in the crude colloquial language of what could be the consequences for his family, in case he met with an accident where he could die or be incapacitated for life. The worst-case scenario was mentioned. This had to be read and signed by the driver before he drove his vehicle out from the unit. By this admonition, we had no accident while I was the CO.

Handing Over of Over 300 APBVs

There were no directions as to which units the APBVs were to be handed over. With great effort, just three days before the CEME inspection, I was able to get the requisite order issued. Normally, handing over of vehicles is an extremely difficult task as the unit taking them over raises maximum defects while the unit handing over wants to show that all is in order. This 'cat and mouse game' went on for five days and only one vehicle was taken over. As all the vehicles had been through the CEME inspection, I knew I was on a strong wicket. I met the CO of the EME Battalion who suggested that I may consider driving the remaining 49 vehicles out of the unit and he would declare them 'BER'. When the ASC Battalion CO came to know about this, he rushed to meet me. He apologised and took over 45 vehicles in one day. The rest were declared BER by the EME Battalion. The remainder vehicles were handed over to other units without any problems. Thus, we were able to adhere to the tight schedule we had set for ourselves.

Handing Over of 350 MT of Bridging Stores

For handing over the bridging equipment, the letter to nominate whom the stores were to be handed over to was issued after a tremendous amount of liaison. They had to be handed over to different establishments. Since we had handed over our vehicles, we got third line transport for back loading the stores. This too was a big exercise as loaded vehicles had to travel between 100 to 150 kilometres, unload the equipment, get the stores checked, and thereafter stack them where the taking-over depot desired. The turn-round time took three to four days. The taking over depot only signed the receipt vouchers when they were totally satisfied. My instructions to the officers and JCO's who went on each trip was to return only with the vouchers duly signed, and with no deficiencies being reflected. Before any convoy left, I used to brief all the ASC drivers on the need to drive carefully and slowly. I told them what our unit drivers were instructed when they went on any duty. This ensured that there were no accidents and the entire stores were handed over without any damage or deficiency. Before the stores were loaded, they were cleaned with soap water and a high-pressure water pump, to give them a new clean look.

Facelift of the Unit

The CWE Guwahati had served under me in the Diploma Wing at CME, while the GE was a civilian officer whom I had never met before. After I met them, the news travelled that the former Commander Diploma Wing was in the station. A few JEs who had done their diploma courses, when I was their Commander, came to meet me. I took their assistance in preparing the AEs of the works I wanted for my Unit and thereafter got them sanctioned from the Col Q, who had become a friend. Once the works were sanctioned, the works commenced soon thereafter. My officers, JCOs and ORs were pleasantly surprised to see the MES doing such good work. In eight weeks, while the entire unit was getting its equipment ready for inspections, the MES worked extremely hard on the roads, drains, barracks, cook houses, offices, etc.

During one of my *langar* visits, where I interacted with the men, one *jawan* asked me why I was getting the unit lines, drains, and internal roads repaired when we were leaving the location forever. I took time to explain to him, and many others who had gathered around, of our bounden duty to look after government assets and the need to leave them in a tip-top condition for whosoever comes to occupy them thereafter. I asked them if they would be happy when the incoming unit speaks well of us for leaving the unit lines in such a good condition. Someone from behind said aloud that, in case everyone in the army does that, then we would have the best assets. I gave them the example of Botswana, and the punishment one got for not looking after government property.

CEME and Arms Inspection

For the arms inspection, I got two excellent armourers attached through the Col 'Q'. As both were guests in the unit and had come to assist us, the men were told to take special care of them and to make them feel at home. The armourers, in turn, went beyond the call of duty and the unit got a very good report from the inspecting officer. Similarly, for the CEME inspection, I had an electrician and vehicle mechanic attached to assist us.

COS Administrative and CEs Technical Inspection

How much the look of the unit had improved in two months was known only when both the COS, Maj Gen SPS Vains, and CE of HQ 4 Corps, Brig SK Mendhiratta, remarked that they had seen the unit lines six months earlier while passing by and since then there was a total change. The COS did ask how I was able to make so many good changes, in so little time. I replied that the unit boys did all the work and they are outstanding. He then asked, "How many discipline cases have you had?"

I replied, "Nil, Sir."

He went back thoroughly impressed and sent a cheque of Rs 20,000 to the unit.

Zero Audit Objections

Over the 16 years, the unit had spent in Guwahati, it had accumulated a large number of audit objections and railway claims whose settlement was pending. I was determined to clear all of them before leaving the station. I had to speak to the heads of these organizations and request their assistance for clearance/settlement of their long outstanding objections. I stressed that, since the unit was moving out, it would be in the interest of both parties to settle them as no other unit was coming to the present location. They assured me that they would pass suitable instructions and that helped. A few smart local NCO's got all the outstanding audit objections settled. The Railways were a little difficult; however, we succeeded in getting all the loss statements settled, two days before the unit was to move out. We thus succeeded in moving out with a clean slate.

Packing Material

As the Unit had not moved anytime earlier, a large number of boxes/ packing material had to be fabricated for the Officers Mess, JCO's Mess, Langars, Mandir, Gurudwara, etc. Through liaison with appropriate authorities, we got a large amount of packing material in two months. With the unit carpenters and two hired carpenters, excellent and properly designed boxes for different loads were fabricated centrally and handed over to the sub-units. Many steel boxes were also fabricated.

Handing Over of Accommodation

I was determined to move the unit with no rear party. The problem was compounded by the fact that the Sub Area HQ was unable to decide which unit/establishment the unit accommodation was to be handed over to.

On our last night in the station, at 2300 hours, I directed my QM NCO to get the BSO to my office. When he was woken up, he was extremely agitated and telephoned his GE who also came with him. Despite the cup of tea offered, the BSO would not agree to take over the assets. His plea was that he did not have locks for each barrack and no *chowkidars* to guard the assets. I had three JEs (two military and one civilian) with me. They told the BSO that in case there were any deficiencies, they would make them up. The Barrack NCO intervened to say that the BSO had been shown the barracks in the morning and he knows there are no deficiencies. There was pin-drop silence. I then agreed to provide locks for all the buildings free and assured him that not one item of the government assets would be removed and all barracks would be left spotlessly clean. The BSO realised that he had been cornered and hesitantly agreed to take over the accommodation. The GE remained silent. The inventory of each barrack had already been prepared and kept ready and signed by the Unit Barrack NCO. The list was placed before the BSO for his signatures, which he did. A bunch of keys, with a tag on which the barrack number was mentioned, was shown to him. This I said would be handed over to him, when we move out at 0900 hours. The

BSO came at the time given, took the keys and we parted as friends. The unit personnel, before moving out, had cleaned their barracks and then locked them. Not a bulb was removed. There was no deficiency whatsoever.

Train Journey

As we had planned our journey well, we got our rations at the stations we had indented them for. After a long journey, we reached Kota, only one hour late where the 2IC had come to receive us. We unloaded our stores and transferred them to the vehicles for the move to Nasirabad. At 2100 hours, the Duty L/Nk came to give me the 'All OK Report' and handed over a chit with the names of four JCOs who would go for a walk with me the next day. I remarked that I had been with all the personnel for my walks. He replied, "No, Sir, not with the persons who had come with the advance party" and thereafter smiled. I laughed in response.

Retrospect

During an extremely short stay as CO 658 Engineer Bridge Unit, I learnt the following:

> Handing/taking over by a unit is a normal activity every three years. However, in this case, it became a tough task as the unit had stayed at the same location for 16 years and when I was moved in there was little time for the numerous mandatory activities. Hence, through planning and proper liaisons at all levels became imperatives to succeed and not get stuck in cobwebs.
>
> Leadership traits have to be suitably modified based on the type of men your command. In this particular case, I had to go for a long walk each day, morning and evening (less Sundays) to know my command intimately.
>
> The solution for my goal of 'zero accidents' succeeded.

In order to have no indiscipline cases, for the type of men under me, suitable punishments have to be devised to break them.

Liaison is the keywords it assists to the maximum.

There is a definite need to institutionalise the training of officers and PBORs of their duty to look after government assets.

Though it was a tough assignment, I enjoyed every moment of it as it gave me great satisfaction to see the results as they happened. I am a firm believer in the dictum, in case one enjoys one's duty, everything else soon falls in place. Only Capt Sunil Moharil rose to the rank of Brig. All three officers who served under me are still in touch with me.

The two months spent at Nasirabad were comparatively restful while we were busy collecting our new equipment and setting up the unit in its new lines. In June 1995, my posting orders were received to move as CE Project Beacon, on promotion. I was given ten days for the move. Keeping in mind the conditions prevailing in the valley, where militancy was at its peak, in the limited time that I had, I decided to shift my family to Chandigarh (my home station) and move alone to Srinagar.

BEACON BOLE CHANGLA

CE PROJECT BEACON (Jul 95 — Dec 97)

Project Beacon during my tenure had two Border Roads Task Forces (BRTFs) under its command – 32 BRTF and 35 BRTF. It was responsible for the construction, improvement and maintenance of all the important roads in the Valley – then NH1A (Jammu-Srinagar-Uri), NH1B (Batote-Kishtwar-Sinthan Pass-Anantnag), NH1D (Srinagar-Sonamarg-Gumri) and also the passes at Zoji La, Pharkiyan Gali, Tutmari Gali, Nastachun and Rajdhan. Zoji La is the gateway to Leh, joining the Kashmir valley with the Indus valley through the 434-kilometre-long Srinagar-Leh road. This road is the lifeline to Kargil and Leh districts. Approximately 2,100 kilometres of roads were under construction/maintenance in Project Beacon. I took over the Project from Brig Satish Kapur, a renowned Sapper.

As this was my first posting to the BRO and in an area where I had not served earlier, I knew that it would be a challenging assignment. As I loved challenges, I was mentally prepared to take them on. With the background of my previous postings, I had prepared an SOP for actions to be taken on taking over any assignment. The SOP, which had to be suitably modified according to the parameters of any appointment, was in three parts viz:

> Part-I. Utilise the period of the handing/taking by going over the handing/taking over notes and briefings. Note down all doubts for

clarifications, after assuming command. Obtain knowledge of the area of jurisdiction, important landmarks, and all details of the topography 'on paper'.

Part-II. Clarify all doubts and thereafter, know my command. Then, get the office working in a methodical, systematic manner to my style of functioning. Simultaneously, see all the infrastructure of the Project HQ and initiate improvement measures which can be implemented in four to six months.

Part-III. List out whom all to meet and develop a rapport with - J&K government officials, HQ 15 Corps, the AOC Air Force, police officials, Principal Engineering College etc. for the betterment of the Project.

Immediate Actions

The aim was to make and implement necessary changes that convince all personnel under my command that the new procedures being adopted are for their good and benefit of the organisation. It is only then that the perception and attitude of your command towards you becomes a topic of discussion and the duty becomes enjoyable.

At the first briefing, in July 1995, I realised that traditionally in the BRO, all roads are mentioned in abbreviations. I requested for a list of all the important roads and their abbreviations along with the maps of the area. By the time the handing/taking over ended, I was aware of the names of all the roads, their abbreviations, their locations and lengths.

On the first day of command, I met all officers in my office, one by one, according to their seniority, for 10 to 15 minutes each. The officer had to tell me about himself, his family, his interests and his problems, if any. Nothing official was discussed. Thereafter I met the Army/GREF equivalent JCO's in the same manner. Through this process, I not only knew each officer but also got a good sense of his strong and weak points. Thereafter, I gave a typed copy of all my doubts/clarifications to the 2IC and TF Commanders for action.

In the afternoon, I went around the office complex with the 2IC and noted what all needed improvement. I also went over the state of the office equipment to ascertain what needed replacement. The 2IC/SO-I (Resources) and the office superintendents were made responsible to plan the improvements decided upon and discuss their procurement plan with the ACE. For infrastructure improvement – beautification and upkeep of the office – a separate plan was to be implemented by another team of officers. I also went over the procedure of *dak* receipt and dispatch to make it efficient and foolproof. Necessary changes were made, after deliberations with all concerned, for the smooth functioning of the office.

On the afternoon of the second day, I got a briefing from the two TF commanders and the RCC commander. It is here that most of my doubts were cleared to a great extent. For the next three days, I went around every nook and corner of the Project – barracks, cookhouses, toilets, religious places, married accommodation, MI Room etc. Directions were given on improvements to be made, after deliberations with those who were to carry them out; including the stores required, how to obtain them and how the improvements would be executed, through a comprehensive work plan.

A week later, I held the first conference with all officers and key JCO's and equivalents. During the conference, I gave the following directions:

> **Office Timings.** The new office timings will be from 0830 to 1330 hours and from 1530 to 1730 hours. All subordinates should enter the office by 0815 hours, officers by 0825 hours and I will come at 0830 hours. In the afternoon also the timings would be reversed and suitably staggered. I will come first. This shall ensure an orderly entry/exit and the importance of time would be understood by all. An electric bell would ring at these times. The name of any subordinate or officer coming late will be noted down and he will host the central weekly tea. His name was not to be announced. After two officers came late in the first two weeks, I do not recall anyone ever coming late. Pecuniary fines for minor defaults work better.

> **Mess Timings.** The new office timings ensured that all officers and subordinate personnel, dining in their respective messes, had their meals together. In turn there was less wastage of food and fuel (in heating & reheating.) Also, the mess staff could finish their work on time. It also enhanced camaraderie. The wives of married officers, likewise, knew exactly at what time their husbands would be home for lunch. With this strict schedule, the ladies too were better organised and expressed their happiness on this arrangement.

Entire *Dak* was seen by me for the first month. This was put up to me, Section-wise, in the evening to carry as 'homework' in three folders – Must See, Could See, and Maybe See. I went over the entire dak every night and wrote my detailed comments on most of the letters for deliberations. The concerned SOs would thereafter discuss their respective cases with me. This ensured all knotty issues were sorted out and there was a definite improvement in tackling all cases. All regular reports and returns were also vetted by me and improved so that authenticated data is always sent to the higher HQs on time. Within a month, all higher HQ's had observed the difference and the SO's work had become easier and simpler. Project Beacon never received a reminder during my entire command. All SOs in HQ DGBR greatly appreciated this change. I also became aware of the outstanding cases which were not a part of the handing/taking over notes/ briefing and could resolve them.

Improvements to the Infrastructure. As the office started functioning in the manner desired, planning commenced on improving the Project HQ area. An officer with a JCO was made in-charge of each zone to plan the work required and the procedure to get it done, similar to the way I did in my earlier appointments. Only those essential improvements were taken up in Phase I, which had the maximum impact and could be completed in three to four months. In the BRO it is easier as there are lesser problems concerning the purchase of stores and hiring of casual labour. However, the standard of the infrastructure in the BRO is much lower as compared to the MES. For this, I took the assistance of the MES by getting in touch with the JEs who had been trained under me as Commander Diploma Wing and a couple of MES officers who had known me earlier. All of them went out of their way to assist me; more than I could have ever imagined. The campus changed to give a clean, neat and military look, which everyone appreciated. Hygiene and sanitation too improved. Littering was not acceptable.

Meals for Subordinates Living in Married Accommodation. Once a month, when a *bara khana* was organised in the JCO's Mess or the OR's *langars,* food was provided free to the married personnel living on the campus at their respective residences. This was essential as, due to the prevailing security environment, they could not go out to eat. This way, the ladies got a day's rest from household chores and the family enjoyed a change in the menu and taste, which was greatly appreciated. For this, from the Project HQ, some amount was given to compensate the OR's and JCO's Mess. The married officers could have a Sunday brunch in the Officers Mess for a token payment. Most families enjoyed the brunch and tombola organised on this day.

Walking. Being a regular walker, it was with a considerable sense of achievement that I encouraged everybody, including families and children, to walk daily in the campus area. The families and children enjoyed walking more than the staff members on the campus amidst the stressful insurgency conditions as a measure of relaxation, improving physical fitness and removing mental stress.

Interaction with Local Authorities

My initial actions also included calling on the local authorities, who were connected with the Project. The AOC of the Srinagar Air Force Station, Air Cmde Ravi Limaye, civil authorities i.e., Chief Secretary (CS), Mr Ashok Kumar Jaitly, Additional Chief Secretary, Mr SS Blowria, the Divisional Commissioner, DC Srinagar, PWD Secretary, DG Police Mr Jagat and IGP (Traffic), Mr Rajan Bakshi, and SP Srinagar. Not to forget the Principal of the local Engineering College and personnel of SASE deployed at the Jawahar Tunnel. The CS, who was generally aware of the Project's vital role to keep the NH1 open and traffic-worthy, said he would appreciate it if I could spare time to brief him on all the works being undertaken by the Project.

In my next formal meeting with Mr Ashok Kumar Jaitly, he had all the concerned secretaries in attendance. This ensured all issues were resolved amicably, and speedily. I went for these meetings thoroughly prepared on all issues, which were flagged. OHP slides to highlight how the projects would assist the J&K State were also used, for easy comprehension. Consequently, time was not wasted in preparing statements of cases and most of the Project's requirements were quickly approved. I became a member of the core group of the CS; whenever a central minister or senior bureaucrat from Delhi visited Srinagar, I was requested to attend. I normally attended these meetings but was careful not to thrust my ideas on them.

This close relationship greatly assisted me in getting a large number of new works sanctioned. Before I left the Project, I had so much additional workload that another TF had to be raised, whereas when I took over, the load had reduced to one Task Force only. Similarly, good relations with the DG Police, the ADGP (Traffic) and the local SP also greatly helped, as they regularly advised me on the security situation. While deployed on slide clearance, they would detail personnel to control the traffic on both ends. This assisted us in speeding up the work.

I met the Hon'ble CM, Mr Farooq Abdullah, once a quarter, to give him a short brief of the work being undertaken by us and an update on the briefings to his CS. He generally knew what the Project was doing and never said no to anything I requested for.

HE General KV Krishna Rao, the Hon'ble Governor of J& K State visited our Project along with Lt Gen DD Saklani, his Advisor. It was an opportunity to give them a formal briefing so that they were aware of the work being done by the Project. Similarly, I gave one formal presentation to the Army Commander, Lt Gen S Padmanabhan (later COAS), who graciously acknowledged the good work being done by the Project in his tour notes. Besides, I maintained close liaison with the Corps Commander of 15 Corps, Lt General JS Dhillon, and his staff. I realised that senior officers are aware of the environment and the work being done under their command.

Zero Accident Culture

In the BRO, due to various reasons, a large number of accidents occur. These are blamed on the difficult terrain on which we operate. Be that as it may, I was determined to reduce them.

Having achieved success in the 658 Engineer Bridge Unit, I was resolute to achieve this here too. I did exactly what I had done earlier. Rather, I made the language more profane. Also, no vehicle could move out without a co-driver, who had to be a teetotaler. This idea did wonders, and during my entire tenure in Project Beacon, we had no accidents.

Amenities for the Personnel Living in the Complex

By interacting with the concerned authorities, I was able to get the following amenities for the Project Complex:

STD Booths. Two were set up to enable personnel to speak to their near and dear ones at home.

Gas Agency. This was a boon for the married personnel living inside the complex.

Plantation of Apples. Through the J&K Government, we obtained saplings of apples (imported from Hungary). They were a miniature variety but gave huge size delicious fruit and needed a steel rod to support the trees. The J&K Government also provided the necessary wherewithal for drip irrigation. Since the trees were planted on a slope, water with manure and pesticide was fed to all the saplings by gravity feed. I tasted these apples before I bade farewell to Project Beacon and they were very good.

Plantation of Fruit Trees. We also planted over 1,000 fruit and almond trees in our area.

Central Heating Plant. The central heating plant in the office complex had not been working for many years. We made it serviceable by carrying out repairs through an expert.

Tube Well for Water Supply. Our tube well was drying up. Boring machines in those days were only available with the J&K Government. Our case, which was pending due to red tape, was cleared after a presentation to the CS.

Enhancement of Electricity Load. With the strength of the project going up, the substation needed to be enhanced. This too was got done through the kind courtesy of the CS. It improved the electricity voltage in our area.

Police Detachment Inside the Complex. A Commission of Inquiry had directed that the CE Project Beacon would convey the status of NH 1A, every day at 0630 hours, to the J&K Radio and TV station. For this, I had a police detachment positioned in our complex, along with necessary radio equipment. This reduced our load tremendously.

Changes to Reduce Cost to the National Exchequer

A few of the major changes made in the system of working, after approval from the competent authorities, which brought in savings to the national exchequer were:

BER Vehicles and Equipment. According to the existing rules, all BER equipment had to be backloaded to the depot at Pathankot for auction. For this, we had to hire suitable-size transport or send our vehicles, with sufficient pioneers. The detachment which went to Pathankot never returned before a month. Through liaison, we were permitted by the Financial Advisor, BRO to auction them at the site on an 'as is where is' basis.

Bitumen and Cement. Bitumen and cement used to come to Pathankot in railway wagons, get unloaded and shifted to sheds inside the depot. As and when these items were required, we had to send our vehicles to lift them from Pathankot. With the considerable improvement in road communication, we commenced getting the cement and bitumen direct at the locations with no trans-shipment; wastage was avoided. It also reduced the overall time in getting them and the cost of the items.

These and many more such changes were brought in with the approval of Mrs Vijaya Lakshmi Gupta, the CDA BRO, who readily concurred with our recommendations if it was in the interest of the BRO. With her guidance and assistance, my Project could not only achieve but exceed the targets set. She was an approachable, dynamic, helpful lady who was always full of life. I learnt a lot from her.

Lessons Learnt

The major lessons learnt in the first six months of my taking over command of Project Beacon were:

> Applying the lessons that I had learnt in my earlier appointments paid the maximum dividends to me since they stood validated. However, though the basic principles

remained the same, based on the situation on the ground, their priorities changed.

To put in the hard work required, one has to remain focussed and be physically, mentally and spiritually fit. For this enough time has to be devoted, till it becomes a habit or a ritual. Most officers are unable to keep this pace for long periods. I used to have a chat with my wife, whenever I received my posting order and tell her that, just when I had got everything in order and the restful phase commenced, I was posted out. My wife would reply, "You should thank God your posting order has been received at the appropriate time. I have observed that the officers under you are getting tired of working at your pace." Today, I realise she was right.

Initially, those steps which could be taken in-house to resolve the administrative problems of the personnel were taken. Thereafter to resolve the measures that were beyond us, I developed a good rapport with the J& K bureaucracy and once they were convinced of my sincerity, they gave me the balance measures. The GREF personnel In turn, gave their best to the Project..

One of the most powerful tools for starting on a new assignment is the creation of a good proximate objective – one that is close enough at hand to be feasible. It is a target that can be reasonably achieved in a short time-frame. It draws power from focussing minds, energy, and action.

In the BRO, I followed the best procedures of combat engineering – teamwork, discipline, camaraderie and physical fitness; of the MES – best engineering practices for new construction and maintenance of assets; and the BRO – practical pragmatic solutions, in tough terrain.

Clearance of the Srinagar–Zojila Road

In August 1995, a cloud burst occurred on the Zojila axis cutting off the road to Leh. At about 0830 hours, I got a call from the GOC 15 Corps asking how long it would take to get the highway to Leh traffic-worthy. I still cannot recall why I confidently said '15 days'. The Corps Commander, Lt Gen JS Dhillon, laughed and said that, based on the feedback he had received, it would take a minimum of two months and put the phone down. I had faltered in giving a timeline without any reconnaissance. As all communications with the OC RCC were down, I could not get the damage report speedily. Thereafter, there was a barrage of calls from HQ Northern Command, the J&K Government and the Hon'ble Governor's office. I stuck to my timeline of 15 days. No one seemed to believe me.

When the calls came to an end, I got a call from the concerned OC RCC that the first Bailey bridge had been washed away and the stream was overflowing with water and ice. There was no way we could cross it. He was trying to establish contact with his detachments on the other side of the stream and would call about the damages as and when he got authentic news. I accepted his plea.

I then sat down with the TF Commander and a SO, who had earlier served in this area, to prognosticate the damages that could have occurred – bridges, culverts, sinking of road, cutting off road etc. We worked out a tentative list of stores, plants, manpower, and miscellaneous items for repairing the damages. We also noted from which locations we could collect these stores and plants. We then went on to make an 'Action Plan' to move the stores where they would be required. Orders were then issued to load them and to move after early breakfast, the next day, with pack lunch.

When the orders for the move of plants and stores from the adjoining TF reached their Commander, he rang me up to say that moving out personnel, vital plants and stores from his area of jurisdiction would create a void in his area which would become vulnerable to any mishap. He also wanted to know who would be the officer-in-charge at the slide area. When I said that I would take charge of the site, he was taken aback and stated that in his two tenures in BRO, he had not seen the CE personally take charge of a site. Having fought all my battles from the front, I closed the discussion by informing him that, henceforth in Project Beacon, based on the damages, the CE would take a considered decision and may take charge, in case the situation so demands.

The next day, early morning the TF Commander with his team moved to set up the campsite, receive the stores, plants and vehicles arriving from various locations and deploy them appropriately. I left for the location after an early lunch and was at the site at 1600 hours. The TF Commander received me, briefed me on how he had set up the camp and had arranged my accommodation at a Brigade HQ located close by. I then took charge of the task at hand.

By 1700 hours, the rain had stopped; however, it was very cold due to the windchill factor. I got all the officers together and briefed them, in detail, on the tasks of each sub-team, and how I expected them to work independently, yet as a team. I could sense their surprise as never before had the CE taken personal charge of an operation. After the briefing, I told them to rest that night and we would commence work the next day, after breakfast at 0800 hours, with a one-minute prayer to God Almighty.

The next morning, when I got up at 0500 hours, it was cold but the sky was crystal clear and a bright sun was shining at 0600 hours. It was indeed a beautiful sight. I saw what nature could do - something I could not imagine in my wildest dreams. The snow was melting fast and the rivulet, which had been overflowing the previous evening, reduced to a small stream and vanished by sunset.

With the situation changed, we could commence work on all sites simultaneously as opposed to tackling them sequentially. The bright sun brought a spring in the feet of the entire force and a smile on their faces. They looked extremely confident in doing their respective tasks. By working professionally, round the clock, and most important greatly assisted by nature we completed the task a day before the target date we had set for ourselves. I left the site after giving a pep talk to all the personnel and thanked them for the hard work put in by each one of them in a professional manner, despite the administrative constraints and without any cribs.

It was nice to be back home. After a well-deserved drink and watching TV for some time, before hitting the bed I instructed the Beacon exchange not to put through any calls to me that night unless they are 'urgent'. I was asleep at 2130 hours when, despite my clear instructions to the exchange, I was woken up at 2230 hours. The exchange operator apologised and told me he had refused a Brig who wanted to speak to me; now, since a Maj Gen wanted to speak and had shouted that it is very urgent, he was constrained to wake me up. It was the GOC in whose jurisdiction the roadblock had been cleared. He initially showed annoyance at my exchange making him wait. I discerned from his tone that he was upset. He then went on to question how I could declare a road that is not traffic-worthy as 'Green'. I curtly replied that he should know that the authority to declare all roads as 'Red' or 'Green' is the sole responsibility of CE Beacon and he has no *locus standi* in the matter. When he realised that he could not browbeat me, he changed to a friendly tone. He told me that his men, after chasing militant's non-stop for over 15 days, had finally eliminated them. He had given his troops a day off for a well-deserved rest. Keeping in view the interest of the troops, I should now declare the road 'Red' and after a day declare it 'Green', I replied softly yet firmly, "Sir, if this request had been put to me before I had declared the road 'Green' I would have considered it. However, now since the state of the road has been intimated to all concerned authorities – the Hon'ble Governor's office, J&K Government, the Command and the Corps HQs, he should appreciate that I am unable to amend the state of the road."

When he realised that I would not agree, he cut off the line in a huff. The next day a huge convoy (mostly of civil vehicles) moved on the road to Leh, without any problems.

The lessons I learnt from this fourteen days tough assignment are:

> My belief that 'nothing is impossible' was strengthened.
>
> The time-frame was correctly assessed by my senior officers. It became feasible to achieve in a lesser time frame mainly by nature coming to our rescue.

Once the CE is at the site, he can get the requisite stores or plants, if essentially required, from any location in his jurisdiction. This is not feasible when an OCC RCC is at the site. Such tasks require detailed planning which we were able to do, hence no time was wasted.

By succeeding in completing my first task in the time frame I had stated brought my Project accolades from all those who matter and I had established myself.

Resurfacing and Strengthening of Srinagar Airfield

The Srinagar airfield serves both civilian and defence air traffic and is strategically very important. The airfield is owned by the Indian Air Force. The Airport Authority of India operates a civil enclave at the airport since 1979. The runway is 12,000 ft long and 150 ft wide with earthen shoulders. Its surface had developed many undulations, cracks and other defects due to prolonged use. The resurfacing work of the runway was planned to be executed by the MES. Project Beacon was responsible for snow clearance only of the airfield, during the winter months, for which it is fully equipped and organised. In October 1996, a sudden decision was taken at the highest level, that the resurfacing and strengthening work at the airfield would be undertaken by Project Beacon. It took us by surprise and I raised an objection that we neither had the expertise nor the infrastructure to execute it. Also, the labour force with us was not trained for the job. My objections were turned down and I accepted this challenging work on 1 November 1996. The requirement was to strengthen the runway to LCN 80 specifications. The parameters were:

For the Rigid Pavement: Concrete of 15 cm thickness having flexural strength = 5 MPa ≡ M 50 Grade.

For the Flexible Pavement: Geotextile layer for impact resistance and crack relief. SDAC 10 cm thick and DAC 5 cm thick.

It was a highly technical work with no scope for error, which required managerial and technical skill. The first task was to have a competent and capable team to take on this unique work to complete it within the allotted time frame. Accordingly, a 'Srinagar Airfield Cell' was created with two technically competent officers, AEE (Civ) Mr AK Mishra and Mr AP Pittule. Both had done their M Tech in Civil Engineering but had never done any airfield work. After the initial briefing, I walked with them over the entire length of the runway explaining to them what I knew, what equipment and plants we would require and how we planned to execute the work. We had to go over the plan repeatedly till we were in sync. The tentative plan was formulated after discussions with my officers in the HQ, viz Col Grover, EE TN Bhatnagar, EE AK Bhatnagar and Dr Panda, all experienced and outstanding officers). It included the following major aspects:

Conduct a detailed survey.

The equipment and machinery required for laying of the 'Flexible' and 'Rigid pavement'; how to acquire it and then have it assembled at the airfield.

Procurement of Geotextile from a foreign vendor. Acquire knowledge of it and understand the process of laying it.

Conduct a study of the drainage system to ensure and sustain the longevity of the airfield.

Setting up a laboratory for testing.

Equipment for cutting of concrete and other miscellaneous requirements.

Stores required, viz. aggregate (various sizes), bitumen, cement, Geotextile, admixtures etc.

Sites where the plants and allied equipment were to be set up inside the airfield complex.

Site where the camps for the labour force were to be set up.

Once clarity on the above was reached, the capacity of the plant, the number of machines etc. was to be fixed based on the design, exact scope of work and the period of execution. We agreed that the aforesaid list would need to be continuously updated. We also had to obtain all relevant IS Codes for the various tests and learn how they are to be conducted.

The runway at Agra was being resurfaced. Mr AK Mishra was sent to see how the work was being executed and to clarify all doubts. Mr AP Pittule was sent to visit the manufacturing site of the Concrete Batch Mix Plant, which was to be inducted in the BRO for the first time, to learn the techniques of its operation and the procedure to take out the desired design mix concrete from the plant. On their return, both officers were confident to take on the work. I also learnt that the airfields earlier constructed by BRO had developed some defects which were being analysed separately. I obtained the reports and studied them for gainful implementation of their recommendations.

The next trip of the officers was to the E-in-C's Branch to obtain the BPs, AEs and design details as well as clarification of their doubts. After the formulation of the AEs, they went to HQ DGBR and briefed them on the project. HQ DGBR took a lot of time to comprehend the task. I also had to intervene at appropriate levels till everyone understood the intricacies of the project. Thus, the E-in-C's Branch and HQ DGBR were brought on the same page. Meanwhile, I ordered the move of one Surfacing Platoon from Awantipur to Srinagar airfield in January 1997.

I shall refrain from writing on all the activities involved, except on one of the tasks, which we thought would be a simple one viz. induction of the labour force. A deliberate decision was taken, after discussions with the Air Force authorities that, keeping in view the security environment, no local labour would be employed. The alternative was to get labour from Bihar. For such a large requirement, a team of three officers (including one doctor) and six subordinates was selected by me and sent to Dumka, in Bihar, to coordinate recruitment of labour with the assistance of the civil administration and State Government. I also had to request the Chief Secretary J&K to speak to his counterpart in Bihar. It was only then that we succeeded in getting the 400 labourers we desired.

The recruitment, despatch, arrival, reception of the labour, and establishment of a labour camp inside the airfield premises with hygienic living conditions was an exercise in itself. Initially, the Air Force authorities did not permit the labourers to stay inside their area for reasons of security and bird problems that could arise. I assured the AOC, Air Cmde Ravi Limaye, that I would personally ensure that the camp is always maintained in the most hygienic conditions. I take pride that we lived up to our assurance.

The work of overlay of the runway started on 15 August 1997. It was organised in two shifts from 0600 to 2000 hours daily to achieve the laid-down target and to reduce the closure time of the airfield. However, work continued round the clock as many preparatory works like maintenance of HMP, bitumen feeding in tanks, heating of bitumen was to be done in the night hours so that the HMP could start at 0600 hours daily. The team of officers were at the plant site at 0600 hours and remained there till 2100 hours on all days including Sundays (being regular work days).

Independent monitoring was essential to ensure that the highly technical work was completed in a tight schedule. The commitment and morale of the hard-pressed working team were stupendous. I also walked on the runway almost every evening and interacted with the team leaders to get first-hand information on the work and boost their morale. I also constituted two separate teams, one non-technical to check on the working team and to extend necessary administrative support. The second team looked into the technical requirements and provides timely feedback. With such continuous monitoring and support to the working team, the initial 2,400 feet portion of the airfield work was completed with the best quality and workmanship on 15 October 1997. Soon thereafter, Air Cmde Ravi Limaye and I were nominated for the NDC course, and we left at end of December. The work was finally completed in October 1998 and inaugurated on 9 November 1998 by the Defence Minister of India

The PCN test of the airfield pavement was done by the SEMT Wing of CME, Pune using a 'Falling Weight Deflectometer.' The results indicated that the PCN value of 120 on flexible and 105 on the rigid pavement was much higher than the designed value. Srinagar airfield was optimally used in the Kargil war as, after strengthening, it was upgraded for use by Mirage 2000 and Sukhoi-30 aircraft.

Lessons Learnt

Having served with the Air Force during my tenure at Chandigarh, I was aware that they take their runways seriously. Further, they do not permit any margin of error. My problem was that no one in the project had worked on a runway. The major lessons learnt were:

Initially, I had to remove the fear psychosis from my thoughts as well as the officers who were to execute the work. Once it was overcome and there was clarity on the way forward, it had to be put in writing.

The two officers who formed the team were good learners. However, being far junior in rank they tended to blindly follow my instructions. I had to remove this senior/junior barrier so that any direction by me which was technically incorrect be brought out. This had to be gradually done. We would always deliberate all issues to arrive at a consensus decision. I also had to build their confidence that I would back them to the hilt, in case anything goes wrong, inadvertently.

Collection of equipment, plants, tools, lab equipment, and stores required setting up the correct QR's in conformity with the relevant IS codes. Thereafter, administrative and managerial skill to get them at the site on time. I took on this responsibility to reduce the workload on the junior officers, so that they could concentrate on technical aspects only.

Training of personnel has to be given due attention and priority. The assistance of various agencies was taken – engineering colleges, other executing agencies of runways, and vendors who were supplying the equipment and stores. However, no short cut was taken or permitted.

No equipment was accepted till it was calibrated from a NABCL-ascribed lab.

Before any store was accepted it had to go through rigorous testing in conformity with the relevant IS codes. I had to get the IOC official to the site, as the packed bitumen was not to the laid down criteria. He accepted the shortcoming only after I had to threaten him. In his defence, he stated that it was the first time that packed bitumen had ever been checked and rejected.

When any fault occurred, it was brainstormed and necessary corrective actions were initiated.

All were permitted to take samples for testing at their labs. CE Srinagar Zone and Srinagar Engineering College were requested to visit as often as they could to check the work. Wherever workable and good advice was given (both on technical and non-technical issues) it was always introduced.

Every day, a different officer from the Project had to visit the site and after his check give his comments in a Register. A 'No Comments' remark was not acceptable.

Documents utilised in MES works like Work Diary, Daily Consumption Register, Daily Work Done, test reports, etc. were introduced and maintained properly.

In retrospect, it was an ambitious, unique and well-executed project undertaken by Project Beacon without any prior experience for airfield construction. It required meticulous work execution plans which had to be well-coordinated with the airport operations. On the technical parameters, it was for the first time that M-50 concrete was used in an airfield pavement runway. Similarly, the Geotextile layer below the bituminous overlay too was a new design concept that was for the first time executed in India.

Slides on NH 1A Between Patnitop and Jawahar Tunnel

There were many locations on the NH 1A which were prone to slides. For clearance of slides in these areas, as and when they occurred, small detachments with dozers were positioned close to these slide areas. The job of clearance could vary from a few hours to two days. When a slide occurred at a location other than the slide prone areas, it was worrisome.

Once, a huge portion of a hill collapsed five kilometres south of the Jawahar Tunnel. I got the message at 0930 hours from the Cdr TF. In his assessment, 400 metres of the road had been washed away and it would take a minimum of two months to rebuild. That day I was to go on four days leave (by the IAF courier aircraft) to Chandigarh. I cancelled my leave and moved to the site. There were more than 150 vehicles lined up near the site. The traffic police were trying to get them into one line. From the Northern end, we could not see the other end of the road. I decided to go to the other end where the TF Cdr was waiting. For this, we had to climb up the hill and thereafter descend to the other side. The climb up, though tiring was easier compared to the descent down the near-vertical slope. From the top, we got a good look at the slide and assess what needed to be done.

On reaching the other end, I got the officers and JCO's together to decide how to tackle the slide. The plan unanimously chosen was that in Stage I, connect both ends of the road by employing dozers from both ends in an inverted V. Thereafter, in Stage-II, bring the level of the road down by demolitions, using bore-hole charges and dozers alternatively. This work would be time-consuming. A list of equipment, stores, T&P etc. was made and instructions issued to move them up.

Work commenced from both ends to connect the road. Working non-stop, in shifts, we succeeded in doing the task in three days. Now, commenced the difficult and time-consuming task of cutting with dozers and lowering the level of the road, with borehole charges. To reduce the time frame further, the digging of boreholes and the dozers working was taken up simultaneously. At this stage, the 'lookout man' blew a warning whistle. Everyone looked up to see boulders hurtling down and ran away. The dozer operator also applied reverse gear and on full throttle moved downwards. In the melee, I was pushed by someone and fell. Before I could get up, the dozer had moved over me. The dozer operator was also hit by a boulder; however, since he was wearing a helmet, he was saved but fractured his arm. I was up without a scratch. Providence had yet again given me a fresh lease of life. Anyway, once the slide stopped, we recommenced the work with full gusto. Working round the clock, systematically and observing all precautions we were able to lower the level of the road to the original level on the seventh day. It took one more day to improve the geometrics of the road. After nine days, we opened the road for two-way traffic.

We helped the passengers stuck in their vehicles on the road with water, tea and *aloo puris*. The traffic police were asked to send back all cars, either to Jammu or Srinagar. Thereafter, the buses too were sent back. The truck drivers always carry ten days of survival ration and have fewer problems to stay on. The little assistance we provided was highly appreciated by them.

One day in the evening, I was gossiping with the truck drivers and started the conversation by asking how many children they had. The first driver said he has a daughter and a son. The daughter was 13 years old and the son 11 years old. I then asked him how often he goes home. The driver said that when his children were small, he went once or twice a month; however, staying alone for long periods made him forget civic life and today he cannot speak without swearing. He further added that he had got habituated to eating spicy food and no longer enjoy home-cooked food. Now his children have grown up and he felt ashamed to meet and converse with them and avoided staying at home. All the other drivers said their lives were similar.

I realised that staying alone in my room in the Beacon House, where everything was quiet, I too had problems when I went on leave after a year. I would get annoyed in case my daughters disturbed me while I was listening to the news. I had forgotten how to converse with them. After I heard the story of the drivers, I made an extra effort to be a family man, whenever I went on leave. I also realised what a tough life these drivers have.

Khunni Nallah Slide

I recall once I was travelling across the 'Khunni Nallah' when a slide struck. It took two hours to clear it. The road was however not opened to traffic till the slide settled down and the geometrics of the road were smoothened. At the other end, I saw a pregnant lady crying. I immediately made her sit on a chair and got her carried across the slide. I sent her with her relatives to the nearest hospital in my vehicle. Later I was told that she had reached the hospital in time and had named her son 'Beacon.' Incidentally, while we were taking the lady and her family across, a CRPF man with a suitcase tried to take advantage and run across; however, he stumbled and his suitcase in which he had over a lakh of rupees fell. I vividly recall the scene as his suitcase had broken while going down the deep valley and the notes could be seen floating in the air. He had to be hospitalised as he became a mental wreck.

I had two opportunities to personally tackle major roadblocks during my tenure. NH 1A, the only highway connecting Kashmir valley with Jammu, has a very large volume of traffic. The vehicles can only move when the road is declared 'Green'. When a slide/roadblock occurs, vehicles pile up at both ends of the slide area. There needed to be a procedure in place to stop traffic at convenient locations so that vehicles do not pile up close to the slide area. Crucial time is wasted to get instructions issued by the IG Police (Traffic) to stop traffic from both ends and to inform all concerned at Project Beacon. If this is done expeditiously, the T&P could reach the site of the slide and clear it in a shorter time frame.

The Governor of J&K, the Hon'ble CM J&K, ministers and many other civilians highly appreciated the efforts of Project Beacon. The IG Traffic Police gave Project Beacon cash awards for looking after the people stuck and seeing our boys working so hard.

Jawahar Tunnel

This 2.85-kilometre-long twin-tube horse-shoe shaped tunnel connects Banihal in Jammu with Qazigund in the Kashmir valley. It was built at an elevation of 2,194 metres, in 1956, on NH-44 (erstwhile

NH1A) connecting the valley with the rest of India. It was named 'Jawahar Tunnel' after the then PM of India, Pandit Jawaharlal Nehru. It was initially partially lined, with a concrete carriageway and it worked on a 'natural ventilation system', which pushed the polluted air outside due to the temperature difference on either portal of the tunnel. Since its construction, it was under the charge of BRO (Project Beacon); however, due to excessive traffic; the natural ventilation system had stopped functioning. Further, in the unlined portion of the tunnel, the leakage of water increased over the years. Overall, the tunnel had deteriorated considerably and I observed that it was in dire need of 'special rehabilitation work'. This was approved by HQ DGBR in late 1996.

The scope of work comprised lining of the unlined portion of the tunnel, including waterproofing of the remaining length using custom made slip form horseshoe-shaped paver; electrification of both the tubes and provision of a mechanical ventilation system using jet fans. The work was entrusted to the Konkan Railways Corporation Limited (KRCL). The carriageway had also to be re-laid after demolishing the existing concrete carriageway as the existing height clearance had to be maintained. The work of re-laying the concrete carriage highway (with PQC M40 concrete) was to be carried out departmentally. It commenced during my tenure and the leakage and the lining work was done. The remainder works were completed, thereafter, providing a new lease of life to the strategically important tunnel.

Miscellaneous Points

Reduction in Loss of Equipment Bridges. A large number of Bailey bridges are in use in J&K. As the streams they cross are not tamed, whenever a heavy discharge of water occurs due to a cloud burst anywhere in its catchment area, these bridges get washed away. To ensure they are not lost during the monsoons, the embankments had to be strengthened before that. For a few bridges which had an alternative route, we used to de-launch the bridge and keep it on rollers on one side after approval of the Civil and the Army authorities. Where no alternative route was available, we used to anchor the bridge on both ends with pulley and block tackles. By these improvisations, Project Beacon thereafter lost no bridges.

Achievement of Targets. Every year, based on the total workload, the targets to be achieved are laid down for each Project by HQ DGBR. I distributed the targets after a confirmatory reconnaissance of the roads, based on the resources allotted, the condition of the road and the weather. The most difficult target was blacktopping of roads due to the weather conditions prevalent. The only simple workable solution was to start the plant at 0400 hours in the working season. The first load of the hot mix moved out to where it is required and was laid at 0900 hours and not at 1100 hours. The additional two hours helped in achieving the blacktopping targets with good work at the site.

Setting up a Monitoring System. A proper monitoring system was put in place during the working seasons. Two teams, consisting of an officer and two subordinates, were selected to check the targets achieved, advise the concerned detachments on how they could enhance their targets and how they could optimally utilise the resources allotted. Based on their feedback, I made course corrections, wherever necessary. I got this idea from working with the Air Force. These teams did what the DASI does in the Air Force. Most of my time was spent on this in the first year and once my command knew I will not accept any laxity in this important task everyone worked as expected. Project Beacon then had 25% to 30% extra achieved each year.

Improvement of NH 1A. This was the most vital road for my Project. I got the history of the road from the J&K Government and had it displayed on huge boards at appropriate locations on the road. It was greatly appreciated by road users. I also had to teach the officers and subordinate executives looking after the different portion of the road how to do even the minor tasks in the best feasible manner. For example, application of chuna; first, the area where it had to be applied had to be cleared/scrapped and thereafter the chuna had to be applied mixed with neel neatly. These small things improved the get up of the highway which was greatly appreciated by all. To get all culverts cleared and repaired, I organised a competition amongst the detachments on the road every month. It resulted in a clean and good look on the road.

Assistance to the Locals. Under the slogan given by Army HQ to win 'minds and hearts' clear directions were issued to all detachments under the Project to look after the minor needs of the locals. During my trips on the roads, I always carried sweets for the children and enjoyed talking with the CPLs. Some of them would call the headman of their village, who would hesitantly request for small embankments to protect their crops and houses from surface water damages. The locals know their land and environment much better than us in uniform, and were attuned to notice the smallest movement of snow on the upper reaches which we could not discern. Their advice during the clearance of slides was also always correct.

Firing at Night. Project Beacon was located in the Old Airport area. Opposite the main gate was a temporary jail where hardcore terrorists and suspects used to be interrogated. On many nights, indiscriminate firing would commence and it appeared as if the firing was directed towards us. To ensure no one died due to stray bullets, clear directions were issued not to open fire without my specific permission. I also got the main switch for the entire electrical system shifted to the 'Beacon House'. The moment the first shot was heard, the guard had orders to switch off the mains and stay indoors. It was a signal for all personnel to stay inside their barracks. The lights were switched on only when the firing ceased for at least five minutes. This 'out-of-the-box' solution ensured that no one in my Project died to cross-firing or a stray bullet, whereas a large number of units in the vicinity had casualties due to the indiscriminate firing.

Permitting Officers to Stay with Families in Field Area. In the BRO, officers were permitted to stay with their families; however, I was staying alone. My family only joined me for short duration visits. Just before Eid, my family had come to stay with me for a week, as I felt that their presence was necessary for the Beacon Day celebrations. One afternoon, just after finishing my work in the office, I was told that there was a call from the OC RCC that their only snow clearing machine had accidentally fallen five metres down in the valley, but it seemed to have suffered no damages. He requested a crane to retrieve it. Without giving a second thought, I directed the workshop officer, Maj Jamwal, to move to the site with the crane and to speak to me on reaching there. After some time, a senior GREF officer came over and asked me to reconsider my decision. When I asked why, he replied, "Sir, last year we lost a GREF superintendent on Eid, who had gone to repair a vehicle." I then told him that both the circumstances and locations are different. "We cannot risk losing a snow clearance machine and the OIC workshop can take my security, if required." After he left, another officer tried to tell me the same story differently. I again refused to change my orders. It did upset me and when I reached my room, there was pin-drop silence. "All OK?" I asked, looking at my daughters. My younger daughter then said, "Papa, why are you so inconsiderate?" I could not fathom what she was getting at. My elder daughter butted in and said, "Aunty had come; she was crying and she told Mama that Sir is sending her husband to sure death." I gave no reply and went for my bath. The girls were told by my wife to go to their room. I knew when the workshop officer had moved out. There were still 20 minutes for him to reach the site. I spoke to the Brigade Commander responsible for the road. He said that I should not at all worry as all ROP's were deployed. When the EME officer did not reach the location at the estimated time, I quickly changed into uniform to go myself to check. Just then, Jamwal rang up to say that he had reached safe and sound. When asked what took him so much time, he said he had to stop for a few minutes as the crane had a minor fault. I then directed him to retrieve the snow clearing machine as there was still sufficient light. I also told him to remain at the location and I would come to bring him back. The day after Eid, I saw the progress of snow clearance work and returned with Jamwal. In retrospect, I feel it is good that the Army does not permit families in the field area as one's decision-making process can get affected by extraneous circumstances. I too had wondered whether I had taken the wrong decision to detail the officer when I saw my children crying.

Retrospect

My two and half year's tenure passed in a jiffy and I was nominated for the prestigious NDC course. I served as Chief Engineer Project Beacon, till the end of December 1997. Some achievements which stick in my memory are:

The National Highway 1A was kept open for traffic for a much longer period during my tenure, which helped the civil administration in maintaining adequate stocks of essential commodities throughout the winter and thereby earned the goodwill of the people.

The quick restoration of the road to the Ladakh region in the wake of the unprecedented floods, in August 1995, facilitated timely winter stocking, which was otherwise causing great concern at one point in time. It set a standard on how Project Beacon reacts to a road closure.

A major bridge at Woyil on the Srinagar–Sonamarg Road, which had been washed away in the floods, was reconstructed in a record time due to the relentless efforts of the Project personnel.

A special drive, in close coordination with the Revenue Department to expedite the finalisation of pending land acquisition cases facilitated the progress of many important projects.

The removal of unauthorised encroachments on the NH 1A with the support of the civil administration, by submitting a consolidated list of encroachments to the State Government.

HE, the Governor of J&K, Gen KV Krishna Rao (Retd) presented a silver trophy (worth Rs 5 lakh) to Project Beacon for the contribution to J&K.

The National Highway was kept open throughout the Amarnath Yatra in 1996 and 1997; the NH1A from Jammu to Srinagar was kept open for 355 days in a year – a record, which I hear has not been broken to date.

The road Srinagar–Leh was opened on 5 May 1997 against the scheduled date of 15 June 1997.

During my tenure, the J& K Government handed over two major roads for development and construction by BRO (Project Beacon). For this, a third Task Force – 760 BRTF, was raised:

Baramulla–Kupwara–Chowkibal: 70.2 kilometres
Kishtwar–Sinthan Pass–Anantnag: 155 kilometres

During the first six months of my tenure, Lt Gen Vimal Shinghal was the DGBR. His successor was Lt Gen RJ Mordecai. Both of these renowned Sappers gave me full freedom of action in performing my tasks. I remain grateful to them.

DISCIPLINE IS THE BRIDGE TO ACCOMPLISHMENT

CE Bathinda Zone (Jan 99 — Feb 01)

After an extremely enjoyable year, in 1998, at the National Defence College (NDC) which was a happy mix of learning and relaxation, the MS Branch, surprised me once again by posting me as CE Bathinda Zone. In a meeting with the Additional MS earlier, I had been told to expect a posting on the staff of a formation HQ around Delhi, but not in Delhi. I once again learnt that the posting was done in 'organisational interest'. I had no alternative but to accept it in the correct spirit. I moved to Bathinda in the last week of January 1999, without my family, as the then CE Bathinda had retained the married accommodation for his child's academic session.

The reputation of the Bathinda Zone had taken a beating with plenty of inquiries and failed projects haunting it. In a way, it was good that I moved alone, as I could devote the first four months totally on the job at hand, except that administratively it was inadequate. I had decided to stay in the ad hoc Officers' Mess of the CE Zone, which had only one other officer, who was a pure vegetarian, dining beside me.

The area of responsibility of the CE Bathinda Zone was vast. It had CWEs at Amritsar, Bathinda, Ferozepur, Sri Ganganagar, Bikaner and Hisar under it.

Exercise Clean-up

On assuming command, I constituted two teams, one under the ACE (Planning) and the other under the ACE (Works). The former team was to check all office equipment to determine what needs to be declared BER, and what was repairable or required to be replaced. Additional equipment to be procured, to assist the Zone to function more effectively was also to be determined by this team. The latter team had to recommend measures to improve the get up of the offices, washrooms, etc., and improvements to the surrounding areas. Both teams were intimated that the measures recommended and the procurement procedure to be followed must be as per the laid down rules and regulations.

I took over the Zone, in more or less the same manner as CE Beacon. In the first two months working 24x7, I knew my command and got them to work in conformity with my 'system'. Exercise 'Clean Up' did take time. However, on its completion, all were extremely happy. The aim was to provide the staff with a congenial environment to work in. The officers and subordinates got equally good washrooms and a proper system was set up to ensure their regular maintenance. In addition, a good music system with speakers in each room was installed. Light instrumental music was played, during office hours. Two coffee/tea machines each were also procured and placed in all the floors and wings.

For cleaning the surroundings, assistance was sought from the local Engineer Regiment. The garden came to be so well-maintained that for the next two years we won the trophy for the Best Garden Office (in the 'Extra-Large' category) in the Bathinda Military Station Annual Garden Competition.

I gave separate talks to the officers and the subordinate staff, where I covered the following:

> Everyone must enjoy the work one is doing; then automatically everything falls in place. To do this, one must be physically, mentally, spiritually and psychologically fit, at all times. Once you do this, you would be liked by your family, friends and office colleagues.

Be on time always and have breaks and meals on time.

Never have negative thoughts or speak ill of anyone. Destiny has brought us together for some time hence we should develop camaraderie and friendship amongst ourselves.

We must keep the offices and surroundings neat and clean.

Anyone who has any personal problems of any kind and wishes to discuss them with me is welcome to meet me before the office commences i.e., from 0815 to 0845 hours. Also, any suggestions to further improve the office working are welcome.

We should never waste electricity and water under any circumstances. Anyone caught wasting electricity will have to pay a fine of Rs 100 in the donation box kept with my SPA. Anyone not knowing what he should know shall also pay a fine of Rs 500, as knowledge is not free.

Visit to Outstations

After my visits to all the stations under my jurisdiction, I realized that to make a visible improvement in all the stations, I desperately needed funds. Since it was the end of January, I was aware that by the second week of February, 'Special Repairs' funds that cannot be utilized are returned by the CE Zones to the Command HQs. Further, the Ministry of Defence (MOD) also allots additional funds for 'Special Repairs' to the Command HQs. The MOD assumes that no one would accept 'Special Repair' funds at his belated stage. I assessed that in case I execute my plan properly, I can procure bitumen and cooling appliances that are deficient and which are on the DGSD list – air conditioners, water coolers, desert coolers, geysers, fans etc. In case this effort succeeded it would be greatly appreciated by the users.

To implement the plan, during the inspection of each station, the GEs were tasked to work out the deficiencies in the cooling appliances and the amount of bitumen that would be required for repair of those roads which were overdue for resurfacing. For this, AEs for all roads due for resurfacing had to be prepared. The CWEs were also directed to vet the

AEs with a team, under an officer, to check all the AEs prepared by the GEs at each station. The GEs were given three days to complete this task and I monitored progress twice a day. I noticed that most of the GEs and CWEs were not fully aware of the latest authorisation of various cooling appliances. I had a copy, since my CWE Chandigarh days, and gave it to my ACE (Works) to authenticate it from the E-in-C's Branch. This was done.

By the time my initial visits were over, I could make a realistic assessment of the funds that we could utilise i.e., close to Rs 10 crore (Rs 9 crore for bitumen and Rs 1 crore for cooling appliances). I then invited both my ACEs for breakfast and we deliberated on my plan. It took some time for them to digest it. Both agreed that it was bold; though full of risks which, they both advised, I should not take. We then analysed the risks and I assured them that I have put in place all risk mitigation measures. They saw that I had done my homework and finally accepted my proposal. However, my ACE (Works), who was a civilian officer who was cool, mature and experienced, remarked, "Sir, you are taking a *panga* unnecessarily." I liked this word and said we will name this 'Exercise *Panga*'. He was made responsible for procurement of the DGSD items and the ACE (Planning) for the execution of the work on 'Special Repair of Roads', in all the stations in the Zone.

Exercise *Panga*

While the ACE (Planning) got the AE's for 'Special Repair of Roads' re-rechecked, I confirmed from the refineries at Panipat and Mathura that they would definitely supply us the requisite quantity of bitumen, before 25 March of that financial year (FY). Both General Managers confirmed that the required quantity of bitumen could be lifted from their respective refineries, provided the supply orders were given to them by 5 March. We rechecked from their head office, at Mumbai, who substantiated it. Simultaneously, the ACE (Works) confirmed that the DGSD items would be available from the vendors before the end of the FY. When the telephone call came from the Command HQ for demands on 'Special Repairs' funds,' if any, my Zone took the entire Rs 10 crore available. All other CE Zones had 'nil' demand. The ACE (Command) did advise me to once again make sure that I would be able to utilise the funds in the little time I had. He added in the same breath that in case you fail to utilise the funds, your neck would be on the chopping block as no return of funds would be accepted.

'Exercise *Panga*' commenced the day the funds were received. The homework had already been done. A formal supply order for bitumen was placed on the Indian Oil Corporation at Panipat, ten days before the target date. The CWEs and GEs commenced receiving their 'handling contracts' and were ready to despatch vehicles to Panipat for collection of the bitumen. Simultaneously, the supply order for the cooling appliances, on the DGSD, which were kept ready, were handed over/posted to the vendors. Thus, we were ahead of the target dates set. Thereafter, progress on all activities was monitored on a daily basis. I gave charge of monitoring the activities within the Zone to the ACEs, and I took on the responsibilities of dealing with the external bodies i.e., the Indian Oil Corporation and the DGSD vendors. All stations were set to go when I was informed by Indian Oil Corporation, Mathura, from whom we had lifted only 20 percent of the bitumen that their Union was going on a strike. This got me worried; I immediately telephoned their head office in Mumbai. I was assured that the problem would be resolved in three days, and it was. Thereafter, the exercise had smooth sailing. On 29 March, the last load of bitumen was inside the various stores, in all the stations.

Once the collection of bitumen was proceeding smoothly, the tenders for the road work, which were simple contracts at the GE and CWE level, were called for vetting at the Zonal level. With our previous experience, we added a number of additional clauses like laying of seal coat with a paver, road furniture etc. This ensured there were no problems at the execution stage. In addition, all GEs, AGEs and JEs, along with the builders who had bid for these contracts, were called to the Zonal Office for a 'one-day capsule' on how to execute the work. This joint training programme played a major role in ensuring that the work was executed in accordance with the laid-down engineering norms. A handout on 'Do's and Don'ts' was also issued to all.

Immediately after the end of the financial year, another exercise to provide external periodical services to all buildings on both sides of the re-carpeted roads was undertaken. For this, a similar training capsule was held at all the stations for all GEs, JEs and builders, to explain the manner in which it was to be executed. These short courses become a norm, thereafter, whenever any work was taken up for execution since most of the officers and builders had little knowledge on how to execute works in conformity with the laid-down engineering norms.

By the end of June, when the re-carpeting road work and the periodical services works were coming to an end, I met the GOC 10 Corps, Lt Gen GK Duggal VrC, and gave him the list of deficient air conditioners, water coolers, desert coolers etc. which had been procured and he could now allot them to the formations and units, as he deemed fit. He was extremely happy and enjoyed acting as 'Santa Claus' while allocating them to the formations. None believed that the deficiencies would ever be made up. The Corps Commander was magnanimous to inform his Commanders that the recently posted-in CE had made up these huge deficiencies.

Finally, the taste of pudding lies in its eating as far the user is concerned. The user not only wants the work to be executed according to engineering norms but the completed work must give a different look, just not nifty and clean. In this case, the roads with road furniture and appealing surroundings gave a different look which the users appreciated.

Good Environment to Work as Professionals

Unconventional yet likeable ideas to make my team function as professionals were devised. A few of them were:

> **20 Minutes 'Your Time'.** Once the music system was functional and playing carefully selected instrumental light music, I decided to give the staff a break of 20 minutes as 'self-time' when everyone was to stop work and shake a limb, do yoga, meditate or any exercise they fancied. I preferred that everyone did a bit of everything, depending upon their mood. The aim was to rejuvenate everyone. During these 20 minutes, fast instrumental music (as heard in gyms) was played. To explain the advantages I got a doctor, who was very popular in Bathinda, to give a talk to all

the officers and subordinate staff. The doctor stressed that they must use this time to exercise and in case they did so, they would never ever be sick and would lead a good life during their old age too. He spoke to the gathering in their local language and dialect with a lot of rustic humour and mentioned that it was the best thing to be done in any office. He was much more articulate than me while enumerating the advantages of 'Your Time'. Everyone liked this and commenced exercising during 'Your Time'. No one ever missed doing some exercise or meditation during this time. That was the craze for 'Your Time'.

Coffee/Tea Machines. Initially, the consumption was high, but once the novelty died down, the average consumption was only two cups per day. This service was on a self-help basis.

Walks. One can only expect the best from your team, when it remains physically, mentally and spiritually active. I also used to take different groups of officers for a walk/work out every evening. This helped develop camaraderie and good relations amongst the staff.

Saving on Electricity and Water. As I always went to the office an hour before others, I was aware of how the sweepers cleaned the offices in the morning. The first thing they would do is to switch on all lights and fans of a room and then commence their work. After cleaning the room, they left them on till the office runners came for the dusting. They too did not switch off the lights and fans. Finally, when the officer came in, he only adjusted the speed of the fan or the air conditioner in the summer or the heater in the winter. The sweepers normally came in one hour earlier and the office runner 15 minutes before the officer and the other staff. I stopped this bad habit of the sweepers. An NCO was detailed to ensure only the minimum lights are switched on while the sweepers did the cleaning and switched off immediately thereafter. The energy saved, just by this action, was mind-boggling. The officers and subordinates were issued strict directions to switch off their lights and fans, whenever they left their room for any purpose and switch them on again when they returned.

To have fun on certain days, my office orderly would ask me, "Sir, which officer is to be called?" I used to say, "Call anyone." He would go around and see an officer who is busy and tell him that the CE wants to see him immediately. The officer would literally run into my office and my question to him was whether he had come to my office, after switching off his office lights. When he would hesitatingly say "No, Sir," the office orderly would bring in the donation box. Everyone would have a big laugh. This habit of switching off lights was carried home by the officers and subordinates and they would often talk about how much their electricity bills had reduced.

Knowledge is Not Free

Whenever a CWE, GE, or for that matter any officer or a subordinate entered my office, they were asked a 'Must Know' question by me. Once he agreed that the question falls in the 'Must Know' category he had to give an appropriate answer. In case he did not give the correct response, he had to put in Rs 500 in the donation box kept with my SPA and then I would give him the correct answer. No one was excused from paying this fine. On the last day of my tenure, when the donation box was opened, there was over Rs 97,000 in it. 35 percent each was given to the Mandir and Gurudwara, 5 percent each to the Mosque and the Church and the remainder 20 percent to the janitors.

I also got Rs 1,500 from the Principal, Giani Zail Singh Engineering College, Bathinda. This exercise was also undertaken with many other engineers (members of IEI Bathinda) who used to come to meet me. Though they were experts in their respective subjects yet their basic knowledge, essential on the application and practical side of engineering was lacking. I too had to work hard to prepare new questions every time which were interesting and not taught in any of the engineering colleges. This practice also ensured that knowledge was shared and passed on.

As CE Bathinda Zone, I was also the President of the IEI Bathinda Chapter. The State Government was not giving us the land to construct a building where we could hold our activities. With persistent efforts, we succeeded in getting a piece of land for making the building. When I became E-in-C, the Institute members invited me to inaugurate it. This is the only time I have ever inaugurated anything. In my opinion, we have no business to dedicate anything built with government funds.

Major Works Programme

On taking over, I had observed that the BP's and AEs of five works recommended to be included in the MWP had not been progressed. They were completed within 15 days and taken 'by hand' to the E-in-C's Branch and thereafter to the QMG's Branch and from there to MOD (Def) for clearance. This was done by two officers who had earlier served at Delhi and had good contacts. They used to give me a daily progress report and returned after getting them cleared at all levels. They were also tasked to move earlier files that had been held up for clearance. They did outstanding work and we got all our works included in the MWP issued by the QMG's Branch.

As and when I learnt that a Work had been included in the MWP, I would get my Planning Team to commence planning three to four months prior to the issue of the Administrative Approval. This advance planning enabled us to issue the tenders within a fortnight of its receipt. It ensured that the works commenced on the ground, within three months of the receipt of the Administrative Approval.

Further, the time period given to the builder, rather than being fixed on an ad hoc basis, was done after taking into account all factors viz. weather, holiday season etc. into consideration. Thus, all works always proceeded ahead of the laid-down schedule. Simultaneously, the list of works planned for inclusion in the next MWP was finalised and the draft BPs and AEs prepared. When the list was issued by HQ Western Command all BP's and AE's were ready and the presiding officers were extremely happy as they did not have to keep requesting MES officials for them. By October in the next financial year, all our BP's and AEs were with the QMG's Branch, after getting them cleared from the E-in-C's Branch. My Zone fully exploited the 'first come, first served' rule' and in 2000, Bathinda Zone had 95 percent of the total works of Western Command. The Zonal Planning team functioned so well that I had to slow them down. They had mastered the art of preparing a tender document with all relevant details and verified in accordance with the prevailing ground conditions.

Progress of Works

For keeping a hawk's eye on the progress of all works, similar to DASI procedures, I selected two officers to check some of the works on my behalf during various stages of their execution. They were given the points to check and give me a verbal feedback. Thereafter the concerned CWE, GE and the builder were called to my office and each of the observations was explained. Our aim was to get the works completed to the laid down specifications with top workmanship without any time and cost over-runs. The message to the builders was clear and consistent that it is not in their interest to lag in the laid-down schedule. They knew that a 'Completion Report' would be given only when the site was left spotlessly clean. On this point, there was no leniency whatsoever. This took time to inculcate but it became second nature to them.

Operation Zero

The MES has many 'housekeeping points.' These are neither known to the users nor are the users interested in them. For this reason, no one pays any attention and they keep adding up. I had tasted blood as CO 658 EBU, CWE Chandigarh and CE Project Beacon where I succeeded in making them zero. I realised that having the housekeeping points reduced to nil, one would not get into a problem at a later stage. It also reduced infructuous work and arbitrations. I wanted to achieve this goal in Bhatinda Zone too.

Though my reputation in this regard had reached the Zone, the ACEs advised me not to rush into it as all officers and subordinates were already overloaded. I knew they were, but I also knew that no one dies of hard work. I took on the easiest task first i.e., submission of all ACRs on time. In the MES, ACRs are normally delayed for one to two years and no one bothers. I called my SO1 (Pers), a dynamic civilian officer, Mr Mittal, and told him my goal. I also spoke to all GEs and CWEs that all ACRs were to be initiated on the due date. Thereafter, the RO got two days to review them and the SRO got one day. On the fifth day, all ACRs of my Zone were handed over to the CE Western Command office by hand. They wondered how this impossible task was done.

'Housekeeping points' targets were fixed for each GE, and progress was monitored by me personally. Backlog, if any, had to be cleared by working on Sundays. Initially, progress was very good but later it slowed down. I then started going to each GE's office on Saturday evening, at 1800 hours, when work to clear the backlog had to commence. This continued at night and recommenced on Sunday morning, till progress was achieved. Just the fear of this made them resolve the objections expeditiously. Once the audit authorities at the GE level knew that I had got the backing of their top officers at the PCDA office; they had no alternative but to resolve all old issues. In six months, we came to zero in all housekeeping points. I can today proudly state that my officers worked extremely hard, though they were circumspect that the targets set were unachievable. When we succeeded, our joy cannot be put in words. In the MES, this was for the first time ever achieved. It was highly appreciated by the PCDA office and brought to the notice of the Army Commander, Western Command, and my Corps Commander.

Year of the Jawan – 1999

After deliberations with the formation commanders, a proper drill was formulated on how all complaints/ breakages of the OTM and married accommodation would be attended to.

Before taking up the repairs, a list of all the breakages to be replaced, and items to be repaired etc. was drawn up. Thereafter, the stores and tradesmen required was worked out and arranged by the concerned GE. On the planned weekend, work commenced at 0900 hours. While the military personnel cleared the surroundings, the roof and the common areas, the MES tradesmen concentrated on the repairs/replacements. The external electrification, water supply and sewerage lines were also attended to. On these two days, tea and *langar* food was provided to the MES personnel by the respective battalion. Over a weekend, the entire unit was made 'defect free'. The AGEs and JEs supervised the works. The GE, with the CO, used to be present when the work ended each day. In case any work was not completed it was done on the next day.

Penalty Imposed by Punjab Electricity Board

A penalty was imposed by the Punjab State Electricity Board on the Zone, in 1994, which was paid without going into the details; accordingly, an audit objection was outstanding. When I went through the case, I observed that the penalty was wrongly charged. We then filed a case in the consumer court and won. The Punjab State Electricity Board had to pay back the entire fine of Rs 1.20 Crore with 18 percent annual interest, since 1994. More important, I came to know that most State Electricity Boards were charging the Defence more in their bills and, due to ignorance, the MES authorities were paying it. As I realised this towards the end of my tenure, I carried forward this issue to tackle as CE of a Command.

Retrospect

The following lessons were learnt by me:

Corrective measures should be initiated only after all data has been collected, properly analysed and a pragmatic and effective plan for implementation prepared.

When work has to be done at a fast pace, one must select the best officer/subordinate for a particular task. For this, it is imperative that you know your command.

One has to make sure the entire team is pulling in the same direction by keeping a constant check. There are always perpetual 'cribbers'. One needs to let them know that they are under observation; to make their mindset change. Man-management is the key. Always be humble, polite, straight-forward, comprehend their problems; yet be firm and resolute to get the assigned task completed in the timelines laid down. Expect the best and you will get the best.

Never hear ill about your predecessor or ever speak ill of him. Never encourage any talk on what happened earlier, in your presence.

My first CO always said that opportunities are always passing by you. It is for you to catch and exploit them. I did this by taking on a huge amount of 'Special Repairs' close to the end of an FY. In such high-risk actions, there has to be no margin of error. Every step has to be checked and re-checked to ensure no errors crop up at any stage. For this, a pragmatic and workable plan has to be prepared and executed with proper checks and balance. Things can fail if they are not closely monitored, on a daily basis. The dividends from the effort are worth it. In my case, it enabled me to change the perception of the MES held by the Corps Commander and his subordinate commanders. We became a dependable, reliable and transparent body, who were seen as thorough professionals.

Pleasure in the job puts perfection in the work.

Never consider any success as your achievement. One is only permitted to say, one performed the assigned duty and nothing more.

With the enhancement of the workload, another CWE (Project) was raised at Bathinda. With zero 'housekeeping' points, we easily won the 'Best Zone Trophy' for the first time since it's raising. Incidentally, from the last position, we got to the first position by a huge margin.

It was a great honour to be conferred with the Vishisht Seva Medal on 26 January 2001and I also stood approved for promotion to Maj Gen.

Lt Gen GK Duggal, VrC the GOC of 10 Corps and the Chief of Staff, Maj Gen CS Panag were outstanding soldiers who demanded the best for their command and nothing for themselves or in their respective residences. They always had a feel of the pulse of their command. When they observed that I was running a happy team and delivering on the ground they backed me to the hilt. It was initially difficult to serve under such coriaceous taskmasters but, once they saw the changes on the ground, I had their total support. I thoroughly enjoyed working under such superiors who encourage you to do better and better. The lessons learnt under them assisted me greatly to perform my duties as CE Command and E-in-C. I am in touch with both of them to date. Maj Gen IJS Dhillon was the CE Command for the earlier portion of my tenure. Thereafter, it was Maj Gen Madhav Aaren. Both gave me complete freedom of action and for this, I remain grateful to them.

I also had an opportunity to make a presentation to the GOC-in-C Western Command Lt Gen Vijay Oberoi during his visit to Bhatinda Military Station. He asked many perspicacious questions on performance of the zone and left extremely satisfied. It gave me immense pleasure to interact with him.

The only military officer from the Zone who has risen to Maj Gen rank is (then) Major Ashok Kumar. He was my SO2 (Design). He has the potential to rise further. Amongst the IDSE officers, Mr Narinder, my ACE, and Mr BK Jain, then DCWE B/R at CWE Bikaner, superannuated as ADGs. Mr PK Sharma, then DCWE B/R at CWE Bathinda superannuated as CE. Mr RP Shinghal, then SSW in my Zone, is presently serving as ADG.

All officers, whether military or civilian, who served with me have remained in touch and all of them worked very hard to get the 'Best Zone Trophy'. They fondly recall the effort we all put in together and achieved what was considered impossible – 'Respect from our Users.'

Overall, CE Bathinda Zone was a tough assignment and one had to be on one's toes throughout, to ensure everyone works in sync. In February 2001, I was posted as DDG (Personnel) at HQ DGBR in Delhi. After a very warm send-off, on a cold winter morning, we drove down to Delhi in our car to assume my new appointment.

COMING OF AGE

DGBR HQ (Mar 01 — Apr 02)

After a hectic, challenging and productive tenure as CE Bathinda Zone, in February 2001, I was posted as DDG (Personnel) at HQ DGBR. When I reported for duty there, in March 2001, the HQ had just commenced moving into its newly-constructed premises, in Naraina. Obviously, settling down in the new building had many teething problems. Having had two assignments in MES earlier, I was experienced in how to interact at appropriate levels with this organisation. As a result, I got busy resolving numerous problems amicably and the DGBR personnel were made as comfortable as feasible in the new environs. The surroundings were also in a sorry shape and the assistance of an Engineer Regiment was taken to clean the area. Where additional office equipment was needed, it was procured in accordance with the existing rules and regulations. A few additional rooms for drivers and visitors, toilets for the guard etc. also had to be constructed. As all the Sections moved in with huge quantities of files, they were advised to have 'Destruction Boards' for files that could be extirpated strictly in conformity with the existing rules. For the first time, the BRO celebrated its Raising Day at its own location.

Having served as CE Beacon, it was clear to me what a CE wanted from HQ DGBR. Accordingly, I set my targets to be achieved. However, once you actually sit in the appointment, one always takes on more than what one has aimed for. When the shifting and settling down at the new location was over, by force of habit, I went on to totally revamp the working of the Personnel Branch. I knew that I would be in my appointment for only one year. Ergo, I had first to be clear on what all I could do in the time available and also progress each of the targets I set for myself.

While I was resolving the teething problems of the building, I was getting briefings from all Section heads. There were a large number of pending Department Promotion Committee (DPC) meetings; and an equally large number of disciplinary cases to be finalised. Further, the posting of officers was not being done in a rational and transparent manner and they were not being implemented by their due dates. Once there was clarity in my mind, I put the points in writing and wrote against each the steps which I would have to take to implement them.

After planning was done and targets set, action began and daily targets were fixed. I continued with my habit of reaching the office an hour earlier than the scheduled time. Every morning, a mini-conference was held from 0900 to 0930 hours and daily targets given to all officers. The primary aim of the morning conference was to get everyone to come to the office on time. Thereafter, I avoided calling any member of the staff to my office. From 1500 hours onward, a 15-minute time slot was fixed for the Section heads to meet me. At this time, progress achieved was reviewed and problems, if any, were resolved. Initially, a rap on the knuckles was given to those who failed to achieve their respective targets. At the end of the week, those who did not achieve their laid-down targets had to attend office from 0930 to 1300 hours on Saturdays with me being present.

Postings of GREF Officers

The existing SOP on posting of GREF officers was more than ten years old and outdated. Necessary draft changes were made after due deliberations. Thereafter, a copy was sent to the CEs (with a copy to their TF commanders) for perusal, with directions to send suggested amendments, if any, or a nil report would be assumed after 15 days. Reminders were sent to everyone through telephone and fax from the tenth day onward. Most of the CEs sent a nil report. After approval of the DGBR, the updated policy was issued for implementation.

Postings of Army Officers

Whatever I learnt earlier, while serving in the MS Branch, greatly assisted me to implement the changes in the prevailing system of postings in the BRO. Before an Army officer was inducted into the BRO, his spoken reputation was obtained from two other officers. A record of their inputs was kept with the noting sheet, based on which the officer was posted to a suitable location and appointment. A feedback on the officer's performance was obtained from the concerned CE, after six months, and a record of it was also maintained.

To ensure that all officers moved in and out on time, in conformity with the posting orders, a proper SOP was issued. Within a week of the receipt of the posting order, in case any change of date was desired, the CE had to speak to the DDG (Personnel). If the request was genuine, it was accepted and the date of the move or the posting was amended. In case the request was not in order, it was put up to the DGBR for a ruling. In this manner, quick decisions were taken, after due deliberations and infructuous work at all levels was obviated. The day an officer moved out on posting, the DDG (Personnel) office had to be informed, both on telephone and fax. Within a month all posting orders commenced being implemented, as issued.

Timely Submission of ACRs

Most ACRs were not being received by their due dates. To ensure timely initiation and submission, a comprehensive SOP was issued. Initially, weekly checks were done by me; later it was fortnightly. The officer-in-charge ACRs did a check, on a daily basis, and wherever delay was noticed, he would call the SO1(Personnel) concerned. No excuse was accepted for delay. Very soon, everyone started following orders, basic discipline was enforced, and infructuous work reduced drastically.

Conduct of DPCs

A very large number of DPCs/Promotion Boards were pending for officers and subordinate staff. As this affected morale of the personnel concerned, I took it up as a challenge. The Secretary BRDB (a bureaucrat) was the head of the DPCs. I first developed a good rapport with him. I also worked out a draft programme of all the pending DPCs and got the chart approved by him.

A lot of homework had to be done for holding the DPCs. All old ACR's had to be collected, and a complete record of the individual concerned made correctly. For this, I had to attach a few officers and clerks from other Sections and work on weekends. Only after the record was fully ready, checked and rechecked, did we start holding the DPC meetings. Secretary BRDB used to come to my office and since our records were complete, they were completed in less than an hour. Earlier they could not be held for want of complete and updated records.

Before I left HQ DGBR a record number of DPCs were held. The entire backlog was cleared. It involved a lot work, but it was an excellent morale booster. A large number of officers and subordinates finally got their long due promotions. With the CEs adhering to the SOPs, discipline was brought into the system. For me, cultivating good relations with the Secretary BRDB and the PCDA was not difficult as I had the earlier experience as CE Beacon and CE Bathinda Zone.

Disciplinary Cases

Long outstanding disciplinary cases had piled up at the DGBR and the BRDB offices. First, a list of all of them was prepared, with the date of initiation of the case and the reasons for it lying pending. Once the list was ready, each case was thoroughly studied and those which, as advised by the legal team in my office, were for minor offences, were separated. To my consternation, out of the hundred-plus list, 53 were for minor offences. I went over each of them and I could remove only one and not put it in the 'major offence' category. I then divided the list of minor offences into various categories according to their nature viz.

misbehaviour, drunkenness, non-performance of duties etc.

Thereafter, in a meeting with the Secretary BRDB, we discussed these cases threadbare and he agreed that they can be disposed of at the DGBR level, and some by the respective CEs. We got his approval in writing and took action accordingly. Within a fortnight, action on all of Phase 1 long-delayed disciplinary cases was completed. The balance of major offence cases was again studied in depth by the legal team. Those which could be finished by collecting additional data, were mortised. Others were disposed by deciding on the punishment to be given. We went in a similar manner as done for minor cases and completed as many as we could with the requisite updated document, evidence etc. Once this was done, we took the easy cases first, rechecked them and wrote our recommendations for each and took them to Secretary BRDB. We gave him a week to study our cases and recommendations with his team and then we would again deliberate, wherever there was a difference of opinion. In two cases, the Secretary desired additional information, which we provided and 14 more cases were completed. In actual fact, no one wishes to touch long-outstanding disciplinary cases with a barge pole, for obvious reasons.

Lessons Learnt

The major lessons learnt while serving as DDG (Personnel) at HQ DGBR were:

The BRO has its strong and weak points. I aimed to instil the good points of MES and combat engineers into the BRO. I think we succeeded to a great extent.

A good rapport with Secretary BRDB and the PCDA BRO assisted in doing my tasks professionally.

A system can only be improved when we reduce infructuous work and bring in transparency and enforce discipline.

It is pertinent to mention that I observed that the GREF officers in the BRO, like the IDSE officers in MES had similar issues regarding additional appointments in higher ranks, equivalency of ranks with the Army officers. However, this was suppressed to a great extent as all their long outstanding DPCs were held.

Posting Out

One year in the HQ DGBR went by in no time and, in April 2002, I was posted as CE Southern Command, on promotion. Three officers who assisted me in my assignment greatly were Col Narasimhan and Col Rajeev Dutt (both superannuated as Maj Gens) and Maj Jham (who superannuated as Lt Col). I also had two coursemates in HQ DGBR - Brig M Swaminathan (who had earlier served with me in 54 Engineer Regiment) and Brig MG Girish from the EME (who superannuated as Lt Gen). In addition, Brig IJ Singh from the EME, who was relief to Brig MG Girish, later superannuated as DG EME, another outstanding officer.

In this short tenure I served under two renowned Bombay Sappers, Lt Gen AK Puri and Lt Gen Prakash Suri. Both were very different personalities, however there was a lot to learn from each of them.

WE DID IT

CE Southern Command (May 02 — Dec 03)

In April 2002, around 1530 hours on a Friday, when I had just commenced my daily conference with the Section Heads of the Personnel Branch, I was informed that the MS (X) at Army HQ wanted to speak to me. On the phone, he congratulated me on my promotion and posting as CE Southern Command, as a relief for Maj Gen NP Aul, who had moved out on posting as COS Northern Command on promotion. I was asked to report at Pune on the coming Monday morning. The extremely short move was due to Operation Parakram, which had been ordered a week earlier. I thanked him but requested one additional day to move. He agreed and our conversation was over.

At Pune, I was received warmly by Brig SS Tejpal, the ACE (Plg) who briefed me on the operational situation and handed me a copy of the handing/taking over notes. The first day commenced in meeting and addressing all the officers about what I expected from them. The Army Commander, Lt Gen GS Sihota, VrC, welcomed me warmly. I requested permission to go on a short operational familiarisation trip. He readily accepted and directed the MGGS, Maj Gen Daljeet Singh, to coordinate the trip so that I could see the maximum operational areas and meet the maximum formation commanders and get briefings from them, in the three days at my disposal.

Operational Familiarisation

The MGGS wanted two days for coordinating and organising the trip. The next day I spent with the BGS (Ops) and the ACE (Combat) Brig Raghu Trivedi for a detailed operational briefing. The operational familiarisation thereafter was hectic but extremely productive. I got clarity on the terrain and the engineer support plan and was also able to meet most of the formation commanders. I was happy to receive positive feedback from them on the multifaceted engineer support tasks being executed, to ensure the operational readiness of the Southern Command theatre. On my return, I gave concise feedback to the Army Commander. He advised me to remain in touch with the formation commanders and sort out their problems if any. I assured him that I would do so.

Conference with all CE Zones

I then shifted my attention to the MES. On two days' notice, all CE Zones were called for a conference at Pune. To prepare for it, I stayed up late at night to list out the points to be disseminated. I also prepared the draft minutes in detail (as the staff at Pune was not aware of my style of working). The conference was held in two parts. In Part-I, all CE Zones together and in Part-II, the CE Zones of the Army, Navy and Air Force, separately, to go over their specific points. I spelt out what all I expected from each of the CE Zones. Targets were laid out and their date of completion given.

While the conference was going on, two staff officers, (one who had earlier served under me) were checking the draft minutes being typed, correcting it and getting it retyped. During the tea and lunch breaks, I checked the draft and, when I was satisfied, I told my SO, Lt Col Naveen Jha, to get it printed, sign it and hand over a copy to each of the CE Zones. Immediately after I left the conference, he walked in and gave the document to them. They were astonished to receive it so fast. Copies were thereafter faxed to all the Zonal Offices, with directions to disseminate it to their CWEs, who were instructed to fax a copy to all their GEs. When the CEs of the Zones reached their respective offices, they were astounded to learn that all officers were aware of what had occurred in the conference. All officers thus not only knew what my KRAs were in less than a week of my taking over as CE Southern Command but had commenced working on them.

The ACEs and the staff in my headquarters were also given a 'Monitoring Plan' on how the results achieved by each Zone were to be monitored weekly and the progress achieved was to be shown to me, every Tuesday, before 1000 hours. The format in which the progress was to be prepared was also formalised. This close monitoring got stricter, as time passed, till the targets laid down were achieved. By this action, the entire MES was brought into sync as my reputation regarding what I had achieved as CE Bathinda Zone had reached the last man. My aim was to revamp, revive and rejuvenate the MES into an efficient force, responsive to the genuine needs of the users.

Industrial and Basic Staff

The CE Command is responsible for all industrial and basic staff of the entire Command up to JE. Their postings and promotions are under his aegis. I observed that their service books, which were held at the GE level, were not being updated and maintained as they should be. I spent two hours every week on this aspect and was able to bring in a quantum improvement in their records by issuing a number of instructions on this vital subject. In all stations, I addressed the officers and subordinate staff (basic and industrial) separately. Problems, if any, were resolved expeditiously. Their morale and motivation were always kept high so that they gave their best to the organization. The first basic rule, 'know your men' must not be forgotten

Visit to the CEs (Air Force and Navy)

I commenced my outstation visits, by first visiting the Naval and Air Force Stations as the Army stations were denuded due to Operation Parakram. These two services have excellent SOPs. A young, dynamic officer is detailed as a LO, who receives a visiting officer and accompanies him everywhere. He also regularly keeps giving feedback on what the visitor was doing in the Station to his seniors. I realised this when I met the FOC-in-C; who was aware of my hectic programme.

My first visit to all stations was for two days each. Those days, there were no flights from Pune at timings which suited me. I had to drive down to Mumbai and stay the night in a room close to the airport, where I normally reached between 2030 and 2100 hours, depending upon the traffic en route. Either the GE or AGE received me. I never had any meals there; only a cup of tea in the morning. I would catch the first flight from Mumbai normally before 0500 hours in order to reach the station I was visiting before 0730 hours. Breakfast was on-board the aircraft. I would change into uniform in the Naval/Air Force guest room and be in the Zonal office by 0830 hours, half an hour before it commenced functioning. I would meet the staff officers and address all officers for 20 minutes and then listen to the briefings of the CE Zone and CWE, which had to be in accordance with the format issued. At 1000 hours, I would address all MES personnel of the station for 20 minutes and hand out gifts to the persons who had performed well. This was followed by tea, with all MES personnel, where I interacted with them for 10 minutes.

After this, I met all the builders, gave them a talk on my expectations and resolved their points. Thereafter, I went around the entire station, inspected its services and important works under execution. This would come to an end by 1900 hours. The next day at 0530 hours, along with the CE Zone, I would walk to see the places missed out. After breakfast, I met some of the local OC units and heard the problems they wished to bring to my notice. Finally, I would call on the FOC-in-C at around 1100 hours. As the FOC-in-C's were aware of my hectic schedule in their respective stations, they hesitantly told me their problems. During these interactions with the FOC-in-C/AOC-in-C, I found that they were acutely aware of their station problems. I would inform them that the CE Zone would give a time schedule and plan on how we intended for resolving their problems, the next day. This was finalised in the afternoon before I left the station. I used to take a soft copy along for my staff to monitor the progress. In addition, in the afternoon, I would prepare my Draft Tour Notes and take a soft copy with me. This ensured no points were missed out or there were any misgivings, as they were shown to the CE Zone. My return evening flight was planned at a time to be in Mumbai latest by 2130 hours. In the car journey back to Pune from Mumbai, I would try to sleep in the back seat of the Ambassador car and, on reaching home at midnight, I was in my study till 0330 hours and saw all the *dak*, wrote my comments on all the letters, and sorted them as follows:

> For action today (in the office in the morning).
>
> For action today (in the afternoon).
>
> For action at the Section level – reply to be shown to me, before dispatch, on the same day.
>
> Action at the Section level – to be seen by the ACE, before dispatch.

After seeing the entire mail, I slept till 0600 hours and reached the office at 0730 hours. My staff knew my routine and would be present at that time. The sorted *dak* was handed over, entries, where required, were made by the staff and I would get on to preparing draft replies on the letters/notings received. The draft tour notes on my visits were typed (in double space) for a final check by me and handed over to my SO to issue to all concerned through fax and email by 0830 hours. The addressees always wondered how I managed to do this. By the time the remainder of the staff came in 0900 hours, most of the handwritten draft letters would be handed over to the Section Heads for getting them typed. At 0930 hours, I would meet the COS for his points, if any, say hello to the MGGS and MG Adm and then return to my office. I would be back in the office, in the afternoon, to complete pending work. The day ended only when action on all letters was completed. This way, there was never any backlog or reminder ever.

After two such visits, in the first six months, there were normally no points from the FOC-in-C/AOC-in-C. I would suggest improvements which they could consider and they always accepted my advice. This ensured an excellent rapport with all our users. As a rule, I did not have any formal dinners or lunches. They were unavoidable if the FOC-in-C/AOC-in-C gave me no option.

I vividly recall that there were three works which the CE Zone wanted to close prematurely, and do a risk and cost tender. I stopped this practice as it is extremely difficult and time-consuming; the work gets unduly delayed and inevitably results in a court or arbitration case. After discussions with the concerned builders and their head, they realised that it was in their interest to complete the work expeditiously. The President of their association was also requested to assist the builder, financially, in order to get the work completed. The CE Zone too was directed to give quick decisions. The builder was also told that, under no circumstances, would substandard work be accepted. All three works got completed while ensuring that both parties, the builder and the executive, were in a 'win-win' situation.

Visit to the CE Zones (Army)

All active units and formations were in their operational area at the time. During my visits, I instructed the CE Zones to concentrate on works under planning and execution. I also emphasised the need to finish the BP's and AE's of the works under planning, expedite the issue of tenders of works that had been released; and finally, speed up the works which were progressing tardily. A proper monitoring system was put in place and the builders whose works were progressing slowly were formally and informally warned. Simultaneously, work to clear the huge backlog on 'housekeeping points' was also being progressed. The constant monitoring by me, every Sunday, had the desired effect.

Army Commander's KRA

After about six months into my tenure, the Army Commander called me to his office and told me that, "In addition to whatever you are doing I want you to achieve my KRA. I want a definite improvement in all the bathrooms, kitchens and dining halls of PBORs and a definite facelift be given to the JCOs Messes. If feasible tile all of them."

I said that it would be done; however, the MG Adm and the Station Commanders would have to take action in consonance with the guidelines given by me. It was only then that I could ensure there would be no problems and the project would be executed with the best workmanship. The Army Commander called the MG Adm and directed him accordingly. I commenced homework to plan the project viz:

> The number of bathrooms and toilets in permanent/temporary buildings in every station with the name of the unit. Similar information was obtained on JCO's Messes. In Stage 1, facilities in permanent buildings would be taken up, where the sizes, hopefully, would be the same.
>
> Each JCO Mess would require thorough planning as they may be in different types of buildings.
>
> To work out the costing, the size of each facility/room, and the height up to which tiles were to be installed was assessed (less the doors, windows and ventilators). The requirement was worked out separately for bathrooms, sidewalls and the flooring.
>
> The work would have to be executed from 'Special Repair' funds. The MG Adm would have to keep maximum funds available for this. The heading of each task would be 'Special Repair' to Building Number ... Also request the QMG's Branch at Army HQ to allot as much Special Funds, as feasible.
>
> To keep the cost of the project down, select one firm to supply the entire quantity of tiles at each of the stations. This was to be done after adhering to a proper bidding procedure.
>
> Only plain tiles of a sober colour were chosen for the flooring and wall tiles. Designer tiles were not used, as they could go 'off the shelf' during the maintenance period.
>
> Lay down the height of tiles in the bathrooms and toilets.
>
> The facelifts of each JCOs Mess to be prepared by the architects, in detail, and thereafter it's costing worked out.

Two officers were tasked to collect all information on tiles. They did a thorough job and we learnt everything there was to know about tiles and the relevant IS Codes. I also nominated a team of three officers, (one officer each from planning, architect and the surveyor's Sections) to assist. I gave them the list of checkpoints I had prepared and directed them to separate the points under the three heads – Planning stage (included collection of data); Issue of Administrative Approval; and Execution Stage including monitoring of the project. I gave them two days for this. They were permitted to add as many points as they wanted and list them under the following heads.

Collection of Data.

Financial Planning.

Issue of Administrative Approval.

Execution Stage.

Monitoring Stage.

With total clarity on how to execute the project, we collected the data on all the bathrooms, toilets and JCO's Mess in all stations. To ensure it came in the manner we desired, proper formats were sent out. Once the data came in, the rough cost of the entire project was prepared.

I then met the MG (Adm) and asked him to get all the station commanders to Pune so that they can be briefed on the project. As an appropriate auditorium was not available in Pune, I coordinated with the CME for using their auditorium and arranged a bus to take the officers there. Only the CEs of the Army Zones were called. After my address, all Station Commanders and all CE Zones were on the same page. A handout on 'Do's and Don'ts' was also distributed.

With the users in harmony with the MES, the project went ahead extremely smoothly and, except for monitoring, I had to make no intervention. Rather, there was a healthy competition among the units and formations and they put in more effort than I had ideated. The project was completed a month before the target date. The Army Commander got a positive feedback from his formation commanders during his visits; he was delighted to see the men ecstatic at what was done for them.

Demining Operations

When Operation Parakram was ordered by Army HQ, to ensure timely operational readiness, a large number of minefields were laid. I was posted after the mine laying was completed in which we had a number of casualties. When a stalemate came about in the political situation, I anticipated that demining would be ordered, at some stage. I gave considerable thought to the idea of formulating a suitable drill for this since it was mainly a Sapper responsibility. It was also imperative to ensure that there were no casualties. For this, I told my staff to collect the data of all the types of mines laid, and their lot numbers, from all the formations and the engineers.

This data was compiled, collated and thereafter verified by the Ordnance Branch of HQ Southern Command. We found from the lot numbers of all mines laid in the Southern Command theatre, that they had long outlived their life. Accordingly, we wrote to the Ordnance Branch at Army HQ for a confirmation whether they can be destroyed in situ, or were still required to be returned to the ammunition dumps. This took time, but a confirmation was received that we need not return the mines. However, a destruction certificate was to be handed over to the ammunition dumps from where the mines had been collected.

In the formulation of a drill for the demining operations, with no chance of any casualty, the following factors were considered:

> 99 percent of the mines were laid in the desert area. The anti-tank and anti-personnel fragmentation mines, by their sheer weight, would remain in their original position where they were laid. However, a few anti-personnel mines could have been shifted by desert rats.
>
> Since all the mines laid had outlived their life and we did not have to return the lifted mines to the ammunition dumps, we could destroy them in situ.
>
> In combat field engineering, we had learnt that all mines (even if fitted with a detonator) do not blast when burning. Thus, we could use kerosene, petrol, diesel and dried camel dung for this.
>
> Since the anti-tank mines would be in the same position where they had been laid, which was known to us, and by virtue of their size, they would be easier to locate, the priority was to locate them first; then the anti-personnel (fragmentation) mines; and finally, the anti-personnel (NMM14) mines. The located mines were to be burnt in situ.

> In case any anti-personnel mines were not found in their original position, the location needed to be marked and the fencing around the minefield was not removed.

During deliberations in planning the demining, the following additional points came up:

> The mines should be located by blowing off the sand near their location by using a compressor, rather than a mine prodder.
>
> As there were a large number of anti-personnel mines, they could be lifted with a long flycatcher and shifted into a pit, where they could be burnt together. This way we could do the activity faster and use less fuel.
>
> For command and control, the same party that had laid the mines should demine the area.

Once the demining drill was finalised in my mind, to the last detail, I deliberated on the plan of action with my ACE (Combat) Brig Raghu Trivedi, who was an intelligent officer and a friend. The recommended drill was accepted after a consensus emerged that the chances of fatality would reduce considerably by adopting it.

In the next brain-storming session, I proposed that for dealing with the anti-personnel mines which had moved from their location, a JCB could lift the sand and put it through a sieve till the mine is located or we can send in a road roller to blast the mine. Many such ideas can be adopted, depending upon the ground conditions.

Thereafter, I visited an engineer regiment and deliberated on the recommended drill with them. They had apprehensions as none of them knew that mines burn. When I burnt one anti-personnel mine before them, they accepted the new drill. I directed them to practice and fine-tune the drill to ensure there are no casualties. The drill was then passed on to all engineer units, with additional directions to not only fine-tune it but also to fabricate protection equipment and safety equipment required for demining actions. Requisite funds were also allotted to them. All engineer regiments practised and mastered the drill. They also trained the infantry battalions on the new drill.

When the strategic relocation of forces was ordered, there were no instructions on the demining of minefields. The GS Branch told me that the Army Commander had ruled out demining till the requisite demining equipment is procured and allotted. I went to meet the Army Commander; he confirmed that since he cannot accept any casualties, he had not permitted demining operations. I proposed that in case the demining operations are conducted by a drill through which there are no casualties, would permission be accorded. He concurred and said, "Yes, with no casualties."

I then conveyed the Army Commander's directions to the MGGS who then wanted me to prepare the draft instructions for the formations. My staff did that and the demining operations began.

The demining operations commenced slowly but then the pace picked up. When progress had reached 98 percent and I was busy in my office, I got a call from the Army Commander who said, "Come to my office immediately."

I rushed to his office wondering what had gone wrong. As I entered his office he asked, "Have you commenced the demining operations?"

When I confirmed so, his next question was, "How many mines have been demined?"

I said, "98 percent, Sir, and we should complete the demining operations very soon."

He then asked for a briefing on the drill being adopted. I, on the next day gave a detailed briefing to the GOC-in-C on the drill adopted in accordance with the terms of reference laid down by him that no casualties were acceptable, during the demining operations. Further the drill formulated by us was best suited for the terrain in which the mine fields had been laid. I also mentioned that since the mines laid had outlived their life they were not to be returned to the Depots. This afforded us an opportunity to deviate from the mine field breaching drill taught to us at the Schools of Instruction to accomplish success and speed in our task. He complimented me on applying my mind on this complex task.

Lt Gen GS Sihota was a very cool, calm and collected personality, who gave complete freedom of action to his commanders. I recall an anecdote narrated to me by him from the time when he did his Staff Course at

Camberley (UK). He was the syndicate leader tasked to prepare a plan to protect a bridge. The plan evolved by his syndicate was in accordance with the standard solution, as taught in our schools of instruction and evoked praise from the instructor. However, an Israeli officer, who was also attending the course, was vehement that the plan would not work in an actual combat situation, for the simple reason that it was a predictable one. This stuck in my mind. When I sat down to evolve the demining drill, I formulated a drill which suited the existing environment. It worked and we were able to carry out the demining without any casualty.

Savings in Electricity Tariff

Over the years, I had observed that the State Electricity Boards were charging the MES electricity tariff on an irrational basis of rates that were much higher in comparison to the civilian counterparts in that particular State. However, I could not take it up till I became CE Southern Command.

Let me explain why I got this impression. In all military stations, we normally have one to three 'takeover points' which are 11 KVA, 33 KVA, 66 KVA or 132 KVA capacity (depending upon the size of the military station). The military spends its own funds to construct these take-over points as well as for the infrastructure required for distributing the power within the military station, through overhead lines/underground lines, transformers and smaller substations, right up to where an electric meter is provided for the consumers. In other words, the MES spends money not only to build this huge infrastructure but thereafter incurs expenditure to maintain it. In the civil, the State/UT incurs the capital cost to install/erect the same infrastructure and thereafter spends its own funds on maintenance. The State Electricity Board gets paid by the Army, in bulk, for the electricity purchased/consumed, whereas for those living in the cities and towns a lot of time and resources are spent for individual billing. This issue had been irking my mind for many years.

There were also other technical points that were not being addressed by the State Electricity Boards. Accordingly, to obtain the most economical tariff rates for defence, from each of the states, a drive was launched in phases:

In Phase-I, all MES formations were directed to critically analyse the tariff schedule applied to them, and compare the rates for the civilian population in the same state. The terms and conditions for the supply of electricity were analysed, in detail, and the anomalies in the tariff schedules existing in each state were identified.

In Phase-II, the Southern Command theatre was divided into state-wise regions and Nodal CEs were appointed for each state.

In Phase III, state-specific petitions were prepared and sent to the Nodal CEs for taking up with the respective State Electricity Boards and State Electricity Regulatory Commissions (SERCs).

After a persistent and continuous effort, a breakthrough was achieved with all the nine states in Southern Command. By this effort, the savings accrued were:

Tariff Revision. This was accepted by most of the states as only veracious points were projected in the petitions, to which the State's Electricity Boards had no cogent answers.

Rebate. In our petitions, we requested all State Electricity Boards to offer a rebate to the Defence as we draw electricity in bulk and always clear our dues promptly. We sought a 10 percent rebate, which was finally accepted at 7.5 percent of the total bill.

Incentives for Power Factor. A number of states offered incentives up to one percent of the bill amount in case of a Power Factor above a fixed level i.e., beyond 0.95 were achieved. As it was in our interest to achieve the desired Power Factor in all stations, suitable measures were introduced by all GEs to avail of this discount. Due to the improvement in power factor, the electricity breakdowns in all stations reduced drastically.

Incentive for Clearance of Bulk Bill. Most states were giving a 0.5 percent incentive for clearing the Bulk Bill within three days of its receipt. By adhering to this, most GE's commenced getting an additional 0.5 percent rebate of their bill amount.

Energy Audit. This was done at both ends. The State Electricity Boards' bulk electricity meters, which were not functional, were got replaced, and re-calibration of the existing bulk meters was carried out to ensure correct and authentic readings. Joint meter readings were made mandatory. All State Electricity Boards bills were properly scrutinized before payment. Regrettably, the audit authorities showed no interest in this as the payment was from one government agency to another and for over-payment, if any, no one is blamed. To reduce wastage of electricity, elaborate guidelines on energy conservation were issued through departmental and staff channels. For this, an energy audit was carried out in all stations, through the Station Commanders, to ensure optimum utilisation of electricity.

Electricity Duty (ED). According to provisions contained in an article of the Constitution, ED is not liable to OTM accommodation. Regrettably, due to ignorance, most of the GEs were paying it. Payments were stopped and refunds were obtained from most of the States.

Connected Load and Maximum Load. This needed to be carefully worked out and reflected in the agreements.

The total savings achieved by this exercise was over Rs 45 crore annually and recurring. This was achieved by September 2003 and would have gone to a much higher figure by the end of the FY.

Interaction with the Chiefs of Staff

For the first six months of my tenure, Lt Gen MA Gurbaxani was the COS. Due to my visits to the Naval and AF Zones, I had missed the PPET. One day, after returning from Chennai, due to the hectic pace, combined with the change in temperature, I had a high fever and body ache. In the morning, before going to the office, I went to the Duty MO at MH Pune. After checking me, he said that I had flu and recommended that I should be admitted to the MH as that would enable me to recuperate fast and all other medical parameters too would be thoroughly checked. I requested the MO not to admit me. I assured him that I would rest at home and in case I did not feel better by the evening I would get myself admitted to the MH. I took the medicines he gave me and got busy in the office routine followed after an outstation tour.

At 0930 hours, when I went to meet the COS, he said, "Tomorrow is the PPET, please attend." I had gone to tell him that I was placed 'sick in quarters' by the MO but I could not say so. I telephoned the Commandant Bombay Sappers and requested him to get white shorts and a half-sleeve white shirt (without pocket) stitched by evening. I sent a shirt and shorts for measurements. I also told my SO to purchase plain white socks and old-pattern white canvas PT shoes from the market. I had my medication and the next morning, though I was running a slight fever, I was ready for the run. As I was exercising daily and going for long walks, I easily stood first in the run and could also do the remaining tests of sit ups, bend stretches, etc. The COS was happy to see me fit. We then went to the range for carbine and pistol firing. I had fired a carbine a number of times earlier. The first test was firing from the hip position on three targets. I alone got all my shots on all three targets to achieve the 'Marksman' category. To our good fortune, once this test was over, the COS had to leave as he got a call from his wife and further tests on pistol firing were not held. For the COS, thereafter, I was a good soldier.

I served under two Chiefs of Staff during my tenure. Lt Gen MA Gurbaxani was a thorough gentleman who expected all officers to be physically fit, mentally alert and properly turned out at all times. He was soft-spoken but expected immediate action on any of his directions. I thoroughly enjoyed working under this so-called hard taskmaster and I learnt a lot from him.

When Lt Gen Gurbaxani superannuated, he was replaced by Lt Gen Satish Satpute, another clear-headed General who had his own methods to test his juniors. Regretfully, he had a bad experience with the MES when he was the Corps Commander at Bhopal when that station was under HQ Central Command and adequate funds for his formation were not allotted. Initially, he would pass snide remarks against the MES. I had to tell him to first see the functioning of the MES in Southern Command before taking a standpoint. He did test me (the MES) a number of times and we always delivered well beyond his expectations. Thereafter, he spoke well of the MES. I learnt a lot from him too – his memory, sense of humour in most tense situations was worth emulating. I vividly recall that soon after he had taken over, he desired to visit the CE Southern Command office complex. (I had spruced it up in the first month of my taking over). After going around the entire complex, he entered my office, and surprised me by commenting, "Where have you brought me? This is an infantry battalion and not an MES setup." I was taken aback for a moment when he commented, "Only an infantry battalion can be so spic and span, please take me to the MES set up." There were many more such one-liners from him.

Army Sports Institute (ASI) Pune and World Military Games at Hyderabad

The Army Sports Institute at Pune was a unique project where the complete planning and construction was done by an external agency, under the guidance of Southern Command. Col Amin Naik, the first Commandant of ASI, who was the officer in-charge of the project came to meet me and requested my assistance, as the project was experiencing delays. I readily accepted but asked for a day to check with the Army Commander. Lt Gen Sihota was aware of the project and the ASI Commandant had met him too. I was directed to provide the requisite assistance.

I went all out to provide the technical assistance required to get the project back on track. It was a complex and challenging Greenfield project, the first of its kind in India. It included training areas, hostels for accommodating the athletes and other allied facilities. The infrastructure was being created for selected sports disciplines, where India had hopes of winning medals in the Olympic Games. This being a turnkey project, all facilities were to be of international standards. Accordingly, one had to make sure that we do not falter, under any circumstances.

I had several back-to-back meetings with international sports experts to check all mandatory items required in the project, were of international sports specifications. We confirmed that the services viz. water supply, electricity, sewerage, and drainage had been correctly planned and included. Necessary confirmations, sanctions, and clearances were then obtained from the competent authorities. Similar action was initiated for cutting of trees and shifting of the open sewage line.

Thereafter, all data was re-verified and corrections-cum-amendments made in the specifications. A thorough ground check of the land where the project was to come up was done by a team of officers. Due to the effort put in during the planning, the tender action phase proceeded smoothly because, during the pre-bid meetings, a detailed brief on the project was given to the bidders, and all relevant important clauses brought to their notice and clarified. The project took off expeditiously. With periodic meetings and timely decisions given to the builder on the site itself, work progressed without a hitch and was completed in record time with no time or cost overruns. Even today, after 20 years, it is still the best sports institute in Asia.

The World Military Games for the first time were being held at Hyderabad in Sep 2007. This took a lot of time to initially plan and thereafter execute this complex project.

Approval of Zonal Plans

Zonal Plans show space allocations for KLP units, including future expansions, amenities, town centres, and external services. They include proposals for the total conceptual development plan of military stations. Zonal Plans (including all amendments) of military strength up to 5,000 are approved by the GOC-in-C of the Command and more than 5,000 strength are approved by the QMG. The Army Commander was gracious to find time hearing the briefings of the architects and, after satisfying himself, he approved a large number of pending Zonal Plans.

Miscellaneous Works

Among other works which I had to undertake to spruce up the accommodations and infrastructure in Southern Command were:

Armoured Corps Centre and School, Ahmednagar.

School of Artillery, Deolali.

Guest Rooms and Officers Mess, Artillery Centre at Golconda, Hyderabad.

Army Clerks' Training School, Aurangabad.

Defence Security Corps Centre, Kannur, and many more

Posting as DGW

The COAS, Gen Nirmal Vij, visited HQ Southern Command in early December 2003. All MGs had lined up to meet him. When he came to me, he said, "You are coming to Delhi as DGW very soon and I have lot of works lined up for you. I am hopeful that you will live up to my expectations." I replied, "Wilco, Sir."

Incidentally, this was the first time in my entire career that I knew of where I am being posted before my posting order was issued.

Retrospect

The major lessons learnt during this tenure are:

The Navy and Air Force Stations in my jurisdiction had to be given a little more attention than the Army formations so that they did not feel they were getting a step-motherly treatment.

Clearance of housekeeping points was made mandatory and no one got a movement order, till they cleared their respective backlog. This had a positive effect on the works and reduced arbitration cases drastically.

Regular updating of zonal specifications ensured that Users were given buildings in conformity with the latest materials available in the market. Non-schedule items were reduced to the minimum. It ensured timely and correct payments were made to the builders.

The unknown MES subordinates who did good work were honoured every quarter. This brought in pride and healthy competition amongst the tradesmen and subordinates.

We succeeded in rationalising the electricity tariff being charged to the military stations by the various State

Electricity Boards. This brought in a huge recurring annual saving.

The Army Commander had clearly spelt out that demining operations can only be conducted provided we ensure there are no casualties. We accordingly applied our minds and based on various factors involved with this operation, innovated a suitable drill by which we not only succeeded in having no casualties, but also were able to accomplish our task in the least feasible time frame.

CE Southern Command was an extremely busy and hectic appointment. I had to work 24x7 as I had set myself difficult KRA's. I was successful as the Army Commander and the COS's had full faith in me and I had to live up to their expectations. Further, I was fully supported by all the officers in my office and in all the Zones too. I need to mention the extreme hard work put in by Brig SS Tejpal, my ACE (Wks) and all other officers. I owe him and the entire team a lot of gratitude. As in previous appointments, I saw that once one commences in achieving success, every member of the team works hard to achieve what seems impossible when you commence the task. I was nicknamed '*Karamyogi*' by my juniors.

It was a great honour to be conferred with the Ati Vishisht Seva Medal in 2004.

NOTHING IS IMPOSSIBLE

Col Comdt The Bengal Sappers

It was a proud privilege and honour for me to be elected as the Colonel Commandant of the Bengal Sappers, in May 2003. There had been a delay of four months in my appointment as the process of ratification took time. Be that as it may, one of my main tasks was to organise the Bicentenary Celebrations of the Bengal Sappers, at Roorkee in November that year. Operation Parakram had wound down and my focus shifted to planning the grand event

First, I had to go to Roorkee, where our group and centre is located, for the formal taking over ceremony. At Roorkee, I came to know that the Centre Commandant stood approved for promotion and was expecting to move out soon. So I heard his presentation and offered no comments. During the two days stay, I went around the Group Centre two to three times and became totally aware of the condition of the infrastructure.

On return to Pune, I got down with a pencil and paper to write down the major points for planning and conduct of the Bicentenary Celebrations. I had read a quote by Mark Victor Hansen, "By recording your dreams and goals on paper, you set in motion the process of becoming the person you most want to be. Put your future in good hands—your own." My points included:

> A suitable Commandant was to be selected who had a good soldierly bearing and could command the Bicentenary parade. By

tradition, in the Bengal Sappers, the parade is always commanded by the Centre Commandant.

The celebrations must be traditional, yet different, and done in a grand and befitting manner.

The three Service Chiefs must be invited. A detailed plan for each dignitary would have to be worked out.

The 'Surya Kirans' the IAF acrobatic team must perform at this mega event.

The history of the gallant Bengal Sappers (pre-independence and post-independence) must be highlighted during the celebrations.

The infrastructure at the Group Centre needs improvement, for which additional funds under 'Special Repairs' must be released expeditiously.

Due to limitations of civil accommodation in Roorkee, invitations to the Bengal Sappers of the British Army had to be restricted to a delegation total of 20.

The action could commence only after a Centre Commandant was posted. I did, however, continue planning for all the activities. The main limitation was the shortage of time and the new Centre Commandant would have his hands full. I had no choice but to take on the responsibility of a number of activities. My experience while organising the 'Golden Jubilee Celebrations' of the CME was a suitable guide.

In the first week of June 2003, the posting of Brig Gautam Banerjee (the Engineer Brigade Commander at Nasirabad) who I had requested for as Centre Commandant was declassified. I rang him up to congratulate him and requested him to meet me at Pune before moving to Roorkee. When Gautam came, I mentioned the broad events I had decided upon. The celebration of 200 years of the glorious saga of service and sacrifice of the Bengal Sappers involved an elaborate framework of programmes and events. From his expression, I could see that he was wondering how so much could be achieved in so little a time. Also, my plan to get the three Service Chiefs appeared inconceivable to him. I told him that the Bengal Sappers have always achieved the impossible. In my view, the word impossible is only used by those who are unwilling to perform a task.

A week later, the E-in-C, Lt Gen Hari Uniyal, who was also a Bengal Sapper and the Senior Colonel Commandant, rang up to say that the veterans and senior serving the Bengal Sappers were getting anxious about the conduct of the celebrations and that I should plan a trip to Delhi and brief them. I did so on a weekend. After hearing the programme, almost unanimously they were of the opinion that the events planned were not pragmatic and practical. They opined that I would not be successful in getting even one Chief for the event and expressed serious misgivings on getting all three to Roorkee. I brought the discussion to an end by requesting them for a month to work on the plan. Many left the meeting full of apprehension of the proposed programme fructifying.

Invitations to the Chiefs

I spoke to the E-in-C separately on inviting the Service Chiefs. He said he would extend an invitation to the COAS, on my behalf, and that the invites to the CNS and the CAS were my responsibility.

I managed to obtain appointments to meet the CNS and the CAS with an hour's gap on the same day. I went to the CAS, Air Chief Marshal S Krishnaswamy, first. I introduced myself as CE Southern Command and as I looked after the Air Force stations, I would like to know from him whether he was happy with the service being provided by the MES. The Air Chief smiled and said, "How can anyone be satisfied with MES?"

I said, "Sir, please reserve your comments till you speak to any of the AOCs in Southern Command or the AOC-in-C. The Air Chief decided to speak to two AOCs and must have got positive feedback as he mellowed down and said, "I am extremely happy to hear that the AOCs are satisfied with the MES cover. Well done General."

I then told him that I wear another cap, that of the Colonel Commandant of the Bengal Sappers and since the first 12 *'hawai sipahis'* were from the Bengal Sappers, it was my honour to invite him and Mrs Krishnaswamy for our Bicentenary Celebrations in November at Roorkee. After a few seconds, he said, "OK." I thanked him and moved out of his office.

In a similar manner, I extended an invitation to the CNS, Admiral Madhvendra Singh. He expressed his pleasure on MES providing good service to the Navy and directed me to take special care of Naval Academy. He was also gracious to accept the invitation. I left for Pune by the evening flight and then rang up the E-in-C to confirm that the CNS and CAS had accepted to attend the event. He said, "Excellent; now go all out to make the Bicentenary spectacular."

Planning the Film and Laser Show

At Bengaluru, I was introduced to Nandish Mariyappa, the Managing Director of Reach Events, an event management firm that specialised in laser shows. I called him over to Pune to discuss the idea of integrating the Army Symphony orchestra with a state-of-the-art laser technology presentation to showcase the history of the Bengal Sappers. Initially, he found the idea absurd and not workable. On my persistence, he agreed but his demeanour reflected his scepticism about the concept succeeding.

After some thought, I homed on to Col Ajay Chaturvedi to make a film on the Bengal Sappers and to coordinate the laser show. He was then an instructor at the CDM in Secunderabad. I rang him up and frankly gave him no choice but to accept this huge responsibility. Fortunately, I knew the Air Vice Marshal HPS Sidhu, having assisted the CDM to complete its Officers Mess before the scheduled date; he gave permission to use the services of his officer. Ajay Chaturvedi is an extremely sincere, dedicated and hard-working officer who knew the history of the Bengal Sappers and had the talent to convert it into a short film. To assist him, I introduced him to Mrs Archana Kapoor, (MD Archana Productions) who had worked with me at the DGBR, for making a film on the BRO. For the laser show, I introduced him to Nandish Mariyappa at Bengaluru, (MD Reach). The film was to showcase the history of the Bengal Sappers in the pre-independence era and the laser show, the history post-independence era

The comperes for the event were again chosen after due thought. I decided on using the services of Col and Mrs Haider Rizvi. The officer was then posted as CWE Chennai. They started work on their script after discussions with Col Ajay Chaturvedi. They both then decided what all was to be shown in the film and the laser show. Simultaneously, the script for the same was written.

Ajay and Rizvi thereafter spent a week at Bengaluru where they supervised the script, voice over, recording and allied actions related for the movie and the laser show. Ajay kept me constantly updated and got everything cleared from me so that the vision of the show was maintained. We used to talk nearly every day and later met mostly at Delhi airport to sort out minor issues.

Sharing of Responsibilities

There were countless other activities connected with the Bicentenary celebrations on which preparations had to be done. I took on the responsibility of memorabilia and souvenirs for the event. In the Centre, I took on the renovation and total refit-cum-redesign of the Museum and Officers Mess. Lt Col Balwinder Singh and Lt Col Shankhyan of the Centre did all the tasks, under my supervision. I used to visit the Centre at least once a fortnight to check on progress and give decisions on the spot, wherever required. There was total unison between me, Gautam Banerjee and his team. There was total harmony and everyone was on the run as so much had to be done in so little time. We spoke often, sometimes many times a day. Though Gautam had my tacit approval to take any decision; as a good soldier, he always brought me into the loop before taking any action. Much later, when the plans were finalised, I decided to include a detachment of veteran JCO's and ORs in the parade. For this, the parade ground had to be extended. I had to intervene to make the MES undertake this task expeditiously.

Trip to London

A large number from the Bengal Sappers Veteran Officers Association of the British Army wished to attend the Bicentenary celebrations. As we could not accept more than 20 guests, due to accommodation constraints at Roorkee, they desired that I should visit

Britain and take out a draw to decide who could or could not travel to India. Accordingly, I went to the UK on a short two-day trip. Fortunately, I was in touch with my NDC coursemate, a British Sapper officer – Brig Chris Sexton – and God bless him, he made all the arrangements. I was received at the airport and driven to the School of Military Engineering (SME) at Chatham, where a luncheon was laid out. It was followed by a detailed briefing and visit to see the Sappers being trained.

Some impressions of my short trip merit mention. I was received by a corporal in civilian dress. Brig Chris Sexton had given him a photograph of mine to help him recognise me. In India, a soldier stands (in uniform) with a placard to receive a senior officer, thereby endangering security. In the SME, I observed there was more stress on practical and application-oriented training. They took maximum care of their tools, plants and material during training. Whatever could be reused was done for the maximum number of times. In the entire SME HQ, there was only one lady employed as a receptionist. All officers did their work on their respective computers. Tea and coffee machines were centrally placed and everyone brewed their own cup. The SME was spread over a large campus. Only the workshops were cleaned by the students, the upkeep of the rest of the area was through outsourcing. For minor mistakes, fines were levied as a deterrent and the money collected was put in the Regimental Fund.

On the first day, I was invited to dinner by Brig Chris Sexton. He had also invited British officers and their wives who had attended the NDC course in India earlier and a couple who were to attend the next course. Chris, again so thoughtfully, had sent me the photographs and names of all the guests who I was to meet along with a few lines on each; hence, no introductions were required. The next day, I visited the Royal Military Academy, Sandhurst, and the British War Museum and had lunch in the Corps of Engineers Officers Mess with the veterans for the draw.

In the early morning, I went around the Officers Mess of the Corps of Engineers, which had a large number of historical paintings. Chris Sexton explained each one of them; he had correctly gauged that I would not be able to see them during the lunch as the invitees would detract my attention. What surprised me was that a single lady and her daughter organised the proper sit-down lunch for over 80 attendees. They had not only prepared the meal but also laid the table and served the lunch. They left after cleaning up the tables and the kitchen. British Army Gurkha pipers were in attendance at the lunch and they were extremely happy to see an Indian Army officer.

Last Push for the Event

A complete facelift was given to the Group Centre and a large number of projects were conceptualised and executed. The Group Museum was redesigned and was a topic of appreciative discussion, finding endorsement from the Service Chiefs. Ten days before the celebrations kicked-off, I with my wife, my staff officer, Maj Nilesh Sawant from my Regiment, a dedicated and an outstanding officer, one JCO clerk and two other clerks, we moved to the Centre to take on last-minute actions and tie up minor details. Col AK Chaturvedi and the comperes of the show, Col and Mrs Rizvi came four days earlier. Nandish with the laser equipment and Mrs Archana Kapoor, with her team, arrived three days earlier as she was the official photographer for the events.

The day after my arrival, the Centre Commandant and I sat down for two hours and went over each event. I had prepared checklists for them and we went over the points where actions were still required. Thereafter, we met only for ten minutes every evening to compare notes. I had to sit late as there were a lot of interactions for the Bicentenary show, rechecking the script, and listening to the rehearsals by Col and Mrs Rizvi. Invitees for the two lunches for the CAS and CNS had to be decided. The checklists for each event were being continuously amended and additional points added so that nothing was missed out. Security too was a big concern as, with the *Surya Kiran* show, everyone in Roorkee wanted to attend the events on all three days. The mornings went in going over the sites and routes where the VIPs were to move/visit/hold press conferences etc. We also arranged for two IAF aircraft to ferry officers from CME to attend the celebrations.

Close to D day, I could easily sense that not many people were hopeful of a good event. Due to force *majeure,* we were not able to conduct a single rehearsal before the show. I took a big risk of doing the laser show without any rehearsals, which seldom happens in the event management industry.

The Event

Organising the Bicentenary celebrations in all its solemnity and grandeur was a task of herculean proportion. It was attended by the three Service Chiefs, over three successive days, in turn, joined in by 316 officers, serving and retired, including the British guests and their ladies, 650 retired soldiers as well as 14,000 recruits, serving soldiers and their families from the Centre. Air acrobats of the Air Force – the *Surya Kirans* – put up a marvellous show, as did the horse and dog teams from the Remount and Veterinary Corps, martial arts team from the Special Frontier Force, Para Gliders of the Para Brigade and the 105-member Army Symphony Band.

On the first day, the E-in-C, Lt Gen Hari Uniyal, was the chief guest and the events went off with clockwork precision. It gave us confidence that the visits of the CAS and CNS would also go well as they were exactly similar and they did too. When we saw off the CAS and CNS after their respective visits, they expressed their happiness and sent congratulatory messages.

The Bicentenary parade, and the *Surya Kiran* show, went off without any glitch. The British officer, from the Scots Guard, could not fault it. Rather, he averred that he had not seen smarter soldiers and better drill anywhere else in the world. Incidentally, the number of people from Roorkee who had come to see the parade and the *Surya Kirans* air show, in particular, came as a great surprise.

After lunch in the JCO's Mess and escorting the COAS, Gen Nirmal Vij, to the guest room, I rushed to the site where the evening 'showstopper' event was to be held. Only Col AK Chaturvedi was there, the rest had gone to see the parade and the *Surya Kiran*s and then moved for lunch. Ajay Chaturvedi was rightly disturbed as the furniture for the spectators seating had not come in, nor had the Army Symphony Band. When the laser show in-charge fetched up, there were only five hours for it to commence. I knew that to keep the expenditure to the minimum, the furniture was being shifted from the other functions. I arranged lunch for Ajay Chaturvedi and cheered him up. Within minutes everyone started coming in and quietly went about doing their respective tasks. As this event was totally my responsibility, I had to stay at the site to ensure all arrangements were complete in all respects. The numbers to be played by the Army Symphony Band had been chosen carefully after discussions with Major Nazir Hussain. The show was to start at 1930 hours. Finally, at 1830 hours, I had a final look, gave a pep talk to all the participants and seeing them confident, rushed to change.

When I returned with my wife, she was not aware of what the show was about; neither was the Centre Commandant or any of the guests. I too had not seen any rehearsal but individually I had seen/heard each portion of the show. In an unparalleled show of class and substance, the film of high quality and content eulogized our glorious past. The unique laser show to highlight our history since independence drew unprecedented applause.

During the show, Gen Vij asked how many rehearsals we had for it.

I replied, "Nil, Sir."

He remarked, "I admire your guts to put up a show for the COAS without any rehearsals."

I said, "Sir, there was no way I could hold a rehearsal, I will explain the reasons at dinner time."

As it happened, I did not get an opportunity to do so.

Organising the laser show was a unique experience. But the bigger issues entailed technical and logistic details. The power needed was not feasible from the MES feeder and no generator set of the requisite wattage was available in Roorkee or any nearby military station. A generator was available at Allahabad and the same was organised due to my personal equation with the COS Central Command, Maj Gen AS Jamwal, who was my coursemate from the NDA. However, it arrived only on the day of the event. Its late arrival made many of us miss a heartbeat or two. When it reached, and I heard the problems which the team had faced, it made me salute them because a lesser mortal would have given up; but for a determined Bengal Sapper, nothing is impossible.

When the showstopper ended, everyone was ecstatic with a sense of euphoria. We had to rush back to see the arrangements for the Bicentenary dinner. At the dinner, I doubt there was an officer who did not compliment me on the show. The COAS wanted exactly a similar show in the Dogra Regimental Centre for their regimental get-together to be held six months later. When we finally saw off the General and Mrs Vij at the helipad, he again complimented us in holding the Bicentenary celebrations in an exemplary manner and felicitated the Bengal Sappers.

Immediately after this, my wife and I rushed back to change and drive down to Delhi and return to Pune, from where I was away for a fortnight. Before moving out I did thank Brig Gautam Banerjee and his team for putting up a great show.

Recording the Events

The Bicentenary celebrations was an undertaking of a complex and wide-ranging scale. More importantly, it was successful beyond expectations in a manner unique in many dimensions. I had, with the unflinching support of Brig Gautam Banerjee, succeeded in organising the event in the scale it deserved. It was achieved without any shifting of focus from training. Be that as it may, it is my experience that once an event is over, there is no urge or necessity felt to compile a record of the events for future generations. There is a dire need to develop institutional memory. I was unable to get any record of the 150th anniversary celebrations and was determined to rectify this mistake. The Centre was directed to store all the matters connected with the Bicentenary, both in hard and soft copy, in the archives. I also created an exclusive enclosure for the Bicentenary celebrations in the Group Museum beside the publication of a special edition of *Faujeshwar*, the official magazine of the Bengal Sappers.

I now turn to later actions as Colonel Commandant towards preserving the past, honouring the present and shaping the future.

Improvement of Training Standards

I conducted an 'open house' discussion with the key officers at the

Centre and the Centre Commandant, Brig AK Chaturvedi (the previous Commandant had been nominated for the NDC course). The aim was to make the training more focused, practical and mission-oriented for each trade. I told them of the need to break the fallacy that the Bengal Sappers have only brawn and the Madras Sappers only brains. For this, they had to train our sappers so well that when they go to attend the Combat Engineers Instructors Junior Warfare Course (CEIJW) at CME they must excel on this prestigious course at the NCO level. I must compliment Brig AK Chaturvedi and the Superintendent of Training, Lt Col Dinesh Gupta, for continuously getting the best results on this Course till I was Colonel Commandant.

Honorary Ranks

Yet another KRA of mine was to ensure that maximum JCO's of the Bengal Sappers obtained honorary ranks. With sensible planning in the posting of good JCO's, we commenced getting more honorary ranks. We had to sensitise the environment for this and the JCO's also strived to achieve this goal.

Officers Website for Bengal Sappers Veterans

After an enormous effort to collect data of all veterans, I launched a Bengal Sappers Officers Association (BSOA) website. It had photographs of the officer on commission and on his superannuation, his service record and a write-up written by the officer himself. From this website, a wealth of information could be extracted for knowing how many officers resided in each city; how many had passed away and of what cause; how many from every course were promoted to each rank etc. The writing of an obituary also became easier. Unclassified news of the Centre and the Corps of Engineers was uploaded to keep them updated. On a personal note, I could easily meet/call the veterans in any place I visited.

BSOA Chapters

In all cities with more than 20 veteran Bengal Sappers, we got the senior-most veteran living there to open a chapter. The officers met once in six months/whenever they wanted to. This contributed to enhancing camaraderie and brotherhood. In towns that had less than 20 veteran Bengal Sappers, we requested the senior-most veteran officer of the Bengal Sappers living thereto contact them and form a mini-chapter. I must mention the effort of Brig Amarjeet Singh, a veteran initially at Pune and now at Panchkula, who in addition to a page on Facebook kept all Bengal Sappers as a big family by sending birthday and anniversary greetings and updating them on the news of the Corps and the achievements of veterans and serving officers. He continues to perform yeoman service to date.

Infrastructure in Roorkee

Having seen the Bombay Sappers and Madras Sappers closely when I was CE Southern Command, I knew that we in the Bengal Sappers had the least infrastructure at our Group Centre, in Roorkee. I went out of the way to fill this void by interacting with everyone I could approach and, in my tenure, got maximum works included in the MWP from the Army HQ. The assistance of the GOC-in-C Central Command, Lt Gen OP Nandrajog, in getting us the best infrastructure in sports was noteworthy.

Selection of Centre Commandant

I ensured that the best officer was selected as the Centre Commandant and he put his best foot forward in the appointment. I take pride in the fact that all the officers selected by me as Centre Commandants were nominated for the prestigious NDC course – Brig Gautam Banerjee, Brig AK Chaturvedi, Brig V Wadhawan and Brig Manoj Kumar.

I handed over the baton of Colonel Commandant to Maj Gen Gautam Dutt when I took over as the E-in-C.

DISCIPLINE REDUCES WORKLOAD

DGW E-in-C's Branch (Jan 04 — Sep 04)

After a hectic, satisfying and rewarding tenure as CE Southern Command, I reported to Kashmir House at Delhi, where the E-in-C's Branch is located, as Director-General Works, in December 2003.

I had visited the E-in-C's Branch only twice earlier during my career. The place was not familiar to me. My first desire, after meeting the E-in-C, Lt Gen Mathew Mammen, was an orientation tour of the premises. When we saw the conference hall, I was totally aghast at its upkeep and glumness. The officer showing me around told me that the Army Commanders conference is held here every six months. My first resolve was to renovate it before the next Army Commanders Conference.

Conference Hall at Kashmir House

In the evening of my first day in the office, I rang up a builder I knew, who worked only on auditoriums and conference halls. They were a husband-and-wife team, a civil engineer and an architect, both professionals. I called them at 1130 hours the next day, to discuss improving the conference hall. They turned up punctually and I showed them around. I stressed that they had limited time and could work only at night; however, on weekends they could work round the clock. I asked them to meet me the next day with an outline plan of how they intended to execute the job with a cost estimate. It took 15 minutes and they stayed back to take detailed measurements and photographs. On the third day, we went over the outline plan and, within 30 minutes, approved all the materials and specifications for the work. The audio and audio-visual systems were precluded from this project, for the Corps of Signals to execute. Thereafter the builder sat down with two officers, one each from the surveyors and planning branch, and the concerned GE to check and verify the costing of the project.

I then spoke to the DGSD about my intention to upgrade the conference hall and the cost involved. He gave the go-ahead and the work was sanctioned, the next day, by HQ Delhi Area. A month later the work was accepted and commenced with full vigour. By rotation, a JE from the GE's office was detailed to check the work being executed at night. I also requested my staff officer, Lt Col AS Malik, to visit the site every night and inform me of the progress, in the morning. When the roof was ripped open it was seen that the main wooden beam had been eaten by termites. When he rang me up regarding the situation, I directed the GE to visit the site, photograph it, and approve its replacement with a steel girder. The work then progressed smoothly. The Corps of Signals were integrated into the project at the appropriate time and the work was completed five days prior to the Army Commanders Conference. The COAS, E-in-C and other dignitaries appreciated the effort put in.

Planning of Major Projects

I was acutely aware that my tenure in this appointment would be for less than one year. Accordingly, to achieve my KRAs, I would have to change my style of working. After deliberate thought, I decided to enhance multi-tasking; be more rigid on time management; delegate responsibilities to officers who I thought were capable; have a flexible and pragmatic monitoring system, and finally, remain cool and composed at all times. My Technical Secretary, Col Ashok Kumar, was of great assistance. Having worked with me while I was CE Bathinda Zone, he knew my style of working and took over a lot of my load. He went well beyond the call of duty and I can state that but for his dedicated hard work behind the scenes, my achievements may not have been there.

My initial work involved listening to presentations, deliberating on concepts and arriving at quick decisions. Further, since all activities were to initially run simultaneously, I could not get more than two hours each day for routine office work and had to carry files home every day. Once the projects got on track, there was more time. While the work on the conference hall was progressing, in conformity with my schedule, three other works were planned. They were:

The National War Memorial.

Manekshaw Centre, Delhi Cantonment.

War Memorial at Jammu.

National War Memorial

Every nation in the world has a national war memorial for the Armed Forces personnel who laid down their lives in the service of the country. In India, the All-India War Memorial (known as India Gate) was constructed in 1931 to honour the 90,000 soldiers of the Indian armed forces who died during World War I and the Third Afghan War. However, there was no national memorial for the Indian soldiers who made the supreme sacrifice for the country after Independence, in 1947.

A national war memorial should permeate an aura of reverence and regard for those who sacrificed 'all' with valour, courage and devotion; radiate a fragrance of that eternal living spirit; inspire a sense of hope and pride for the future, and create a will for the supreme sacrifice. To achieve this aim, the war memorial must be at a site that is prominent, central and visited by a large number of important foreign dignitaries, sections of society and visitors.

After considering a number of alternatives, the Armed Forces had identified the empty canopy (*chhatri*) near the India Gate as the most suitable location. The canopy, which is 500 feet to the east of India Gate was not part of the original Lutyens' plan of Delhi. It was constructed later as a homage to King George V, on his demise. The statue of King George V was removed from the canopy and shifted to the Coronation

Park (Kingsway Camp), New Delhi in 1968 as it was considered to be a symbol of the British Empire/Imperialism. The spot, contiguous to India Gate, where all our national-level functions like Republic Day etc. commence by paying homage to the martyrs at Amar Jawan Jyoti, would not disturb the existing architecture, aesthetics and pristine beauty of India Gate. Construction of a National War Memorial in the area contiguous to the India Gate, our existing war memorial, would not only update the historical saga of martyrdom inscribed on the India Gate but also enhance its pristine glory and further reinforce its status as the most important and sacred monument in the country.

Despite the cogent reasoning offered, initially, the Municipal Corporation of Delhi and the Urban Affairs Ministry were not even ready to consider the site and wanted to construct the war memorial elsewhere in the National Capital Region. The Army remained adamant. Finally, permission was accorded to plan a war memorial at this location, with the following main limitations:

> There would be no change to Central Vista.
>
> No cutting of trees was permitted.
>
> There would be no obstruction to the line of sight from any direction to the Central Vista after the war memorial comes up.

We took the assistance of Mr Charles Correa, a reputed architect in the Delhi Arts Commission. After many meetings with him in which we gave our terms of reference, an outline design was decided. It was conceived in the form of a landscape without constructing any new structure above the surrounding ground. The lawns around the canopy were to be raised towards the canopy by nine feet with a very gentle gradient of 1:40. It was also planned to have a 12-feet-high retaining wall (including a three feet parapet) for inscribing the names of martyrs. All roads in the vicinity (except the one connecting India Gate and the canopy) were proposed to be raised by 4½ feet, and thereafter sloped down in a 1:40 gradient to meet the canopy perimeter at the existing levels. Thus, there was neither any obstruction to the view of India Gate (145 feet high) and the canopy (74 feet high) from the outer C Hexagon; nor was any change envisaged to the existing pattern of traffic flow. Before obtaining approval from the Municipal Corporation of Delhi and the Urban Affairs Ministry, we had to make a 3D model, a walkthrough and a large number of photographs of the actual site from all four sides and a video film to show that there would be no obstructions to the view.

In subsequent phases, it was also proposed to have an underground tunnel connecting the war memorial to a museum to be built in the present Prince's Park accommodation space (which had outlived its life.) In addition, at the opposite end i.e., the Jodhpur Hostel (which too had outlived its life) was to be connected with a tunnel to an underground vehicle parking area.

A large number of presentations had to be made to the three Service Chiefs, politicians and to the Supreme Commander. They all approved the design and the project; however, there was no further progress during my tenure. Most of the work was done by Brig Rajeev Gupta, the DDG (Air Force), a competent and dependable officer, working under me. The National War Memorial was completed in 2018. It conforms to over 90% of what was planned in 2004.

Manekshaw Centre

Gen Nirmal Vij, the COAS, was very clear of its location in Delhi Cantonment and what it should encompass. The journey began in end-December 2003 when the Centre was conceptualised. He wanted it to be an edifice with modern architectural design. It was conceived as a multi-utility, state-of-the-art convention centre, spread over 25 acres of landscaped area.

Once the non-negotiable parameters were fixed, the planning and execution was our responsibility. Once again, there was a competition held for architects on the conceptual drawings. M/s STUP Consultants planned and designed the project. It was executed by the MES with the contract awarded to M/s K-Tech Engineers and Builders.

The elegant interior decor of the building showcases the rich ethos and glorious traditions of the Indian Army and also reflects the diverse and remarkable cultural heritage of our country. It was inaugurated on 21 October 2010.

Jammu War Memorial

It was conceived in end-2003 by Gen NC Vij, the COAS, as a homage to our war heroes and to immortalize their sacrifice for posterity. The project required finding a site of suitable size which was elevated, as compared to Jammu city. Once the site was selected, at Sunjuwan, a competition amongst architects was held to choose the best design. The selected design was by the College of Architecture, Chandigarh. Once the design was approved, tendering action began for acceptance at the CE Zone level. The pillar, now called *Balidan Stambh,* is shaped like a bayoneted rifle surrounded by three layers of water bodies. The curved structure attached to the side of the tower depicts the sling. The height of the pillar is approximately 60 metres from the base, which required necessary clearance from the Air Force. At the base is an eternal flame. An inscription wall, wherein battle accounts of each war fought in J&K has been inscribed, stands as a backdrop to the tower which is encircled by 52 memorial pillars. Two musical fountains, pathways and a landscaped garden add to the ambience and beauty. The memorial is unique in design and, when illuminated, it is visible from afar. It was inaugurated on 24 November 2009.

Interaction with Ministry of Defence (MOD) Officials

The functioning of the MES, in general, is totally based on the MOD as all procedures which have financial repercussions have to be cleared by the latter. It is a tedious and time-consuming process. If one does not follow an issue on a daily basis, and with tact, it will never see the light of the day. For this, there is a need to develop good relations with the concerned officials and know the subject thoroughly. In a short time, I realised it and got the following long outstanding cases cleared:

> **Discontinuation of Cement as Schedule 'B' Stores.** Important construction materials viz. cement and steel in the bygone years were 'stores to be issued by department' under 'Schedule B', for incorporation in MES works, since the availability of these items was restricted in the open market. However, with the opening of major industries, the availability of cement and steel in the civil

market had increased. A case was taken up with the MOD to remove these two items as 'Schedule B' and make them builder's supply items completely. The MOD accorded approval on 15 July 2004. Thereafter the practice of issue of cement and steel was discontinued and the responsibility to procure these two items was shifted to the builder.

Maintenance Grant Enhancement Revision in norms of Maintenance of Buildings by MES. Buildings in military stations, under the charge of MES, are maintained on a grant, based on the area of maintenance. The norms are laid on the basis of annual repairs for civil engineering/electrical loads. The earlier norms were issued in 1998. Due to issues like the price of materials, labour and other effects, they were insufficient. A case for revision of norms for military buildings was issued on 2 July 2004. An average increase of 40 percent in the rates ensured better satisfaction for the maintenance of buildings. The plea for the grant to be automatically amended every year, based on inflation and other relevant factors, as was being done in CPWD, was not accepted.

Miscellaneous Tasks. In addition to duties as laid down in the charter of duties of the DGW, my office had to provide technical support to the Married Accommodation Project (MAP), Army Welfare Education Society (AWES) and Ex-Servicemen Contributory Health Scheme (ECHS). Planning and costing of all their projects had to be cleared by my office. It was tremendous work, though for one time. For this, I had to interact with the MOD officials on a regular basis. They would only accept logic and reasoning when it was put across humbly and without any ego. This technique assisted me tremendously when I came back as E-in-C.

Retrospect

The major lessons learnt as DGW were:

> At higher ranks, one is generally aware of the length of time one would have in any appointment. KRAs must, therefore, be set on this primary factor.

Planning vital projects require interaction with a number of consultants. Time management was most critical and had to be given necessary emphasis from the outset. My experience with consultants was that they do not adhere to the timelines mutually agreed upon. I had to adopt pragmatic solutions, based on the personalities involved, motivating them and check progress daily. This was time-consuming but it made them work to complete a task on the accepted timelines.

At higher ranks, there is no choice but to delegate responsibilities. However, one has to be very careful and so should only be done by a capable and reliable officer; otherwise, things can go wrong. For this, my 'third eye' worked. The concept of multi-tasking also proved very effective.

In the MES, all contracts are 'lump-sum contracts.' For a lump-sum contract to work, all contractual drawings have to be complete in all respects well before the project starts. In the civil, where consultants are employed, they only provide detailed drawings in conformity with the stage of work. Thus, the lump-sum contracts are difficult to execute. Such contracts have then to be executed as 'item-rate contracts.' To do this, the permission of the MOD is required, which they are hesitant to give.

The MES functions strictly in conformity with the MOD policies issued from time to time. The MOD has its own rationale to determine the conditions of working. Further, they do not take timely decisions. At one level it is justifiable as, during the time taken to arrive at a decision, all aspects of the case are dissected. To overcome this, one has to develop a good rapport with the MOD officials and, only when they are convinced, they accept your point of view.

In mid-September 2004, I got my posting-cum-promotion orders to move to Pune as Commandant CME. Yet again, after a hectic and short tenure in which I had succeeded to achieve all the KRAs I had set for myself, I moved to my *alma mater.* I would be failing in my duty if I fail to record the total support the entire Works Department and the Surveyor of Works Section accorded me. Each one of the officers and subordinates posted under me worked relentlessly to assist in my endeavours.

THE ALMA MATER BECKONS

Comdt-CME (Oct 04 — Apr 06)

The CME at Pune, is a premier tactical and technical training institution of India and the *alma mater* of the Corps of Engineers. 'First into the battle and last out of it', the Corps of Engineers comprises of the Sappers, MES, BRO and Survey. The college traces back its existence to the erstwhile School of Military Engineering established in 1943 at Roorkee. It moved to the present location at Pune in 1948. In view of the increased responsibilities and in keeping with the higher status of the degree engineering courses being conducted by the School, it was re-designated as CME in November 1951.The College is presently affiliated to Jawaharlal Nehru University (JNU) for its B Tech and M Tech degrees. Its graduate and post graduate courses are recognised by the All India Council for Technical Education (AICTE).

The CME has a sprawling, lush green campus with abundant flora, fauna and water bodies. It is a self-contained institution, with complete infrastructure required to train and accommodate all its students and staff. It has all the facilities for imparting theoretical as well as practical training, sports and administration. It offers an ideal environment to enhance technical and tactical brilliance and to pursue all kinds of adventure activities.

The CME is responsible for training of personnel of the Corps of Engineers besides imparting instructions in combat engineering, CBRN protection, Works services and GIS matters to personnel of all Arms and Services. It conducts a variety of long and short courses. It also houses a Cadets Training Wing (CTW) for training of Gentleman Cadets under the 10+2 Technical Entry Scheme. The CME has also assisted the local administration in disaster relief/rescue operations on numerous occasions in the past.

It is generally understood that the functions of the Commandant of a revered institution like the CME is more of a continuum, and a work in progress. Each of the Commandants have added value to the institution, as a truly modern, syncretic temple of learning in sync with the ethos and traditions of the Army and the customs of the Sappers fraternity. Be that as it may, my inner heart was always impelling me to think what I could or would do, if I ever had an opportunity to head this hallowed institution. That day came on 1 October 2004.

As I drove in through the Buland Darwaza and the HQ came into sight; the clock on the tower reminded me that my time had already begun ticking on the race I had resolved to run, to enhance the pristine environs of this paradise – all on 3,600 acres of land situated on the banks of Mula river – and awaken the human intellect of the Engineers within, in every sphere so that together, mentally, physically and emotionally, we could improve its standards and outlook, albeit at a brisk pace. At the back of my mind was the Serenity Prayer.

My previous tenures at CME, together spanning nine years had already created a repository of ideas in my mind on what could be done as the Commandant. This thought effaced in a jiffy what many told me when I was on my way to take up this assignment – *"Enjoy your tenure and don't try to change much out there as it runs in self-mode by an unwritten code."* The conflict of these two divergent thoughts lasted for three days leading to sleepless nights; and when it reached a crescendo, the volcano in me erupted and I decided to bash on regardless and follow my instincts and resolve.

Fortunately for me, the three days were the handing/taking over period. Once the decision was made, I had a deep and sound sleep at night (which I always normally had). I got up next morning with a spring in my step and my wife noticed the change and said, "I am seeing you as your usual self after three days; please remain like this." I smiled and went to the office. At 1000 hours, I joined the college in giving the traditional warm farewell to my worthy predecessor, Lt Gen Yash Malhotra. After the send-off, I commenced actions in conformity with the plan I had mentally drawn up. That day, I met the HQ staff and told them about the arrangements to be made for the next two days.

In my address to the officers (staff and students) I stressed on my mission to give back to our alma mater and convert it into the best training institution in India. Further, I told them what I expected from each one of them to achieve it. After the 20 minutes sermon was over, my third eye told me what the audience was thinking. Those who knew me thought, 'we better tighten our belts as he makes sure no one gives him anything less than the very best'; while those who did not know me were saying, 'nothing has ever changed in the CME, this General too will see it for himself soon.'

On similar lines I addressed the JCO's, civilian staff of CME and held the *sainik sammelan* for the PBOR.

Facelift to the Campus

Having gone over the handing/taking over notes I was aware that they were limited funds; hence, I first took up those tasks which could be executed without funds and within own resources. After a reconnaissance of the entire campus, both during day and night in my own car, and gathering information from my personal staff, I listed out all the tasks that could be done and the resources required. The first priority was to give a face lift to the campus. Over the next two days, tasks were allotted to the commanders of Faculties, Wings and the CO of the Engineer Regiment. They had to conduct their own reconnaissance and thereafter work out the resources and methodology to execute their task. Thereafter, the OIC nominated for each task was to present his plan of action to me. Since I knew CME better than them, I could not resist from intervening and advising them.

All task forces went about their allotted work with the necessary tools and plants to clean and repair the entire campus with full gusto. The list of works was endless. Tree pruning to ensure illumination from the street lights falls on the road; cutting branches of the trees along both sides of all roads so that they do not touch the overhead electric lines and thereby prevent short circuiting. This reduced the electricity failures drastically. Another task force constructed berms on both sides of all roads inside the campus, while yet another repaired all storm water drains; at some locations the existing road was widened or raised to prevent accidents. Standard sign postings with the Corps colour were installed. The wild grass and shrubs all along the roads were removed to give a clean and neat look to the entire campus. Simultaneously, all major buildings, built with stone blocks, were washed with high pressure pumps with water and fine sand. This not only gave a clean look, more importantly, it enhanced the life of the building as the pores of the stones opened up and they were able to breathe. Brainstorming sessions threw up more suggestions which were implemented. A student officer drew a cartoon in the CME Weekly '*Sabh kuch dikhta hai*'. From one end of the CME, one could see the other end. The campus became litter free and the waste commenced being dropped at the appropriate locations. Everyone, down to the janitor took pride in keeping the campus spruced up and spotlessly clean. This activity continued as there is no end to improvement. The emphasis was to maintain the campus with minimum resources.

Physical Fitness

Physical fitness was high on my agenda and obesity was to be curbed. To ensure this, all officers had to go through a weight check at the MI Room. During the first weight check a large number of married officers, attending the degree course, were found to be overweight. Accordingly, I directed the Colonel Administration to assemble the officer's wives at the Officers Institute for a talk. He was also directed to keep a paper and pen at each table. After wishing the ladies a warm good morning, I gave them three minutes to write their mother-in-law's name and address on the paper and walked out. Everyone began speaking to each other animatedly with a question mark on their startled faces. I was greeted by pin drop silence when I returned. I noticed that one of the youngest amongst them was gathering courage to speak. I said that I know she wants to ask a question and should please do so. She got up and said, "Sir, why do you want the name and address of my mother-in-law?" I replied that I wanted this information as I want to write to her that you are not looking after her son and he is unable to perform. One of the girls giggled and I responded that it was not in the sense she was thinking, but to perform his assigned duties both during peace and war. Hearing this, their laughter brought the roof down and the ice was broken. One of them got up and said, "Please give us one month and we will ensure that by then our hubbies are no longer overweight." I readily accepted their timeline and believe me, thereafter, no degree course officer was ever overweight. Bicycles replaced two and four-wheelers at a fast pace, for moving within the campus, and it soon became the order of the day.

Improvement of the Environment

Initially when an activity starts, there is anxiety and resistance to change. To cross this hurdle without creating ripples, one needs to include some element of humour. Then everyone begins enjoying the activity and progress gets better every day. To add a fun element, I started evening walks with the Commandant which contributed to the release of tension.

I was always in a hurry to get the work done by the officer to whom it had been assigned. When I observed things not moving at the desired pace, I asked the concerned officer to accompany me for my evening walk. The fifth or sixth officer who had to accompany me on the walk was Col Rawat, the Adm Wing Commander. After discussing mundane issues, I asked Rawat why he was not able to complete the assigned task. With an amused look, he asked me if he could be candid, to which I nodded. He said, "Sir, whenever a car from the neutral gear is put in to the top gear it gives a jerk. We were all in reverse/neutral gear and you have put us all into the fifth gear, obviously there would be jerks and not a smooth transition." We had a hearty laugh but his task was completed soon thereafter. I knew Rawat from 1976 when he was doing his EODE course and I had picked him up for rowing. It also sent a signal to the rest that they would have to take a walk with me (pun intended), if they were sluggish in performing their assigned tasks. I got very few partners for the evening walk thereafter, as all assigned tasks got completed well before the target date/time set for them. Thereafter, to keep the fun alive, from a walk in the evening with me, I amended the previous order. The defaulter had to give a beer party on Saturday afternoon in the Officers' Mess. These parties were initially twice a month and subsequently reduced to once a month. I must add that I too had to give one such party and, on that day, the one glass of beer norm was broken.

It is during this stage that I was nicknamed 'Tsunami' and there was nothing I could do about it.

Rowing Channel

I vividly recall that, from my YO days, the golfers dreamt of 'greens' in lieu of 'browns' on the CME golf course. Their wish was fulfilled in 1994 when the golf course got its first 'greens'. The rowers, I being one of them, too dreamt of having a rowing channel way back since 1969. As this was a mammoth project and since there were many other works which had greater priority, there was little chance of getting it sanctioned, despite all my efforts. Close to the end of my tenure at CME, when I had literally given up hope to get it through, an official from the MOD (Finance) rang up and requested me to get the final bill of a builder, who was his relative, cleared. The builder was working with an MES establishment in Odisha under a civilian officer who had served under me when I was CE, Southern Command. The bill was cleared in a day and the bureaucrat could not believe that it had been done so quickly. He rang up and thanked me profusely as, despite his best efforts and speaking to everyone concerned, no progress was forthcoming. He added that, if there was ever anything, he could do for me I should not hesitate to ask. I requested him to find time to visit CME which he willingly did on a Sunday. At our meeting I convinced him that we badly needed a rowing channel. He spontaneously agreed and requested for a detailed statement of case with the costing which should not exceed Rs 150 lakh (which was within his financial powers to sanction). We had in anticipation prepared the statement of case, which mentioned that the rowing channel would be dug through own resources. Much to his surprise, I handed over the statement of case on the spot. He carried it along to Delhi and hey presto; we got the Administrative Approval in three days. I later moved as E-in-C and could mobilise all the earth moving plants that the CME required for taking on this difficult assignment. The rest is history and today, the rowing channel, an engineering marvel, is a reality.

Today, the Army Rowing Node has been established at the CME with a magnificent eight lanes rowing channel. It also has a boathouse, a gymnasium and an indoor rowing facility for training. Construction of the rowing channel commenced in October 2006 and was completed in March 2009. The first of its kind in the country, it complies with international standards. It involved construction of a channel of 2.3-kilometre length and 150 metre width, requiring major excavation and filling.

Today, the CME regularly trains the National Rowing team. 19 out of the 22 rowers that formed part for the Indian team in the Incheon Asian Games were trained here. CME has also hosted the Amateur Rowing Championship of the East Rowing Association, a prestigious international event. The improved performance of Indian rowers at the Asian Games and regular representation at the Olympics is a strong indicator that rowing as a sport is gaining momentum in India.

Reclaiming the Glory of the Corps in Competitive and Adventure Sailing

The CME had always been home to the Corps of Engineers Sailing Club. I wanted to revive sailing and reclaim the glory of the Corps in the sport. As pioneers of sailing in the country, the Corps had achieved impressive milestones in both competitive and adventure sailing in the past. However, over the years, this impetus had slackened leading to the Indian Navy and civilian sailing clubs dominating the sport. The CME was also under pressure from Mumbai-based sailing clubs to hand over to them the reins of the National Optimist Association of India (NOAI) of which the Corps was the founder and the Commandant CME, the elected President.

CME's vintage Sailing Club, housed in a wooden hut alongside the Mula River which had once bustled with activity with officers jostling to get a yacht to sail, was more or less a relic with few taking to the waters. Procurement of contemporary yachts and equipment was minimal and mostly vintage yachts were available to those who evinced interest in the sport. The enthusiasm amongst officers, ladies and children to enjoy and partake in the frolic and competition had withered away over the years as officers grappled with their heightened academic curriculum and fiery ambitions.

It was my good fortune that a keen sailor, Col Uberoi was posted at the CME. I gave him a mandate to revive the sport. Various means were adopted. Officers, ladies and children were encouraged to hit the waters. Weekend sailing in HBTC Marve was started. A bus was arranged for officers and families for overnight weekend stays at Marve for coaching in sailing in coastal waters. Yachts for both learners and competitive sailing were moved to Marve and safety arrangements put in place. The initiative saw a good response from young officers and ladies. Sailing was included in the watermanship training curriculum of the CTW and made mandatory for cadets on a bi-weekly basis. Children of JCOs/OR were also encouraged to sail, train and participate.

The Sailing Club hut was spruced up and unrepaired yachts were serviced to create a sail-worthy fleet. Funds for procuring new boats and equipment were arranged and a record number of yachts were procured. The ball had been set in motion and more procurement fructified, even after my departure, on the basis of the proposals we had got approved.

Several expeditions had been undertaken in the flagship yacht of adventure sailing of the Corps – the *Seabird.* This diminutive yacht was a harbour sailing craft, not one to sail the open seas. Our two vintage *Seabird*s were no longer seaworthy and procurement of new *Seabird*s would entail considerable time. Accordingly, two *Seabird*s were chartered from Mumbai-based clubs to undertake our first expedition in coastal waters.

The risks involved were considerable and the process to obtain numerous sanctions, organising training of the crew, putting safety and communications in place and tying up logistics was tedious and cumbersome. The crew were mostly greenhorns with practically no experience in coastal water sailing. No meaningful training could be imparted since the chartered *Seabirds* were obtained at the last moment. The ensuing monsoons also limited the window of opportunity for undertaking an expedition. Preparations were undertaken on a war footing and sanctions from the E-in-C's Branch, DGMT Directorate, HQ ARTRAC and HQ Southern Command were obtained in record time. On 29 March 2005, the FOC-in-C, Western Naval Command flagged off from Colaba the first amongst several expeditions that would follow destination Goa. The event was well covered by both the print and electronic media.

An expedition from Mumbai to Cochin followed in October-November 2005. It was the first ever Corps of Engineers expedition to be recognised by the Army Adventure Wing and to be funded by it. This expedition was undertaken in two new *Seabirds* procured by CME. The entire crew of this expedition were awarded the COAS Commendation Card.

It was time to raise the bar further. The first ever 'All-Women Crew' sailing expedition from Mumbai to Goa in *Seabirds* was conceived. Since only two lady officers had experience in sailing, we co-opted two experienced lady naval officers and two civilians to ensure adequate experienced hands-on board and to increase the bonhomie between the Army, Navy and civilian sailing fraternity. However, even the sole naval volunteer fell out in the attrition process leaving only lady sailors from the Corps to undertake the expedition. The expedition was flagged off by me on 30 January 2006. Much lay at stake but the crew performed creditably. A new benchmark indeed had been set. In 10 months, the Corps had undertaken three successful expeditions and had set the stage for more to follow, as they indeed did.

The keenly contested *Thimmaya Trophy* was bagged by the Corps. Setting up of an Army Adventure Node at HBTC, Marve under the DGMT for training all ranks of the Army in coastal sailing was subsequently sanctioned.The NOAI became a beehive of activities. The Inland Water Championships conducted by Southern Command saw a record participation of children. The children of one of our JCOs emerged as the national champion and represented India in various Asian championships. A record number of some 40 odd sailors received COAS Commendation Cards during this period. Singlehandedly, Mickie had achieved the impossible, both in competitive and adventure sailing. Hat's off to this officer.

EODE Courses

In my address to officers undergoing the EODE courses, I emphasised that, as Sappers, they had no choice but to be fully trained soldiers foremost. In their three years at CME, they needed to keep on developing skills in soldiering too, besides gaining technical knowledge. They were advised to indulge in self-study to clear their promotion examinations. It was expected that the officers would have cleared their Promotion Examination Part 'B' in their regiments/units. In the CME, they should try and clear the Promotion Examination Part 'D' in their first year of the EODE course.

After clearing their promotion exams, they were provided with pamphlets of the Junior Command (JC) course and counseled to prepare for the DSSC/TSOC entrance examination. They were advised to prepare for them during their second and third year of the EODE course and appear for the competitive examination at the earliest after completion of the course. For this the students were formed into groups and each student officer taught all others in his group one subject each. Instructors from F Combat were made available for guidance 24x7.

Sapper officers before proceeding for JC Course serve in BRO, MES and Combat units. It was imperative that all such officers were put on the same grid before they went for the JC Course so that they speak in a common language. After interacting with the Army Commander ARTRAC, DGMT and the Commandant of the War College, Mhow, we succeeded in getting the ECC Course to precede the JC Course and the ERC Course to precede the SC Course. This vastly improved the performance of our officers and the Corps reaped spectacular results in these courses. It was also extremely gratifying for me that the Corps of Engineers got the best result in the DSSC entrance examination in 2006.

I was also convinced that classroom or blackboard teaching was outdated. It had to be replaced by focused, application-oriented and practical training. Students learn more by seeing and listening. Accordingly, the students in CME had to be provided with the best infrastructure. For EODE courses, as part of the application-oriented training they were asked to check an existing building, and list out all the faults in its construction. Thereafter, against each fault they had to write why it had occurred and how it could be rectified. Initially, the results were discouraging, but with an increased focus on practical aspects, an incisive eye was developed by them. The students were also taken to a number of construction sites in and around Pune, where work was on at different stages, and at 'special repair' works sites inside and outside CME. A short one-week capsule on MES and BRO was also given to the EODE course. Actions were also put in place to streamline the syllabi of EODE courses. New engineering disciplines were added keeping in view, the current requirements of the Corps which included nuclear, chemical, electronics, computer and communications aspects.

My focus was on a multi-pronged development of the haven of the Corps, be it personal, infrastructure, combat training, engineering or works training and welfare activities. The success mantra was very simple. The entire team of officers, both staff and students, JCOs, ORs, civilian staff and most important the engineer regiment at CME, under Col Lobzang Neema, were amalgamated into all these activities and they rose to the occasion and willingly put their shoulders to the wheel, with determination, intensity, hard work, commitment and dedication for the CME to become a spectacular abode of excellence in the years to come. I would be failing in my duty if I do not thank them for contributing immensely towards my vision and dream.

I shall refrain from writing about the milestones achieved in infrastructure development, training aspects (tactical, technical, general knowledge, physical fitness, sports, adventure, character building, and camaraderie), as that is etched in the annals of the history of the CME and for others to comment upon. My one and half years at the helm zipped by and the clock on the tower seemed to move too fast as we were always trying to stay ahead of time, having opened up many facets of work simultaneously. The entire team worked as a well-oiled juggernaut onto the path of development, making the impossible, possible and I dare say we breezed ahead of our times.

Soil Engineering and Materials Testing (SEMT) Wing

In the CME, we had a well-equipped R&D facility in the SEMT Wing. During my first inspection visit, I was disappointed to see that the lab equipment had not been calibrated from the competent authority. Also, the lab did not have the mandatory ISO (NABL) accreditation. I got Lt Col Manoj Tipnis posted in as Director of the SEMT Wing and gave him the specific charter to check and confirm that all the procured testing equipment was fully functional. During the check it was observed that the state-of-the-art, imported Heavy Falling Weight Deflectometer (HFWD) machine, which had been procured for evaluating the strength of airfield pavements and determining the PCN value required for aircraft operations on the designated airfield pavement, was lying unused. Commissioning it required expert analysis and bold decisions for moving it by air to different airfields. It was finally proven and commissioned; and thereafter deployed in testing of a number of airfield runways. It facilitated meeting a major demand of all our military airfields. The lab was also used extensively during the construction of the 'rowing channel.' Manoj deserves kudos for achieving both these KRAs.

Works Projects

Once requisite funds were arranged through liaison under all heads (Minor Works, Revenue Works, Low Budgeted Works and Special Repair Funds) in FY 2004-05 and FY 2005-06, work started expeditiously, as thorough planning had been done for all of them. Auditoriums, classrooms, conference halls, *Aagosh* (the main guest room), the HQ building stairs and main corridor, reception centre, Officers Mess and Institute were the focus of improvement. Their execution was overseen by selected officers from the staff. The CWE, GE and the builders to whom each of these works was allotted were aware that I would not accept anything other than the very best and no time/cost overrun was acceptable. In office contingency, we managed to get Rs 1 crore allotted and this assisted tremendously in improving the class rooms.

By moving BP's and AE's 'by hand' though nominated officers we got the OTM accommodation for the Diploma Wing, Faculty of NBC and Bio Chemical Lab works etc. included in the major works programme in FY 2004-05 and 2005-06. Works worth over Rs 82 Crore were sanctioned, something done never before in the CME for a long time. For this a GE (Project) had to be raised in the CME. All these works now stand completed.

Welfare Activities

The CME is the only institute which has no uniformed Mess staff (all are civilians). They have been doing a yeoman's job to look after the Officers Mess, Guest Rooms, etc. The staff literally spend their entire life in CME and they do have various health problems. I was aware of their medical requirements as well as of their families (having been PMC of the Officers Mess in an earlier tenure). With permission from the Southern Army Commander, a number of medical camps were organised. Both the Command Hospital and MH Khadki assisted in this welfare venture. The entire Mess Staff were covered under an insurance scheme, which gave them a lump sum amount on retirement.

Ecology

Everyone was fully aware of my ardent love for nature. During the monsoon season, we planted over one lakh trees (which were most suitable for the area). This incidentally, is always done every year in CME. For the first time fruit trees were given for planting in all married accommodation. In addition to the existing lakes in CME, we constructed yet another lake on the CTW side, in the first six months of my stay in CME. After the next monsoon season, we were happy to see it filled and looking beautiful. In addition, in the catchment areas of the CME campus, small *bundhs* were made to collect rain water, rather than letting it discharge into the Mula river.

Retrospect

It is to the eternal credit of all officers (staff and students), PBOR's and civilian staff,down to the janitors,who pitched in to improve the CME. A few names that come to mind are my faculty and wing commanders Brig Naozar Patel (in particular), Col Manoj Pande (presently the Chief of Army Staff), Col Manik Sabharwal, Col Mickie Oberoi, Col Bajpai, Col EJ Sanchis, Col SK Tiwari, Col Manoj Tipnis, Col Repswal, Col Neema, Col Rikhi, Col Sanjeev, Lt Col PKG Mishra, Lt. Col Kumeri ... (the list is truly endless). Not to forget my SOs, Col Ashok Kumar (who came from Delhi, leaving his family behind to assist me) and Col B Ghosh. Each one went well beyond the call of duty towards achieving my goals with their unique capacity to understand large challenges and conceptualise solutions. I remain eternally grateful and feel blessed by my association with them.

I feel that I did make the CME step out of the shadow of its past and walk down new vistas. It was amusing to be referred to as a 'tsunami' for my efforts. The CME Weekly of 21 April 2006 and 22 April 2006, took out a very adulatory 'special edition' bidding me farewell as Commandant.

WEAR THE CROWN WITH APLOMB

E-in-C (May 06 — Aug 07)

It was a great privilege and honour to become the head of my service and be appointed the Engineer-in-Chief, in May 2006. In higher ranks, it is important to have a very good support staff. I had selected Col B Ghosh as my TS; a very capable officer, who could put in continuous hard work, and was totally dependable and reliable. I had Lt Col Pawan Chadha, as my SO; he had a meticulous sense of professional organisation, coupled with a cultured and refined ability to decorously interact and work with others. To assist me with MES, I selected Mr Gurdev Singh, SE. He was soft-spoken, hardworking, remained cool, and had unimpeachable integrity. These three officers were a tremendous asset to me in this appointment.

My predecessor was Lt Gen Ranjit Singh. According to tradition, tea is organised on the central lawns of the Kashmir House with all ranks and civilians of the E-in-Cs Branch. After the tea, the superannuating E-in-C is pulled in an open jeep to the gate of the Kashmir House. Thereafter, the new E-in-C assumes his office, in the presence of the ADG's.

Once the ceremonies were over, I told the officiating ADGE (Personnel) that I would address all officers (both military and civilian) together, in the central lobby, the next day at 0930 hours, for 20 minutes. Then, after a 15-minute break, I would address the subordinate staff. The major points I stressed in my talk to the officers were:

> I would come to the office daily at 0800 hours i.e., one hour earlier. Anyone who had any personal problem of any kind could meet me then. Many did come and their problems were resolved. This also assisted me in keeping a finger on the pulse of my command.
>
> Once a month, all officers, Directorate-wise, would attend a meeting in my office at 0800 hours. Progress on targets would be reviewed then. The agenda of the meetings would be intimated in advance. No conferences would be held during working hours. Anyone who could not keep pace with the team would be prematurely posted out of the E-in-C's Branch.
>
> We should never forget that we all are officers and gentlemen. I expect everyone to be punctual, and remain physically, mentally and spiritually fit to perform his duties with sincerity, dedication and in concert with each another. I did not expect officers serving under me to forget basic manners and etiquette and no one should ever do anything they would regret later. We need to work like a well-oiled machine; hence, everyone has to assist each other.
>
> Whatever dress we may be wearing, our primary goal remains the same – keep the flag of the organisation at its pinnacle. All officers would be treated equally by me, irrespective of the dress he or she wears.

I gave a similar talk to all subordinates and JEs in Hindi.

I had gone over the handing/taking over notes several times and was fully aware of the state of affairs. However, no list of the reminders which were pending for reply was mentioned. Accordingly, all ADGE's were directed to check this aspect personally and submit the list of pending reminders, under their signatures, by 1530 hours that day. In the evening, I saw that there were a large number of pending cases to which no reply had been sent. It took me a day to resolve/send interim replies to the concerned authorities. Thereafter, no reminders were ever received by the E-in-C's Branch.

On the third day, I went over to pay courtesy calls to the COAS, VCOAS, and similar appointments in the Navy and Air Force and the senior officials of the Ministry of Defence. That day, I also issued instructions to CE Delhi Zone to improve the entrance to the Kashmir House (the foyer and central lobby which leads to the conference hall). The work was completed before the next Army Commanders Conference.

The Difference in Status of MES and Army Officer

The misunderstanding on the status of civilian and army officers was at its peak when I took over as E-in-C. I was determined to resolve it in the first week itself.

During the farewell tea for my predecessor, I observed that the MES officers were wearing black bands. Most of them, who knew me, removed it after the previous E-in-C left. I warned them that, in case I see an officer wearing a black band after I take over, he would do so at his peril and a 'show-cause notice' would be served to all such officers. At the same time, I mentioned that it was my duty to resolve all their issues amicably. Good sense prevailed. Thus, in the first week itself, there was total harmony amongst the MES and Army officers and it remained so throughout my tenure.

Meeting with Corps of Engineers Officers in other Branches of Army HQ

In conformity with my agenda points, I called all the Corps of Engineers army officers, serving in different branches of the Army HQ, and spoke to them in the conference hall. I requested their support for the Corps on genuine cases. I also told them that they are welcome to request me for any assistance from their Corps and assured them it would be provided without any inhibition.

When I asked the gathering about their problems, if any, one officer stated (and others joined him) that they normally get belated or no replies from the E-in-C's Branch to any of their queries. I apologised and assured them that it would never occur in my tenure. I told them with a smile that a bottle of scotch would be sent from my side, in case any reply is received late henceforth. This short interaction went a long way to get a number of our cases resolved and incidentally, no complaints of a late reply were ever received. Rather, I recall about two months after taking over as E-in-C, I got a call from a Sapper officer from the MO's Branch to say, "Sir, please direct your officers to give us some time to examine the requests of the E-in-C Branch."

I replied, "Wilco."

At that stage, I knew the ES Directorate was on the move.

Human Resource and Personnel Management

I considered it my prime responsibility to look after the human resource and personnel issues of both the uniformed and the civil cadre officers of the Corps of Engineers. I believed that unless the aspirations of the officers' cadre were looked into, you could not expect them to give their best to the organisation. For this, I initiated a number of measures to improve the issues concerning the strength and career prospects of the uniformed officers.

Strength of Officer Cadre. The overall strength of officers in the Corps of Engineers was declining over the years. I highlighted this issue with the AG and MS and ensured that we get our proportionate share of officers at the time of commissioning from the academies, including a fair share of ex-NDA officers.

Officers in Military Survey. The permanent secondment of Corps of Engineer officers to the Survey of India and their reverse deputation to Military Survey had stopped since the mid-1980s', resulting in an extreme shortage of officers in the Military Survey. With great difficulty, the process was revived and we got an additional 25 officers commissioned in the Corps over and above our *pro rata* induction and we were in a position to provide five officers every year to Military Survey, for the next five years, to tide over their shortages.

Schedule of Selection Boards. Holding the promotion selection boards of the Corps of Engineer officers in time was another KRA of mine. With regular liaison and interaction, we were able to bridge the gap between the selection boards of Infantry, Armour, Artillery and Engineers. It also resulted in bringing the nomination of Engineer officers on career courses such as HC, LDMC (now HDMC) and NDC at par with their batches in other arms. In fact, we ensured that No. 2 Selection Boards (Cols to Brigs) for the Corps of Engineers was held twice a year to cater for the lesser strength of officers in 1979-81 batches and the vacancies available for them.

Transparency in Postings of Brigs and Above. The postings of

Brigs (including Cols on promotion) and above are issued based on the proposals sent by the E-in-C's Branch to the MS Branch. I ensured that all postings recommended by us were based on organisational and not on individual interest. I do not remember any instance when our proposals were not accepted. If there was any difference of opinion, it was resolved mutually and no arbitrary postings were issued by the MS Branch.

Management of Officers in Combat and Works Appointments. The management of officers in Combat and Works appointments was balanced to meet organisational interests over-riding individual aspirations. Cols, on promotion to Brig, would generally aspire to be posted as Engineer Brigade Commanders or Strike Corps CEs, CEs in Border Roads, Corps CEs and CEs in the MES, in order of preference. I tried to change the perception by posting officers to these appointments based on their age profile. Officers who had age on their side were posted in the MES and Border Roads so that they had sufficient works experience to assist them later in higher ranks. Officers posted as Zonal CEs, for the first time in the MES, did the Corps proud by not only proving themselves professionally but were suitably acknowledged and recognised by being nominated for the NDC course. I kept motivating such officers by frequently talking to them and interacting with their formation commanders regarding their performance on the ground. This not only improved the image of the Corps but also of the MES. In addition, the posting proposals of officers were forwarded after due discussion with the officers and convincing them, in case of differences. This mutual interaction also helped in officers' personnel requirements being met within organisational constraints.

Orientation Capsule for CEs Command. Another initiative that paid rich dividends was starting an orientation capsule for officers moving on posting as CEs of Commands. Brigs approved for promotion as Maj Gens were called to the E-in-C's Branch for a three-day capsule to update them on the current issues and the challenges faced by the Corps in combat and works side. They were given a detailed briefing by each Directorate in E-in-C's Branch. I got very encouraging feedback from the officers who attended this capsule once they reached their respective Comd HQ. It was surprising to know that some of them had come to the E-in-C's Branch for the first time in their career and were not aware of the functioning of the various Directorates in E-in-C's Branch. I also got an opportunity to interact with them. Thereafter, a similar capsule was started for Cols posted as Brigs.

Interaction with Officers in Formations. I made it a point to regularly speak to CEs Commands, Engineer Brigade Commanders, Corps CEs, Zonal CEs and CWEs looking after important works. This interaction helped me understand their problems and I could intervene by talking to their formation commanders. I could also hold their hand if I found the formation commanders too demanding. The officers also felt that they had a direct channel of communication with the E-in-C, whenever required.

M Tech Courses. The various disciplines of M Tech courses in IITs and other institutions were rationalised, in consultation with the DGMT, to cater for those which were actually required by the Corps. A few foreign courses were started and our officers did exceedingly well in them. I remember apprising the COAS about the performance of our officers and he was very happy with this score. After M Tech, the officers were posted to appointments in which they could contribute with their technical knowledge and expertise.

Differences with IDSE officers of the MES. With the re-designation of MES civilian officers, based on a letter issued by the MOD in November 2003, there were differences between the IDSE and the uniformed officers on their equivalence in the MES. Things were getting difficult and the civilian officers went to court for resolving the equivalence issues. I ensured all such cases were defended properly and the equivalence based on designation and pay scales was not accepted, as was sought by the IDSE officers of the MES.

MES Civilian Officers. MES civilian officers comprise various cadres drawn from diverse backgrounds. They have their own aspirations regarding their career and growth in the organisation. Handling civilian officers and IDSE officers in a mixed organisation like MES which is staffed by uniformed officers in large numbers remains a challenge for every E-in-C. There were a host of issues that I had to deal with regarding their cadre structure, promotions and postings. I spared no efforts to ensure that the civilian officers were given a fair deal within the organisational constraints. I never discriminated between the officers whether they were civilians or in uniform. During my visits to various stations, I used to jointly address the military and the civilian officers and shared my thoughts and vision for the MES and what was expected from them. This proved to be a great morale booster and they were happy in putting in their best to meet our goals and objectives.

Cadre Review. The cadre review for the civilian officers in the MES did not occur in the specified time periods leading to a lot of resentment amongst the officers and the IDSE officers' cadre, in particular. There was a long gap between the first and second cadre review of the officers. The IDSE officers were also not happy with the number of CEs and ADG level posts authorised to them over the years. They felt that the promotion of officers in other Government organisations, like the CPWD and Railways, to higher posts, was in much larger numbers as compared to the MES. After detailed deliberations, a draft cadre structure was prepared with an increased number of senior posts recommended, which the organisation could sustain without creating an imbalance. I promised that I would push the case, which made the civilian officers satisfied to a great extent.

DPCs. Timely DPCs ensured that there was no stagnation in various cadres. I could ensure this as the Chairman UPSC was known to me personally since the days I was CE (P) Beacon and he was the DGP, J&K Police, in Srinagar.

Posting of Officers. I tried to maintain absolute transparency in the postings of MES officers. I directed the DG (Personnel) to be considerate in meeting the genuine personal requirements of officers, within the framework of laid down policies.

Accommodation for MES Officers. It was sanctioned on the lines of MAP accommodation for defence services officers in stations where there was none or largely deficient. Officers' messes for CE Zones, which did not have them, were also sanctioned. The allotment of guest rooms in MES IBs was controlled by the station authorities; as a result, MES civilian officers never got to stay in them while visiting various stations on temporary duty. I got the QMG's Branch to issue instructions to earmark guest rooms in MES IBs for civilian officers.

Prevention to ensure the MES has a clean image. My mantra was 'Prevention'. For this to be a success the whole organisation had to know me and the fear factor ensured they did not err. It

> worked beautifully. I also stopped vigilance teams from the E-in-C's branch going to the zones for checking, as they never reported any defaults. As a result, there was no major disciplinary case during my tenure. It meant keeping my eyes and ears open, through various means.

Dining in by the Air Force and Subsequent Interaction

The then CAS, Air Chief Marshal SP Tyagi, with whom I had interacted earlier as CE Southern Command on Air Force works when he was AOC-in-C, graciously invited me and my wife to their Officers' Mess for a dining-in. After an enjoyable evening, when the dinner was over, the CAS took me aside and mentioned that he was worried about Jamnagar airfield. I wondered what the problem was but confidently replied, "Sir, I shall go there tomorrow to check."

The CAS offered a service aircraft for my travel. A Dornier aircraft was ready at the tarmac, the next morning, and we were airborne at 0605 hours. At Jamnagar airfield, after the pleasantries, I told the AOC that I would brief him around noon and asked to be left alone till then.

For the next three hours, I inspected the quality of the work executed. It became clear what had gone wrong. The builder had earlier done only building works and had no experience of any airfield project; hence the workmanship was poor which was very evident in the construction methodology. My 'on-the-job training' on the Srinagar airfield runway, as CE Beacon, stood me in good stead.

The CWE and GE wanted to do a 'risk and cost' work, so did the CE Zone. I told all of them to come to my office at 1000 hours after a day, fully prepared, after discussions with the builder. The AF LO was requested to inform the AOC that he would be fully updated after 48 hours and, hopefully, we would give him a fit airfield soon.

We were back in Delhi before lunch and I called Col Manoj Tipnis, the airfield expert in the E-in-C's Branch and directed him to proceed to Jamnagar that same day or by the early morning flight the next day, and return by the evening flight. He was to check the airfield thoroughly and confirm that it can be repaired. I told him that I must get a firm answer, in person, before 0930 hours on the day after. His opinion tallied with my prognosis. I then requested the President of the MES Builders Association and a builder, who had executed several airfields, works previously and had no airfield work at hand, to come for a meeting.

At the meeting, I told them that the basic fault was that the present builder who had been allotted the work had no previous experience in runway construction. Further, he had deployed a greenhorn team to execute the work. I added that I will not go for risk and cost, provided I get an assurance from the President Builders Association and the builder who had the experience of airfield works that they would guide and assist the present builder to complete the work within the requisite specifications.

I also stated that I was aware that the present builder would suffer some loss. However, as his self-respect is involved, he should accept my proposal. Before waiting for an answer, I told my TS to escort them to the conference hall, serve them tea/coffee and when they arrived at a firm decision, they could inform me. The CE Zone and his team were also with them. They came back after about 30 minutes and assured me that all relevant details had been tied up and a new team will commence functioning at the airfield within a week, and they shall work 24x7 to complete the work. They assured me that the work would be better than the specifications given and the Air Force would be satisfied. I accepted their offer in good faith and emphasised that they should not let me down, under any circumstances. They all confirmed in unison that they would do what they have accepted.

Thereafter, the work was monitored daily and quality ascertained periodically by the airfield experts in my office. I too kept in touch with AOC Jamnagar. In three months, the airfield work was completed to the satisfaction of the users. The CAS then wanted to see the airfield and desired that I accompany him but I had to decline due to a prior engagement. However, I did receive from him, in Air Force parlance, an 'air telegram' from Air Force 1 that said:

> Good Work, Well Done!

Ongoing Runway Works

Alongside Jamnagar airfield, I took up corrective actions on other runway works under execution and for future runway works in the pipeline. Two other runways, which were under execution, were also facing problems. As I had assured the CAS that I would resolve them, I called all the executives to the E-in-C's Branch with complete details of their problems. First, they had a meeting with the DDG (Air Force) and the CSW. Each point was deliberated upon and a solution recommended. Thereafter, I was briefed. Once the executives and my staff were on the same page, the builders who were executing the works were called in and a suggested solution was presented to them. On two points, where the builders were to do extra work, at no additional cost, I had to intervene and convince them to accept it as a *fait accompli*, so that we could move ahead. I assured them that all inadvertent errors would be removed in future tenders. After some coaxing, they accepted our request and these works got back on track. Manoj had to make a number of trips to confirm that the quality of the works was of an acceptable standard.

For all new runway works, a number of corrective measures were introduced. The major ones were:

> A new clause under the 'pre-qualification criteria' for runway tenders was introduced i.e., the builder should have satisfactorily completed at least one runway work earlier, in addition to the other eligibility criteria.
>
> A list of machinery, tools and plants which had to be deployed at the work site, before the commencement of the work, was prepared and mentioned in the contract document.
>
> Before the tender was issued, the CE Zone had to make a 'tender presentation' at the E-in-C's Branch, which was attended by the heads of the relevant Sections. The Air Force representatives were also invited to attend this presentation. All approved suggestions/ recommendations were thereafter incorporated in the tender document.
>
> Posting of runway construction qualified officers as GE's was made mandatory.
>
> A manual containing all the latest relevant instructions on construction and repair of runways was issued. In addition, a handbook on maintenance and upkeep of runways was prepared. This manual and handbook became useful guides for officer and

subordinates posted to air force stations.

Subsequently, the Air Chief called me to ask the number of airfields works I could undertake. I had 18 builders qualified for runway works and five of them were already involved in projects. I had seven more, and he confirmed that his staff would sanction additional works, and get the funds transferred from the Capital Head as the cost of resurfacing the runways was much less than the cost of a fighter aircraft.

On another occasion, the Air Chief called up to inform me that he was sending a team to Europe to have a look at their airfields and find out how they were maintained. I requested him to include two officers from the Corps of Engineers on the trip to which he readily agreed. After the trip, the report brought out that, in India, we maintained our airfields much better. Further, we could not adopt their system as European countries, being small as compared to India, picked up the aggregates from one quarry location only whereas this was not feasible in India. Further, we could move the equipment for resurfacing the airfields on the road infrastructure as available in our country. The cost would be prohibitive and time-consuming if we had dedicated equipment for each airfield. Not to mention the cost to purchase so many sets of equipment to resurface airfields simultaneously.

The AOC-in-C Western Command, Air Marshal A K Singh, was my NDC coursemate. One day, he rang up and requested me to sort out a problem at Kargil airfield, where the BRO and the MES were palming off the responsibility to maintain it, on each other; as a result, the airfield was not operational. I told him I would go there the next day and sort out the problem. He offered an IAF aircraft for my trip. He had heard that I moved early and confirmed the door closing at 0600 hours. The MES and BRO representatives were there to receive us. The BRO officer had served under me in Project Beacon and the MES officer had served under me when I was CE Southern Command.

The AOC took me to the site where a retaining wall had fallen. I directed the BRO officer to take on the work 'on priority basis'. He confirmed that it would be completed in 15 days. There was also some repair work of the runway to be done; the GE too said that he would finish the work in 15 days. The AOC kept requesting me for a cup of tea;

I had to turn it down as I had piles of work waiting for me in Delhi. I told the AOC that he has got very good engineers and he could relax, as the work would be completed within 15 days. I could see both the officers' chests go up more than two inches when I praised them in front of the AOC. I gave both officers a bear hug and entered the aircraft. My SO noted their mobile phone numbers. The captain of the aircraft, while seeing me off at Delhi, said this was the shortest halt during a VIP's trip he had experienced in his career thus far and enquired whether the work would be completed in 15 days. I asked him to check after 15 days and rushed to my car after thanking him for a good trip.

I did not speak to the AOC-in-C on my return, as I knew the Air Force would have given him the feedback. However, on the fifteenth day, I got a call from him to thank me and a request to visit all the airfields under his command. I said that I would definitely do so for a friend and, as I was going for a short foreign tour, said that we could do so after ten days in case it suits him. He replied that it would be perfect. I called my TS and SO (MES) and told them to plan my visits to the Air Force stations. The SO(MES) was told to inform the concerned CEs Air Force that they should, over for the next nine days, visit their respective Air Force stations and ensure that when I visit them, there should no complaints from their AOCs. During my trip abroad, the SO (MES) closely monitored the progress with each of the concerned CEs, who then sent me a brief before my visits to each of the Air Force Stations. On return from my trip abroad, the CEs confirmed that most points of their respective AOCs had been attended to.

On the due date, I travelled in the same aircraft in which I had flown to Kargil and the same pilot welcomed me. I asked him if the Kargil work had been done in 15 days. He smiled and confirmed it as he had flown the AOC-in-C to Kargil subsequently. Before taking off, the pilot gave me a copy of the tour programme of one hour in each Air Force station except the first stop, where it was for seventy-five minutes, as it included time for breakfast.

The AOCs at each stop said that their GE's had sorted out most issues and the remainder were resolved by the CWE and the CE who had visited them twice in the last ten days; hence I was given a short list of points that needed attention at my level. In this short trip, all AOC's were requested not to take me to their office but to take me directly to their problem sites and to give me 15 minutes with the MES officials and subordinates. I had carried with me the list of works running behind schedule. The builders whose works were tardy were present. I warned them to speed up their works or else they should be ready to face action. I also gave a motivational talk to the MES officers and all subordinates and gave gifts to sincere workers. The whirlwind tour in each station ended with a short tour of the station in a car. I had specifically instructed that I would not have a meal at any of the stations; however, sandwiches at an appropriate time were welcome in the aircraft.

We were back in Delhi around 1530 hours, after a tiring trip, visiting seven AF stations. Before we broke off for the day, the tour notes were issued and faxed to the AOCs, CWEs, GEs and the AOC-in-C Western Command.

The AOC-in-C was impressed with the speed at which things moved and said that henceforth there would be negligible MES points for my attention. Everyone in the MES knew the speed at which I worked and had reacted accordingly. I had rarely to check action on the tour notes as the points were always completed and a confirmation sent to all concerned. At locations where I observed outstanding work was being done by an MES employee, a DO letter requesting that his services need to be recognized was sent to the AOC-in-C. They always obliged me by conferring the individual a Commendation Card.

A similar trip was made by me at the request of AOC-in-C Central Command, Air Marshal JS Gujral. Due to time constraints, I could not do similar trips to other Commands though I did go to meet all AOC-in-C's. I also visited some of the airfields where resurfacing works were ongoing.

Interaction with the Navy

I have always had a soft corner for the Navy, since my cadet days at NDA, when I got interested in 'Skin Diving'. As E-in-C, I had an equally good relationship with the Navy as I had interacted with the CNS,

Admiral Arun Prakash, when he was FOC-in-C Western Naval Command and I was CE Southern Command.

When I was Commandant of the CME, in my capacity as Colonel Commandant of the Bengal Sappers, I had invited Admiral Arun Prakash (he was then the Chairman of the Chiefs of Staff Committee) as the Chief Guest for the Junior National Rowing Competition at the Bengal Engineer Group and Centre, Roorkee. For the return trip, I took a lift in his helicopter to Delhi and got an opportunity to explain the problems being created by the MES civilians. He comprehended the problem and was able to convince the then Defence Minister that their demands were unjustified.

Admiral Arun Prakash had also requested me to keep a close check on the Naval Academy being constructed at Ezhimala. INA Ezhimala is the initial officer training establishment of the Indian Navy and the Indian Coast Guard, located in Kannur district, Kerala.

In 2006, the Navy had lost a couple of 'Marcos' in J&K, due to militant action. The CNS gave funds to the MES to construct a hospital in the village of one of the Marcos who had been martyred. When it was completed, Admiral Arun Prakash wanted me to accompany him for its inauguration. Unfortunately, I could not do so due to another engagement, which I could not cancel. However, the CNS was benevolent to confer his Commendation Cards to the GE, the AGE, and JE.

Manual of Contract Management

This book is the Bible for contract management, as it a compendium of the latest policy letters issued by the E-in-C's Branch under appropriate heading/chapters. The existing manual was of 1974 vintage, thus outdated, and there was a dire need to update it. It required colossal effort and hard work as it required going through all files after 1974 and culling out from them all policy letters and then sift them into relevant chapters, which was time-consuming. The manual was formally released on 1 January 2007. A big void was thus filled up.

Pre-Qualification Criteria for Works Costing more than Rs 20 Crore

In the MES, builders of Class 'SS' had an unlimited tendering limit and could submit quotations for any work. However, not all 'SS' class builders had the capacity to handle high-value works and some of them had failed to complete the works due to lack of financial capacity. In order to overcome this problem, I introduced pre-qualification criteria in line with CVC guidelines for all works costing more than Rs 20 Crore, were both listed as well as unlisted builders meeting the eligibility criteria could bid for the work. This brought in a marked improvement in the selection of builders with sound financial and technical capabilities.

Housekeeping

Housekeeping had always been an important KRA with me throughout my career. Clearing backlogs was essential to have a realistic appraisal of the state of projects and to stop arbitrations. Once the 'Final bill' is paid to the builder on time the chances of a builder requesting for arbitration reduces drastically. To ensure that officers clear all outstanding 'housekeeping points' before they move on posting, the Zonal CEs were made responsible to oversee this aspect. In many cases, I had to personally intervene in such cases. This sent a clear message to officers that they cannot shirk their responsibilities. It resulted in clearance of cases pending for over 40 years.

Improvements in MES

On taking over as E-in-C, an email was sent to all the CE Zones that they would have direct access to me. They were directed to send me an email daily for the next one week before 0915 hours on anything they desired to bring to my notice. One or two CEs faltered initially and were spoken to. Thereafter, emails were received on time and regularly. This got any apprehensions out of their minds. All their emails were replied to after obtaining my approval. All the formats on which the progress of works and housekeeping points would be monitored were approved by me. In the first month itself, there were tremendous improvements. A clear message was sent to the environment that the MES was being closely monitored. Where any CE delayed a reply, I would not hesitate in speaking to him directly.

Lest anyone get the impression that the works were not being monitored earlier in the E-in-C's Branch, I need to clarify that it was being done through QPRs. For this there was a Maj Gen – ADG (Army) – monitoring Army works and DDGs (Brigs) were monitoring Air Force and Naval works.

The CE Commands were kept in the loop through a quarterly DO letter in which progress achieved in both combat engineering and MES had to be sent to me on the targets set. To send a detailed reply to the DO letters from each CE Command, I had to attend office on Saturday's. In short, the entire chain was working in total harmony with one another and no choice was given to laggards.

For a change, the MES was no longer a flogging horse. I recall the COAS, in his opening address during the Army Commander's conference, saying that he does not know what his E-in-C had done but he sees the infrastructure looking much better in all stations he visits; and he receives positive feedback on the MES from the environment. I had my presentation on the second day of the conference. I changed the slides and included a large number of details of recent works completed under various heads. I mentioned that despite the positive feedback there was still a feeling in the Army that the Navy and Air Force stations are much better looked after. I stressed that the Navy and Air Force allocate more funds to the MES vis-à-vis the Army. I displayed slides in which details of the total strength, the total area under each service and funds allotted by all the three services to the MES were shown. This was examined at various levels and our ceiling was enhanced considerably.

Col B Ghosh, my TS, was a maven on computers and he made the necessary software for all progress reports on all facets of works which could be shown in different formats and styles. The Secretary Defence (Finance), Mr Vinod Mishra, used to come to my office often to see the improvements on a large screen and return thoroughly impressed. Back in his office, he would tell many officers in the Finance and Audit about our audio-visual presentations and they would come to see the presentations and return startled. They found it hard to believe that the software had been made in-house, and more important, how such huge progress had been achieved on all facets of works management and clearance of housekeeping points in so little a time. Progress of all major works was available in real-time.

Tours and Visits to Outstations

In the first month after taking over as E-in-C, I met all the Army Commanders, and a few FOC-in-Cs and AOC-in-Cs. These meetings brought home to me their fears and apprehensions about the MES and also gave me an opportunity to clarify their misgivings. Also, I ensured prompt action on all points they gave me and followed up with a feedback report. This went a long way towards creating a working rapport and quickly changing their impressions about me and the organisation under me. When it was not feasible to meet them, for any reason, I would telephone and check whether they needed any assistance. This two-way communication paid great dividends and helped in improving the image of the MES and gave me clarity on a number of issues. Over time they began speaking well of the MES when they saw positive and immediate responses to all their genuine requests.

I also spoke regularly to the Corp Commanders, in whose jurisdiction there were maximum MES works in progress, and generally updated them. Every visit was followed up with detailed tour notes on all the points deliberated. They were monitored diligently till actions were completed. The tour notes to Zones were framed in two parts. Part 1 was applicable to all Zones and was circulated to them accordingly. Part-II related to points particular to the Zone I had visited. In this way, common points, which were applicable to all Zones, kept reducing with each Zone that I later visited. The entire environment in the Corps of Engineers soon realised that I take the tour notes seriously and that progress on the points was monitored closely by my staff. No one dared to submit their report late after I sent a Show Cause Notice to one CE Zone who had faltered. I had asked him to explain why I should not endorse in his ACR that he was 'Not fit for executive appointments'. This spread like wildfire, after which no one sent a half-baked or late reply. This single factor improved the functioning of the MES as it taught them to function on time.

Points with MOD—Plinth Area Rates

Estimation of construction cost is worked out based on the authorised areas and the average cost of construction per square metre. The average cost of construction per square metre of the constructed area is called the plinth area rates (PAR). After a great amount of effort, the plinth area rates for married and OTM accommodation (based on the standard schedule of rates (SSR) 2004 and specifications as per Scales of Accommodation 1980) were finally got approved by the MOD in 2007. This enabled us to work out realistic costs (AEs) of the various projects being planned.

Points with MOD—Defence Works Procedure (DWP)

The existing DWP was of 1986 vintage. We had initiated a case way back in 2004, when I was DGW, that in view of the numerous charges which had taken place over the years, there was an urgent need to issue a new DWP suitable for the present environment. The case was accepted by the MOD and work on it had commenced in July 2004. Since it involved the MOD, MOD (Fin), CGDA, QMG's branch, the E-in-C's Branch and the three Service Headquarters, it was taking a lot of time. I requested the Defence Secretary (Finance) to come to my office with his team of officers for a formal presentation. For three hours, we went over each clause and I answered all the queries raised by his team to their full satisfaction. The Defence Secretary (Finance) was very kind to tell me three days later, that the DWP-2007 had been approved and it would soon be issued by the MOD. One more near impossible KRA was thus achieved.

Points with MOD—Furniture for Married Accommodation Project (MAP)

Though all the buildings were being constructed by the MAP, for reasons I could not fathom, the MOD gave the responsibility for the provision of the furniture for these buildings to the E-in-C. For this, I set up a team of selected officers to re-design the furniture in keeping with our requirements and within the ceiling laid down. Our intention was to procure maximum furniture from reputed and branded furniture manufacturers – Godrej, Durian etc. After tough negotiations, the manufacturers agreed to supply most of the items of furniture at the ceiling price fixed by the MOD. Samples and detailed drawings of all the furniture items were then prepared. They were shown to representatives from all three Services and MOD officials. After their approval, CE Zones in whose jurisdiction the MAP was located, procured the furniture (in conformity with the approved samples) through competitive tendering and handed them over to the MAP on time. I take pride in the fact that there have been no complaints about MAP furniture. It was a time-bound exercise but, by putting in dedicated hard work, we adhered to the timelines laid down by the MOD.

Points with MOD—Scales of Accommodation for Defence Services - 2009

Scales of accommodation for defence services is a basic document, which serves as a guide for the planning of military infrastructure. It defines authorized scales of accommodation, fittings and fixtures, broad specifications and allied services for planning and provisioning for various types of accommodation and is applicable for all three services. The scales, last published in 1983, were in operation for over 20 years and were overdue for revision.

With new technologies and equipment and the requirement of operational readiness, changes in an organisation, induction of new equipment, and other functional needs amongst which were increased aspirations of users for improved living standards, there was a strong requirement for revision of the Scales of Accommodation, 1983. An inter-services committee was constituted in April 1999 for revising and updating it. The committee had submitted its report in July 2000. A large number of deliberations were held between E-in-C's Branch, Services HQ and Ministry of Defence.

I tried my utmost to get them through during my tenure as E-in-C, however, I did not succeed. One KRA of mine was not achieved. The scales were duly revised after factoring in all relevant inputs and Scales of Accommodation, 2009 was finally approved by the MOD on 24 July 2009.

The revised scales contributed towards enhanced user satisfaction levels, better conditions for living and working for the troops and also enhanced capabilities of MES in terms of works services support for the Armed Forces. The scales for married accommodation were brought at par with MAP scales. Incidentally, though the inter-services committee completed the colossal task in 14 months; yet, despite regular follow up with the MOD, it took the latter nine years to accord approval.

Combat Engineering

After perusing the handing/taking over notes, briefings from the ES Directorate, and from my own perception, I knew that hardly any new equipment had been inducted into the Corps of Engineers. I first tasked the ES Directorate to give me the list of the equipment ordered on DRDO for development under two heads - offensive and defensive operations - since 1966 (the year of my commission) and what we had got from them, along with the payments made. It took over 15 days to compile the data. Re-check and confirmation took another five days. It became clear that very little equipment had been inducted into service, and whatever had been inducted had problems.

While the list was being prepared, I commenced the 0800 hours meeting with the ES Directorate. After three such interactions, back-to-back, and perusal of the files, I pinpointed two main reasons for the slow progress. First, the practice was to move each case 'on file' rather than moving it 'by hand.' Second, once each case was forwarded, there was no personal interaction with the concerned officer in the South Block.

Accordingly, I gave targets to each officer with no choice other than to move the file 'by hand'; soon cases commenced being resolved. I recall that I had to speak a number of times to the concerned officers for progress. The ES officers realised that they would have to give me results or perish. With urgency, many cases were brought to their logical conclusion through noting's to the VCOAS. A number of equipment statuses were amended from 'develop' to 'buy' and we obtained funds to purchase critical equipment within the financial powers of the VCOAS.

While actions were being taken at the higher end of the spectrum, at the unit level a paper on 'weaknesses in the training of combat engineers' was issued. All were aware of these lacunae, but no one had put them in writing; hence no progress was being achieved. Once the paper was issued, automatically targets were set and progress achieved began being monitored.

Good headway was made in this matter in my tenure. Decent accommodation came up at the ITC and BTC sites etc. Stress began to be laid to train on engineer support operations which each unit anticipated to perform, in their respective area of operations, rather than on common engineering subjects.

Retrospect

We could take out two coffee table books on 'Sappers in Disaster Management', and 'Sappers Contribution in Nation-Building'. Their publications put into perspective the role played by the Corps of Engineers in these spheres.

The COAS, General JJ Singh, honoured the Corps by presenting a silver trophy on our Corps Day.

On the personal front, I was awarded the Golden Peacock Award on Eco-Innovation – 2006; Most Eminent Engineer award by the Institution of Engineers, Delhi Chapter in 2006; and the Admiral Kohli Trophy for Life Time Contribution to the Sport of Sailing.

It was also an honour to be conferred the Param Vishisht Seva Medal, in 2007.

End of the Innings

Before I knew it, the day of my superannuation – 31 August 2007 arrived. That day I was extremely happy since I was fortunate to have had the proud privilege to be a military engineer and to rise to the highest rank of my chosen arm of service. It had been an incredible journey, on which I have had an opportunity to serve with honour, made innumerable friends, created wonderful memories, travelled across the length and breadth of our great country and visited many foreign lands while endeavouring to always accomplish any task and assignment given to me with conviction, confidence and commitment. It was a journey of teamwork with many joining hands with me to complete the task. I was blessed by the cooperation and support I received during my entire career from all Sappers, MES, GREF officers and PBOR and civilians who willingly put their shoulders to the wheel. I do not think I can ever repay them for keeping their faith in me.

To the lilt of 'Auld Lang Syne,' I was pulled on a jeep for one last time. I had a lump in my throat and despite my resolve to not show any sentiments, my determination about which I have been always proud of, failed me for once and my eyes clouded over. Truthfully speaking, my innings in Olive Green had been so good that I could not have asked God for anything more.

In the end, I can only acknowledge the contribution of the remarkable soldiers who have moulded, mentored, befriended, influenced and commanded me to meet their expectations of my potential. I remain eternally grateful to them.

Old soldiers never die. They simply fade away! So ends a soldier's memoir. I hope that I have lived up to its title and accomplished the tasks, which came my way, to the best of my ability and shown the torch for others to carry forward.

Postlude

The Genesis of the Corps of Engineers

The history of the Corps of Engineers is inextricably tied up with the history of warfare, in general, and the military engineering requirements of the time, in particular. In early times, in order to protect their townships/settlements from the enemy, military commanders utilised the engineer's ingenuity to develop their own defences and to erect obstacles to impede the movement of the enemy. With the passage of time, they came to be known as mobility and counter-mobility tasks. This role has stayed on with the Corps of Engineers to date. With the development of science and technology, there has been a rapid metamorphosis in the strategy and tactics of waging war. Accordingly, the conceptualisation, planning and successful accomplishment of engineer tasks in support of operations, at the strategic, operational and tactical levels, need to undergo systemic and exponential changes.

The word 'engineer' is derived from the Latin, *ingenarius,* which originally meant a person skilled in the art of constructing defences for the protection of settlements or towns. This word was later applied to all those who constructed works of public utility. The military engineer was a precursor of the civil engineer. The military engineer is also known as a 'sapper' – a versatile genius who condenses the whole system of military engineering and all that is useful and practical for accomplishing a task.

Military engineering, in essence, is civil engineering undertaken in a military environment. The need of the hour is to augment its potential, to keep pace with the rapidly changing technology being utilised in warfare. Away from the combat zones, *the military engineer must continue to be capable to take up all kinds of development and construction as may be required by the services or in nation-building.* The ideal military engineer thus will remain to be a composite engineer, *who uses the knowledge and techniques of any or all engineering disciplines in solving engineering problems encountered both in peace and wartime situations.*

Present System and the Way Ahead

In the three-year degree course at the CME, it has only been teaching three disciplines of engineering – Civil, Electrical and Mechanical – mainly through classroom instruction. The time has come to give a fresh look to both the content (disciplines) and methodology of training to be imparted to our military engineers so that they remain ever ready to exploit the dynamic situations in an era of rapidly enhancing technological changes. Their skill sets need to be honed through modern training methods which need to be practical and task-oriented. Their knowledge base has to be widened by imparting broader engineering skills, whilst not for a moment forgetting the development of an innovative mindset as the bedrock of their training regimen. Our training doctrines and philosophies need to be flexible in their content and their methods. The CME must be the cradle of home-grown innovations leading the way for the military and our country.

A few vital aspects to be kept in mind while formulating the syllabi and teaching methodology are:

> **Technical Content.** The technical content must include basics of computer engineering, 5G Internet, Digital Technology, Nanotechnology, Self-Monitoring Analysis and Reporting Technology (SMART) AI, Blockchain, Robotics, Drones, Satellites, and 3-D Technology etc.
>
> **Professional Content.** It is to be kept in mind that while pursuing the EODE course, an officer has to continue to maintain the

mindset of a soldier who is fit, imbued with the spirit of adventure and prepared to excel in his promotion and competitive examinations as well.

Teaching Methodology. The teaching must focus on objective-oriented facets, based on the dictum *'Education is not learning of facts but the training of the mind to think.'*

Creative Thinking. More emphasis has to be on 'creative thinking'. Ability-driven education has to be the key feature for success. This is important as the pace of change today is greater than the pace of learning. Innovation-led technological development should be encouraged, ingrained and institutionalised in its curriculum.

Flexibility in Streams. We need to incorporate flexibility for students to cross over different streams or take subjects in other disciplines. Critical infrastructures are more than just technology. To increase their resilience, engineers should view them as socio-technical systems.

Entrepreneurial Outlook Around Projects. Engineers will need communication skills, the ability to work in teams, and global knowledge. They have to be prepared to solve real-world problems and engineering courses have to be organised around projects and less of lectures.

Specialisation

Specialisation in various disciplines of M Tech courses in IITs and other institutions must continue, as hitherto, to cater for those disciplines which would be required by the Corps for its role (based on the technological developments).

JCO's and OR Training

A rationalisation of the trade structure would have to be done based on the requirements to execute the engineer tasks in support of operations, at the strategic, operational and tactical levels. JCOs and OR who have a flair and aptitude for computers will have to be trained in different aspects of computer engineering based on the evolving technology.

Conclusion

While a degree course for engineers needs to continue, it has to be a tailor-made course, keeping in mind that a military engineer is primarily a professional soldier with the *jugad* (innovative) mind to deliver always and every time. The officer thus must undergo practical, focused and application-oriented training to function effectively in any of the major pillars of the Sappers after attending the EODE. It is, for this reason, the CME decided not to change its name to 'Institute of Technology'.

> *The great liability of the engineer, compared to men of other professions, is that his works are out in the open where all can see them. His acts, step by step, are in hard substance. He cannot bury his mistakes in the grave like the doctors. He cannot argue them into thin air or blame the judges like the lawyers. He cannot, like the architects, cover his failures with trees and vines. He cannot, like the politicians, screen his shortcomings by blaming his opponents and hope the people will forget. The engineer simply cannot deny he did it. If his works do not work, he is damned.*
>
> — Herbert Hoover

Hear it from Them – His Colleagues!

Today the relevance of a '360-degree feedback' is well known. It serves to make a comprehensive assessment of the person under scrutiny. His traits, strengths and weaknesses come to the fore in a true manner.

In the military service, those who serve under you do form an opinion about you and a lasting impression in their minds. Individual perceptions may have a bias, yet collective perceptions are nearer to the truth.

With this in mind and to provide the readers of the book, a balanced and correct perspective, I thought it would be appropriate to include what a few officers, who served under me in each of my appointments, have to say in a few lines, 14 years after my superannuation.

This would also serve to corroborate the experiences in various chapters.

Capt AK Joon (Veteran): 658 EBU, Retd as Col.

In the six months that I served under him, I learnt more than what I learnt throughout my service. Truthfully speaking, he achieved the impossible by moving the unit without a rear party.

Mr AK Sharma (Retd as CE Delhi Zone): GE AF Chandigarh under CWE Chandigarh

The General oozed confidence and was a role model who always carried the entire organisation with him and looked after them. He set standards in each of his appointments, which need to be emulated.

Mr MM Bhatia (Presently DG Pers): AGE under CWE Chandigarh

I learnt from him that to be successful one has to be disciplined, systematic, and focused. Further, his dictum was, 'One is as good as his Team.' For this, one has to always look after one's command.

Lt Col KK Parmar (Veteran): Diploma Wing at CME

The General's innovative methodology to make teaching interesting, focused and tailor-made for the duties the students were to perform later was his hallmark. He was a leader, who was accepted by all.

Capt JS Brar (Veteran): Diploma Wing CME, Retd as Col

After my retirement, I can say with conviction that he is unmatched in 'out-of-box' solutions. He was full of foresight, candour, farsightedness, prudence, compassion and was a godfather to all his juniors.

Mr AK Bhatnagar (Retd as CE): Project Beacon

Though it was the General's first tenure in BRO, he in no time picked up the nuances of its working. Thereafter, by leading from the front, he confidently led the Project Beacon to its pinnacle.

Mr TN Bhatnagar (Retd as SE): Project Beacon

The General had a unique style of working which always gave excellent results. His ability to carry along his team was the icing on the cake.

Mr Misra & Mr Pitule (Presently CE & SE): Project Beacon

We were young officers, yet the General made us responsible for the 'Strengthening and Resurfacing Project of Srinagar Runway'. He then taught and guided us on how to execute a complex technical work flawlessly from ab initio. Thank you, Sir, for having faith in us.

Mr Narinder Kumar (Retd as ADG): ACE Bathinda Zone

The General had the foresight to plan, execute, and monitor each of his tasks thoroughly. Hence, he achieved success in what he set out for. His leadership and man-management traits were awesome.

Mr RP Shinghal (Presently ADG): SW at CE Bathinda Zone

The General had a unique trait to get personal with everyone. One day, I saw him breaking bread with a 'mali'. The 'mali' thereafter worked so hard that our garden won the best garden competition.

Mr BM Mittal (Retd as DG Pers): SO1 (Pers) Design and Planning at CE Bathinda Zone

With his unique style of functioning, he made his team right up-to the janitor to take pride in their respective duties and put in their best. He thus achieved the impossible. This was as per me his 'Magic Wand'.

Lt Col S Nautiyal (Veteran): SO1 (E&M) CE Bathinda Zone

His most outstanding traits were his unique management techniques; his time management; his ability to multi-task, and his ability to put in sustained intelligent hard work. Rest is history.

Col Gurnani (Veteran): CWE Amritsar under CE Bathinda Zone

The General had a knack to make everyone perform and deliver. To win over the users, he introduced a strategy of 'pro-active approach' rather than 'counter offensive' and it worked marvellously.

Maj Naveen Jha, (Veteran): GE Amritsar, Retd as Col

The General was a true example of 'Karma hi Dharma hai'. His achievements were 'Na bhooto na bhawishayati' (it never happened in the past and it will never happen in the future).

Brig S Tejpal (Veteran): ACE (Wks) under CE Southern Command

A General who led by personal example and had no ego. His doors were always open to all. He had an uncanny ability to find simple and workable solutions to all issues.

Brig KJ Singh (Veteran): CE Chennai Zone under CE Southern Command

I have seen first-hand his capacity to multitask, yet remain cool, composed and focused. No wonder he succeeded in doing what he did. He hence remains matchless, different and incomparable.

Col KT Gajaria (Veteran): ACE Mumbai Zone, Retd as Maj Gen

The General represents SARVATRA in all its ramifications His persuasive, target oriented approach in dealing with varied issues is worth emulating by all. The likes of this 'Karamyogi' are indeed rare to find.

Col Haider Rizvi, (Veteran): CWE Chennai, Retd as Brig

A General, who genuinely cared for his command and who had full trust in them. He had the knack to get the best from everyone- a rare quality. No wonder he became a legend in his lifetime.

Col AK Chaturvedi (Veteran): Instr at CDM, Retd as Maj Gen

I was entrusted by my Colonel Commandant with a task, (which at that stage seemed impossible). However, with his guidance, we executed it with military finesse. That was leadership.

Col IS Rekhi (Veteran): Col Adm CME

A few of the General's qualities which impressed me are his professional competence, clarity of thought, speed of execution and a go getter albeit with honest intentions and a humane touch.

Col Manoj Tipnis (Veteran): Director SEMT at CME, presently CEO L&T Infrastructure Engineering

The General is a perfect example of a man with perseverance who never gave up, and with a never-say-die attitude once he set himself a KRA. A truly inspirational leader, with a visionary mind.

Col Mickie Oberoi (Veteran): Instructor F Combat CME

I am convinced the General was born to take challenges. He succeeded as his intentions were noble. Three cruises in 10 months and what he did in all his appointments and for the Corps stands testimony.

Col EJ Sanchis (Veteran): F Combat CME

The General came to CME like a Tsunami, tossed and turned every aspect and left everything spick and span and dressed to the nines. He could revive a dead horse and make it work.

Col Badri Vital (Veteran): Instructor at F Civ CME & HQ DGBR

The General was a very meticulous, structured, focused and passionate man on a mission, who despite that was always concerned about his juniors.

Lt Col PKG Misra (Veteran): GSO1 (SD) CME, Retd as Brig

The General was way ahead in his thoughts and his actions than us. It was his innovative approach that brought in innumerable changes in all facets of the CME which no one before or after him, dreamt of.

Lt Col Gagan Narula : GSO1 Trg at CME, presently a Colonel

The General was an officer and a gentleman. Though a tough task master, yet everyone enjoyed working under him as his style of working was unique and success was guaranteed.

Brig Gautam Banerjee (Veteran): Cdr 475 Engr Bde & Comdt, BEG Centre & CE Western Command, Retd as Lt Gen

A General, whose commitment and achievements cannot be listed out on paper. Suffice to say that the Corps reached its pinnacle, whenever he had the position to steer its course.

Maj Gen Naozar Patel (Veteran): CE Northern Command & Commander F Combat

His incredible deeds as Commandant CME and E-in-C were truly endless. In retrospect, had I not been there in this era and actively participated in each one of them, I would not have believed the same.

Maj Gen BB Sharma (Veteran): CE South Western Command

An energetic General, whose singular aim was to elevate the status of the Corps of Engineers. He succeeded as it was a noble mission, accordingly everyone worked with him relentlessly and in unison. He also gave a new definition to the post of the E-in-C.

Maj Gen Ashok Sinha (Veteran): CE Southern Command

The General was a fountain head of positive energy who with his multi-pronged and interactive management style addressed so many diverse fields simultaneously which gave unbelievable dividends.

Mr Satish Chander (Retd): Jt DG (Contracts) at E-in C's Branch

During my tenure in the E in C's Branch, I served four E-in-Cs. However, my tenure with Lt Gen B S Dhaliwal, from May 2006 to August 2007 was the most satisfying period of my whole career in MES

Col Bhupinder Singh (Veteran): Col Coord at E-in-C Branch

A quote by Jim Rohnaptly describes the great General:

> *"The challenge of leadership is to be strong but not rude; be kind, but not weak; be bold, but not a bully; be humble, but not timid; be proud, but not arrogant; have humour, but without folly."*

Col B Ghosh (Veteran): TS to E-in-C, Retd as Brig

Working with him was insanely difficult but immensely satisfying. In the limited time that he had at the helm, he decided to use it to the fullest and I dare say - he did. He was both, a man with a mission and of the masses, two sterling qualities few possess.

Lt Col Pawan Chadda: SO to the E-in-C, presently Brig and stands approved as Maj Gen.

The bestseller 'What Generals Are Made Of' by Major General Aubrey Newman could add a chapter on one of the most dynamic Engineer-in-Chief's the Indian Army has seen. He was fired by a missionary zeal and a rare enthusiasm only matched by the sparkle in his eyes, yet full of humility. DHALIWALISATION – is a proverbial noun now.

Brig Anand Thakur (Veteran): Instructor CDM

A General who with his distinct aura forced the environment to notice the remarkable changes he ushered in at all the appointments he served in. To which all would say, "How has he done this?"

Lt Col Sherry: Architect in MES

Though the General has superannuated 14 years ago, yet tales about his capability, efficiency and his contribution to Corps of Engineers continue to be a topic of discussion in all social gatherings till now.

Nandish Mariyappa: MD Reach Events

I found his concept for the show absurd, yet the General made us put up an unbelievable show which is remembered even today, after over two decades. This was feasible as he was a perfectionist and confident of what he was doing.